D1459380

Thinking Skills

John Butterworth and Geoff Thwaites

LEARNING RESOURCE CENTRE
FILTON COLLEGE
FILTON AVENUE
BRISTOL BS34 7AT
TEL: 0117 909 2224

Return on or before the last date stamped below.

3 0 OCT 2006

1 8 FEB 2011

02/11/16
RF

CAMBRIDGE
UNIVERSITY PRESS

CAMBRIDGE UNIVERSITY PRESS
Cambridge, New York, Melbourne, Madrid, Cape town, Singapore, São Paulo

Cambridge University Press
The Edinburgh Building, Cambridge CB2 2RU, UK

www.cambridge.org
Information on this title: www.cambridge.org/9780521521499

© Cambridge University Press 2005

This publication is in copyright. Subject to statutory exception
and to the provisions of relevant collective licensing agreements,
no reproduction of any part may take place without the written
permission of Cambridge University Press.

First published 2005
Reprinted 2005

Printed in the United Kingdom at the University Press, Cambridge

A catalogue record for this publication is available from the British Library

ISBN-13   978-0521-52149-9 paperback
ISBN-10   0-521-52149-1 paperback

ACKNOWLEDGEMENTS
Cover design by Tim Elcock

The authors would like to thank the members of the UCLES item writing teams over a
number of years, especially Anne Thomson and David Parry.

The publishers would like to thank the following for use of their material: Harvey
Abrams: pp.166–170; BP: p.248; NCVO: pp. 245–246.

Past examinations questions on pages 44, 72 and 77 are reproduced by permission of the
University of Cambridge Local Examinations Syndicate.
Past examination questions on pages 33, 56, 57, 80, 81 and 151 are reproduced courtesy
of OCR.

Photographs: p. 50 © John Butterworth; p. 95 © Cambridge University Press

Cambridge University Press has no responsibility for the persistence or accuracy of URLs
for external or third-party Internet websites referred to in this publication, and does not
guarantee that any content on such websites is, or will remain, accurate or appropriate.

Contents

Introduction
Thinking as a skill

This book is about thinking. But it is not about any thinking. It is about those kinds and levels of thinking that take some measure of *skill*.

As human beings we think all the time. Most of our thinking takes little or no conscious effort. We just do it. You could almost say that we think without thinking! For example, if I am asked whether I would like coffee or tea, I don't have to stop and carefully weigh up the reasons why one would be preferable to the other. I simply choose. I may think about it briefly, but it is not an exercise of skill.

Similarly, if someone asks you what time it is, and you reply 'It's 6.30', no one is going to burst into applause because you got it right (unless, perhaps, you are very young and have just learnt to tell the time). Moving up the scale a little way, if you have to decide whether 6.30 is a good time to phone someone in Beijing (or Toronto or Manchester), then at least you would have to make some mental effort, to add or subtract the time difference, before making your decision.

These demands on your thinking are not what you would call high level. They require simple *arithmetical* skills, together with some geographical understanding, that you probably learnt at primary school. It is only when we are faced with some problem or obstacle that 'thinking as a skill' becomes an appropriate term to use. Adding and subtracting, once we have learnt to do them, are routine. The thinking is largely done for you and you simply follow the procedure. The kinds of thinking this book is concerned with – critical thinking and problem solving – are not routine in this way. They require you to think independently: for example, to think of the procedure for yourself.

Reasoning

It has often been said that what makes the difference between humans and other animals is the ability to *reason*. The famous apes studied by the psychologist Wolfgang Köhler learnt ways to overcome problems, such as using a stick to get at food that was beyond their reach; but they discovered the solution by trial and error, and then remembered it for the next time. This is evidence of animal intelligence, but it is not evidence that apes can 'reason'. As far as we can tell, no animal ever draws conclusions on the basis of observable facts. As far as anyone can tell none of Köhler's apes did anything like thinking: 'That banana is further from the bars than the length of my arm. Therefore I need to find a stick.' In other words the apes, though clever, are not necessarily being *rational*.

Reasoning is the process by which we draw a conclusion or reach a decision on the strength of reasons. The reasons may be facts or beliefs or observations. Being rational is understanding that from some facts or beliefs others *follow*, and using that understanding to make decisions or form judgements.

Reflection

Another ability that evidently belongs only to human animals is the ability to *reflect*. Reflecting means giving deep or serious or concentrated thought to something. When someone is thinking reflectively, she does not just make up her mind on impulse, but carefully considers alternatives, thinks about consequences, weighs up available evidence, and so on. Critical thinking and problem solving are both forms of reflective thinking.

Thinking about thinking

One very valuable form of reflection can be described as 'thinking about thinking'. The reflective thinker does not just think about the problem to be solved, the decision to be made, or the argument to be won, but also about the reasoning processes that go into those activities. Reflecting on the way we think allows us to evaluate how effective our thinking is, what its strengths are, where it sometimes goes wrong and, most importantly of all, how it might be improved.

Using this book

This book is designed to encourage students to reflect on the processes of thinking, as well as practising thinking skills. At regular points in the text you will find activities to think about, talk about or undertake. Below these activities you'll find a discussion on the activity and, if appropriate, an answer or solution. By comparing the discussion/answer/solution with your own reflections and responses, you can judge whether to go back and look at the section again, or whether to move on to the next one.

Keep a piece of card inside the book and when you see this symbol **use the card to cover up the passages that follow the activities until you have completed them.**

The book can be used either for a school or college course in thinking skills/critical thinking, or by the student for individual study. It is divided into 44 units or lessons that will require around an hour each to read and discuss, and additional time will be needed to complete the exercises.

Introductory activity

By way of introduction, here is a puzzle that illustrates the use of reasoning. You may have seen it before, in which case keep the answer to yourself. If you don't know the answer, have a go at working it out before you read on. We will come back to it more than once in the following units, so get to know it well.

The puzzle

Imagine that four prisoners have been buried up to their necks in desert sand, as in the drawing. Each man can see only what is in front of him, and the wall completely blocks his view of the other side. Their captors place hats on their heads. They are told that there are two hats with black bands and two with white, but none of them is allowed to see the colour of his own, and the brim hides it from view. The buried men are given two minutes, in which time one of them must correctly call out the colour of his own hat-band. If the first one to speak gets it right, inside the time limit, they will all be freed. If not, they will all be left there to die. No communication is allowed, and an incorrect call means they all lose. In short, one of them has to make a life-and-death decision for all of them.

After about one minute, one of the prisoners calls out the colour of his hat-band correctly. He doesn't guess, and there is no trick to the question. He works it out purely by reasoning.

So this is *your* question:

Which one of the prisoners answers, and how does he know he is right?

The man who calls out correctly is Sancho. His reasoning is as follows: he can see that Pedro's hat-band is black, and therefore knows that one, and only one, of the others can be black. But which? He cannot see his own, but he reasons that if his was the other black hat-band, then Carlos would see *two* black hat-bands. He would easily be able to conclude that his own was white, and would quickly call out. But after a whole minute Carlos still hasn't called out, leading Sancho to conclude Carlos must be looking at one black hat-band and one white hat-band, and that his (Sancho's) must therefore be white.

The key point here is that Sancho uses reasoning, and not guesswork. But he has to make an imaginative move in his thinking as well, just as you did to solve the puzzle – if you solved it. The problem, for Sancho and Carlos, is that neither of them has enough *visual* information to supply the answer. There has to be another clue, and it comes from Carlos's silence. Sancho is smart enough to realise that Carlos's silence, *plus* the one black hat-band they can both see, means that his own is white.

This kind of move is often called 'lateral thinking', because it involves stepping aside from the most obvious line of reasoning. If you simply consider the obvious visual clues, you will not solve the problem. It takes a lateral (or sideways) move to be able to see the alternative route to the solution.

Did you make the move that Sancho makes in your attempt to solve the puzzle? Or did you solve it some other way? Did you go about it methodically, or did you just 'stumble' onto the right track by chance? (Be honest.) Or did you not solve it at all?

Whichever applies to you, the important thing to learn from this is how you reached the solution – or why you didn't. That is the way to improve your thinking skills. The more you practise, the more you talk and think about *thinking*, the better you become and the better your chances of success in the future.

Argument

The word that is often used for a piece of reasoning is argument. Sancho uses an argument to conclude that his hat-band is white. This might not be the meaning you would normally associate with 'argument': you may be more familiar with the idea of an argument as a dispute or quarrel. But it also has this special meaning:

> An argument is a reason (or reasons) leading to a conclusion.

Sancho's reasons, as we have seen, are the colour of Pedro's hat-band and the silence of Carlos. His conclusion is that his hat must have a white band. As the saying goes, he 'puts two and two together', and comes up with an answer. In doing that he constructs an argument. And because it is a *good* argument, it enables Sancho (and you) to solve the problem.

PART 1 Critical thinking

1 What is an argument?

Until a few hundred years ago it was generally believed that the world was flat. This was a natural belief to have because the Earth's surface *looks* flat. However, people had also observed (and been puzzled by the fact) that ships sailing away from land appeared to get lower and lower in the water, as if they were sinking, and to rise up again as they approached. Some argued – from this and other observations – that the Earth's surface could not be flat, but was curved. They drew this conclusion because if the Earth were flat, a ship would just appear to get smaller and smaller until it was too small to see. Put very plainly, the argument went like this:

[1] Ships appear to drop out of sight as they sail away. *Therefore* the earth cannot be flat.

This is a very simple argument. It consists of just one reason and a conclusion, and the connecting word 'therefore'. The words 'therefore' or 'so' are typically used before the conclusion of an argument, and are often called argument indicators for that reason.

However, this is not the only way to construct an argument. For example, [1] could have been written:

The Earth cannot be flat *because* ships appear to drop out of sight.

It is not even necessary to include an argument indicator at all: the reasoning may be perfectly clear without it, for example:

The Earth cannot be flat. Ships appear to drop out of sight as they sail away.

In each of these examples the argument is expressed and arranged differently. But it is still the same *argument*, with the same reason and same conclusion. All three could be written out as follows with the parts of the argument labelled R for reason and C for conclusion.

R Ships appear to drop out of sight.

Therefore

C The Earth cannot be flat.

'Oh yes it can!'

Of course not everyone has to accept an argument. Sometimes, even when you have given your reasons, people may still disagree with your conclusion. This certainly happened hundreds of years ago when the first 'Round-Earthers' began trying to persuade people that the world was spherical, not flat.

There may have been conversations similar to the one below. Read this conversation, preferably aloud with a partner, and then answer the questions that follow.

[2] 'Did you know, the Earth is really a large ball?'
'Don't be ridiculous. The Earth is a flat dish.'
'It can't be.'
'Well, it is. I'm telling you. And if you used your eyes you wouldn't need telling.'
'I am using my eyes, and they tell me the Earth is round.'
'Then I'll tell you something else. If you go round talking this kind of nonsense, someone is going to lock you up and throw away the key.'
'But just listen.'
'No, you listen. The Earth is flat.'
'It's round.'
'Flat. F-L-A-T, flat!'
'ROUND ... '

Activity

Is [2] an argument? If it is, is it the same kind of argument as [1]?

The answers are: yes to the first question, no to the second.

The problem with the English word 'argument' is that it has several meanings. Two of them are given by the following dictionary entry:

argument *noun* **1.** a reason or reasons supporting a conclusion; a case made for or against a point of view. **2.** a debate or dispute, especially a heated one.

As you can see, example [1] is an argument of the sort given by definition **1**. [2] matches definition **2**. The main difference is that the second type of argument is a disagreement or quarrel between two or more people. It may involve some reasoning from one side or the other or both, but it doesn't have to. In [2], for example, there is no attempt at reasoning. The two speakers are simply exchanging opinions, without giving any supporting reasons to back them up.

Critical thinking is generally more concerned with arguments of type [1] than type [2]. But the main thing is to be aware of the different meanings of the word and to be clear which one you mean when you use it.

More reasons

Argument [1] might seem like a strong argument to you now, because you already accept that the Earth is round. But, as we also know from history, it was not enough to convince the general public. They needed more reasons than this if they were going to give up a belief that had persisted for centuries.

Imagine you were sent back in time several hundred years and had to convince people that the Earth was not flat. What would you take with you: pictures from space; stories of people who have sailed round the world? These would be a good start. Armed with such evidence, and more, construct an argument with three or four reasons instead of just one.

To show that it is an argument, write it out with the reasons numbered R1, R2 etc. and the conclusion marked with C.

There are many arguments you could come up with. The following is just one example.

> [3] Ships appear to sink lower and lower the further they are from land. But they cannot actually be sinking, or they would not come back. Also, sailors have proved that if you keep going in one general direction, for example, east or west, you arrive back where you started from. These facts show that the Earth cannot be flat. Besides, photographs have been taken from space that show the Earth's curvature.

Here three reasons are given in support of the conclusion, which begins with the phrase: 'These facts show that', another way of saying, 'Therefore'. Two of the reasons are given first; then the conclusion; then a further, seemingly indisputable, reason. So the structure of the argument is:

R1 Ships appear to sink.
R2 They can't actually be sinking or they wouldn't come back.
R3 Ships sail away in one direction but return to their starting point.
R4 Pictures from space show the curvature.

Therefore

C   The Earth cannot be flat.

Obviously [3] is a much stronger argument than [1]. Whether it is convincing or not will depend on the willingness of the audience to accept the evidence. But *if* they believe the claims you are making, then it would be very difficult for them not to also accept the conclusion.

Claims

But this 'if' is always a big if. In all probability the audience from that time would *not* accept your claims. They would lock you up – or worse – and carry on believing what they had always believed and could see with their own eyes: a flat Earth surrounded by flat sea.

This is why 'claim' is the right word for the statements of the kind that appear in arguments. Some of the claims made in an argument may be known facts, but others may be forecasts, suggestions, beliefs or opinions. They may also be *false*. It is perfectly possible to construct an argument from false claims, either out of mistaken belief, or deliberately in order to deceive. (That is probably what people hundreds of years ago would have suspected you of, as they slammed the dungeon door.)

This point is important in understanding what argument is. An argument presents reasons and a conclusion. It does not guarantee that either the reasons or the conclusion are *true*. It is still an argument even if any or all the claims in it turn out to be false.

Premises

Another word for a reason, as used in arguments, is 'premise'. Literally it means 'put before', because logically a conclusion *follows from* the premises that are used to support it. 'Premise' is the more technical term, and sometimes more precise, since 'reason' has a wider range of uses. Both words will be used in this book, and you can use either or both yourself.

Summary

The key words in this chapter are: argument, reason, conclusion, claim and premise.

A reasoned case consists of reasons given in support of a conclusion.

End-of-unit assignments

1 Think of a suitable conclusion that you could add to the following to make it into an argument:

Ice ages last for around 100,000 years. Interglacials, the periods between ice ages, are normally between 10 and 15 thousand years long. The present interglacial has lasted around 10,000 years. *Therefore...*

2 Think of one or two reasons that could be used to support the following viewpoints, and use them to construct arguments:

(a) It is wrong to charge foreign students higher fees than other students.

(b) Private cars with fewer than four occupants should be banned from city centres.

(c) The stars of football, baseball and other popular sports deserve the huge earnings that they get.

3 Find a short argument published in a newspaper or magazine or on the Internet. Copy it down and underline its conclusion.

4 Write a short argument of your own consisting of two or three reasons and a conclusion that they support.

Answers and comments are on page 254.

2 Recognising arguments

As we have seen, an argument consists of a conclusion based on one or more reasons. In order to test whether or not a piece of text is an argument, we need to ask whether there are reason(s) and a conclusion. This can be harder than it sounds. A string of claims is not automatically an argument, even if there is a strong connecting thread between them. For example, it is not an argument to say:

> [1] Photographs from space show the Earth's surface as curved. The curvature does not show when a photograph is taken from ground level.

How we can establish that [1] is not an argument is by asking if either of the two claims supports the other, or states a reason for accepting the other. A useful clue can be gained from placing 'therefore' or 'so' between the sentences and asking: does it make sense? If it doesn't make sense, then there is no argument. Here is the test applied to [1]:

> Photographs from space show the Earth's surface as curved. *Therefore* the curvature does not show when a photograph is taken from ground level.

> The curvature does not show when a photograph is taken from ground level, so photographs from space show the Earth's surface as curved.

Neither of these makes sense. So [1] is not an argument.

The same test can be applied to the next example, only as there are more claims there will be more rearrangements to try out.

Activity

Is the following an argument?

> [2] Completed tax forms and payments must be received by 31st July. Late payment may result in a fine not exceeding 100 dollars. Your payment did not reach the tax office until 12th August.

 No. It is simply a string of claims. None of the claims really makes sense when preceded by 'therefore' or 'so'. For example:

> Completed tax forms and payments must be received by 31st July. Late payment may result in a fine not exceeding 100 dollars. *Therefore* your payment did not reach the tax office until 12th August.

Late payment may result in a fine not exceeding 100 dollars. Your payment did not reach the tax office until 12th August. *So* completed tax forms and payments must be received by 31st July.

Completed tax forms and payments must be received by 31st July. Your payment did not reach the tax office until 12th August. *Therefore* late payment may result in a fine not exceeding 100 dollars.

In each rearrangement the attempt to use an argument indicator sounds peculiar, which shows that none of the sentences is even the *kind* of claim that could follow from the others in the way that a conclusion follows from reasons.

Activity

Using the 'therefore/so test', and the definition of an argument as reasons supporting a conclusion, decide which of the following are arguments:

A   The Tokyo train leaves at 16.24. It can take up to 40 minutes to get to the station if the traffic is bad. We should leave for the station by 15.40.

B   Raisa is the only person with a key to the safe. The police are bound to treat her as a suspect. The money went missing when she was in the building on her own.

C   You can expect a fine. Completed tax forms and payments must be received by 31st July and people who miss the deadline are usually fined $100. Your payment did not reach the tax office until 12th August.

D   From the fifteenth century European sailors reached the lands of the east by sailing west. Those who sailed on and survived eventually arrived back in Europe. When they claimed they had sailed around the world, few people believed them.

E   There are only three possible causes of the leak in your washing machine: the pump could be worn, a hose could be split or one of the connections could be loose. I've checked the hoses and tightened all the connections, but the machine still leaks.

A is an argument. The first two sentences are reasons for believing that we should leave by 15.40.

B is also an argument. The conclusion is that the police are bound to suspect Raisa, firstly *because* she is the only key-holder, and secondly *because* she was alone in the building.

C is also an argument. The conclusion is: 'You can expect to get a fine.' The main reason for concluding this is that payment did not reach the tax office until 12th August. However, this would not be much of a reason on its own: the first and second sentences are needed to establish that the payment was late and that late payment usually results in a fine.

D is not an argument. None of the three sentences makes sense with 'therefore' in front of it – e.g. 'From the fifteenth century European sailors reached the lands of the east by sailing west. Those who sailed on and survived eventually arrived back in Europe. *Therefore* when they claimed they sailed around the world, nobody believed them.' The connective that makes most sense is 'but', not 'therefore'. None of the claims is a conclusion drawn from either or both of the other two; and it is the same whichever order the claims are placed in.

E is not an argument either, because, like D, none of its claims is a conclusion. However, E does *point towards* a conclusion, even though it is not stated. In fact there is really only one conclusion that you could draw from E – that the pump must be worn – because both the other possibilities are ruled out. What we can say about E is that it is not complete. It is left to you (the reader or listener) to draw the conclusion – though in this case it leaves you in little doubt as to what the conclusion should be.

Who wants an argument?

In the last unit we discussed arguments of different kinds. Read the following passage – preferably aloud with a partner, taking a part each – and then answer the questions that follow:

SCENE: a table for two in a restaurant

A What are you going to have?
(Sound of a mobile phone)

B Just a minute. I've got a text message.

A Not another!

B Be quiet, I need to answer it.

A Why don't you just switch it off? They're a menace, those things.

B *(Texting at the same time)* You wouldn't say that if you had one.

A I wouldn't have one as a gift.

B Oh yes you would.

A I would not. In my opinion the world would be a better place if they had never been invented.

B How can you say that?

A Easy. I just did.

B Don't be childish. You know what I meant. What *grounds* have you got for saying that? You haven't got any, have you?

A Oh yes I have. Firstly, you can't sit quietly anywhere without having to listen to one end of someone else's shouted conversation. Secondly, mobile phones are a health risk because they pour out microwaves that cook your brain. Thirdly, they distract drivers and cause road accidents. Therefore, like I said, the world would be a better place without them.

B Well, I disagree. For a start there is no evidence that they are a health risk. They don't distract drivers unless the drivers are stupid enough to have them switched on in the car. Not everybody shouts into their phones, and not everyone finds them irritating. They help people to keep in touch. They save lives in emergencies. So it is wrong to say we would be better off without them.

A *(Shouting)* Well, I'm sorry but people *do* shout into them. They don't know they're doing it. And drivers do use them when they are speeding down the road. If someone crashed into you at a hundred kilometres per hour because he was reading a text message, you would soon change your tune.

B Hang on, you're blaming mobile phones, when you should be blaming the owners. Of course there are always some idiots about who misuse things. It's like guns, isn't it. It's not guns that kill people, it's the people who fire the guns. You're making the same mistake.

A I'm not making any mistake. I agree, guns don't shoot people unless someone fires them, but nor can a person shoot someone if there are no guns to do it with. And people couldn't answer their phones in the car if there were no mobiles in the first place. Therefore the world would be better off without guns *and* without mobiles.

B Rubbish!

A It's not. You've lost that one.

B No I haven't. You're just old-fashioned.

A I'm not.

B You are. You need to get into the twenty-first century.

Activity

Is this just a quarrel, or is there reasoned argument going on here as well? If there is, find some examples.

Overall, this conversation is an argument in the form of a dispute or debate. A lot of it is just quarrelling – stating an opinion, disagreeing, making personal remarks, etc. But in the course of the debate there are examples of reasoned argument as well, coming from both sides.

The clearest example is A's first long paragraph. This is a very obvious, tidy argument, with three numbered reasons and a conclusion indicated by 'Therefore'. It is replied to by B who comes up with a second argument. This gives three reasons which challenge or contradict A's reasons, then two further reasons – the value of keeping people in touch, and of saving lives in emergencies – to support a conclusion which is the complete opposite of A's.

In the three paragraphs that follow we hear A and B each trying to reinforce their arguments with further reasons and objections. Then, as their tempers begin to fray, they go back to quarrelling and making personal remarks; and reasoned debate goes out of the window.

Argument and counter-argument

An argument that opposes another argument is called a *counter-argument*. The first two long paragraphs from A and then B are an example of argument and counter-argument. As you have seen, a counter-argument can challenge the reasons given in the original argument, or take a different line of reasoning; or, like B's counter-argument, it can do both.

Summary

In this unit we have practised recognising reasoned arguments, and distinguishing between arguments and other forms of expression.

We have seen that reasoning can be used in order to argue for or against a viewpoint, using argument and counter-argument, in the form of a debate.

1 Out of the following passages, only one is an argument. Which is it, and what is its conclusion?

   A   Since the last earthquake in California, engineers have been investigating what happens to man-made structures during a large seismic event. They were surprised that a section of the Bay Bridge, which connects Oakland to San Francisco, fell like a trap-door. They also discovered that in some of the older double-decker freeways, the joints that connect the lower column to the upper column may be suspect.

   B   The public should not expect the safety of drugs to be guaranteed by animal testing. Aspirin, which is a safe and effective painkiller for most humans, is fatal to the domestic cat. Penicillin poisons guinea pigs. These examples alone show that differences do exist between species with regard to drugs.

   C   If purchases that are paid for by credit card are to cost more than purchases paid for with cash, people will be discouraged from using credit cards, and the credit-card companies will lose profit. On the other hand, shoppers will be wary about carrying large amounts of cash.

2 Is the following a complete argument? If it is, what is its stated conclusion? If it is not complete, what conclusion could you draw from it?

Announcements to passengers on the prestigious Hong Kong MTR system are at present bilingual: Cantonese and English. There are many Mandarin speakers regularly using the MTR. The KCR corporation has shown the way forward by having had trilingual broadcasting for some time.

Answers and comments are on page 254.

3 Responding to arguments

So far we have been mainly concerned with identifying examples of reasoning. But critical thinking does not stop there. Once you can confidently recognise an argument, the next skill is to respond to it in a critical way.

What exactly does this mean? The best way to find out is to *do* some critical thinking.

Activity

Look again at the debate you read in the last unit (pages 16–17). Who do you think wins the argument? And what does it mean to 'win' an argument?

Think about these questions carefully – or better still discuss them with other students – before coming to your decision.

 You cannot really give a straightforward answer to the question, 'Who won?' – without first deciding what winning *means*, in the case of an argument. So we will pass to that second question first.

Winning an argument is not like winning a race or a game of chess, where there are clear rules that determine the winner. Some people seem to think winning an argument means having the last word, or making a fool of the other person, and in some cases it does appear to mean those things – for example, in many debates between politicians and/or journalists. In some circumstances argument becomes almost a form of entertainment, like a boxing match. But that is not how a critical thinker should view it. Critical thinking means looking at the reasoning and asking: 'Who came up with the better argument?'

The trouble with this question is that it is no easier to answer than the original one. That is because we still have to decide what it means to say that an argument is a *good* argument, or that one is a *better* argument than another. Does a 'good' argument have to be clever, logical, persuasive, convincing … or what? Can you say you've *won* an argument (like A seems to think he has) even if the other person still disagrees with you (as B does)? Or is a necessary part of winning an argument getting the other person to admit defeat?

Let's rephrase the question again so as to come at it from a different angle:

Activity

What is a 'good' argument? How do you decide whether one argument is better or worse than another?

Again, there is no single, straight answer. You may have said that a good argument is a 'strong' argument: one that is difficult to argue against. Alternatively, you may have said that a good argument is one that has a number of strong reasons to support it. Then again you may have decided that good means 'sensible' or 'believable' or 'plausible'.

All these answers are fine, and help us to get straight what we mean by a good argument. They also put us in a much better position to answer the specific question: Who won the mobile phone argument? So return to it now and decide whether your original answer still stands, or whether you need to revise it in the light of the discussions you have had about what a good argument is.

One answer to beware of is that a good argument is *true* or *right*. Sometimes people mistakenly use the word 'true' about an argument. An argument is not the kind of thing that is either true or false. The statements or claims made in an argument can be true (or false), but not the argument itself. For example, it may be true – i.e. a fact – that mobile phones sometimes cause health problems; it may also be a fact that some car accidents have been caused by people using phones. If these claims are known to be true, that *strengthens* the argument against mobile phones, and helps to make it a better argument; but it does not make the argument 'true'.

Pros and cons

It is often not clear which of two arguments is the better one because they both have strengths. This is very much the case with A's and B's arguments: they are more or less balanced in strength.

In fact it is true of the whole debate about mobile phones that there are good arguments for both sides. We can say about mobile phones that there are pros and cons. (These terms come from two Latin words: *pro*, meaning 'for' and *contra*, meaning 'against'.) A's argument consists of a list of *cons* – points against mobile phones. B replies with a list of *pros* – points for them. Deciding whose argument is better is really a matter of whether the pros outweigh the cons, or vice versa.

Take A's claims that mobile phones are a health risk, and that they distract drivers and cause accidents. If true, then these are quite serious blows to B's argument that mobile phones are a good thing. However, B does have a counter-claim, which is that mobiles can also *save* lives, for example by allowing someone to call the emergency services. Similarly, A's claim that mobile phones are anti-social is countered by the claim that they help people keep in touch – a convenience versus an inconvenience.

So in a lot of ways the two arguments *balance* each other. If you wanted to decide which was the stronger argument, you would need some kind of evidence: possibly statistics on how many lives are saved and how many accidents are caused. In fact, one of B's counter-arguments is that A has no evidence. However, no information of that sort is available on either side: there is no more statistical support for B's claims about lives saved than there is for accidents caused.

Refutation

If you refute an argument you show it to be wrong. 'Refute' is a word that is often misused. People say: 'I refute that', when what they mean is 'I disagree.' You have to do more than just disagree to refute an argument. Coming up with counter-claims is one way to attempt a refutation, and we have just seen B's attempt to refute A's case by that method. Another way to refute an argument is to find fault with the reasoning itself, to expose a flaw or mistake in it. This is what B tries to do next.

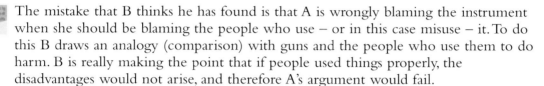

Activity

How does B attempt to refute A's argument in the paragraph beginning, 'Hang on'? How does A respond? Who wins the exchange, in your opinion?

The mistake that B thinks he has found is that A is wrongly blaming the instrument when she should be blaming the people who use – or in this case misuse – it. To do this B draws an analogy (comparison) with guns and the people who use them to do harm. B is really making the point that if people used things properly, the disadvantages would not arise, and therefore A's argument would fail.

Not bad! If you accept that the comparison is a fair one and that it really is the user, not the instrument, which is responsible for the downside of mobile phones, then the conclusion that the world would be better without them seems badly damaged. But A does not take the attack lying down. She comes back with a further counter-argument, and you can judge this for yourself.

Evaluation

A key skill in critical thinking is considering how good, strong or effective an argument is. It is called evaluation. Without evaluating the arguments we read and hear it is impossible for us to make our own minds up in an informed way. Many arguments are very weak when you come to examine them carefully. That doesn't matter if you can recognise the weaknesses and see the argument for what it is worth. But that takes skill and understanding, and practice. Not all bad arguments are easy to spot.

Even when an argument is strong it is not necessarily the last word. The two arguments we have been considering are *both* strong, and that is what our evaluation has revealed about them. What it hasn't revealed is who is right, because the subject is an open one and the two sides both have points in their favour. But at least now we are in a better position to make our own minds up, instead of jumping to conclusions.

Further argument

You are also in a position to bring further arguments of your own. The end-of-unit assignment is to prepare for a continuation of the debate between A and B by thinking up some further arguments.

Summary

In this unit we looked at some of the responses that can be made to an argument: counter-claims, attempted refutations.

We saw what is meant by considering the pros and cons.

We saw what is meant by evaluating argument to decide whether the reasoning is strong or weak.

End-of-unit assignment

You have been asked to speak in a debate either supporting or opposing the statement: 'The world would be a better place without mobile phones.'

Decide which side to take. You can use and extend the arguments you have read in the dispute between A and B and/or raise further arguments of your own.

4 Analysing arguments

Before you can respond critically to an argument, by evaluating it and bringing arguments of your own, you need to have a thorough understanding of it. This means being able to recognise its structure: the way in which the reasons support the conclusion.

'Unpacking' arguments

A lot of furniture and other goods that you buy these days comes packaged for do-it-yourself assembly. When you get the package home you have to unpack and check out all the parts; then put them together.

In critical thinking the same expression – unpack – is often used to describe what you do to an argument when you identify its parts and its structure. Another less colourful word that means the same is analyse. In this unit you will learn some of the techniques that can be used to unpack, or analyse, an argument.

The simplest kind of argument has one or two reasons followed by the conclusion, so that is what we will start with, before moving on to more complex, less obvious examples.

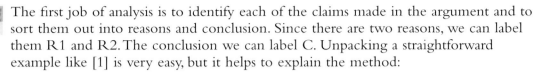

Activity

How would you analyse the following argument?

> [1] The Tokyo train leaves at 16.24, and it can take up to 40 minutes to get to the station if the traffic is bad. We should leave for the station by 15.40 to be on the safe side.

The first job of analysis is to identify each of the claims made in the argument and to sort them out into reasons and conclusion. Since there are two reasons, we can label them R1 and R2. The conclusion we can label C. Unpacking a straightforward example like [1] is very easy, but it helps to explain the method:

> R1 The train leaves at 16.24.
>
> R2 It can take 40 minutes to get to the station.
>
> *Therefore*
>
> C   We should set off by 15.40 to be on the safe side.

Notice that in [1] there is no argument indicator, such as 'therefore', 'so' or 'because'. That is because none is needed. It is obvious which of the claims is the conclusion: it is *because* of R1 and R2 that the speaker claims C, not the other way round.

Also notice that there may be more claims in [1] than there are sentences. The two reasons are connected by 'and' to form a single sentence. Part of the job of unpacking is to identify each of the individual claims and list them separately.

How the reasons work

Once you have located and labelled all the main parts of the argument, the next task is to observe how they fit together. We know already that the reasons give support to a conclusion, but there are various ways in which they can do this. In some arguments, the reasons work independently of each other, each giving its own support to the conclusion. Each of the independent claims may strengthen the argument, but if one of them were removed the conclusion would still have the support of the other(s). In other arguments the reasons work together and depend on each other, so that if one of the reasons were shown to be untrue, the whole argument would collapse.

In [1] the reasons depend on each other. It is the train time *together with* the time it can take to get to the station that leads to the conclusion. If either one turned out to be untrue, then the argument would fail. For example, if the train were not due until 17.24, then R2 on its own would not be enough of a reason for setting off at 15.40. Or, if it were only a five-minute walk to the station, R1 on its own would not be sufficient.

The structure of the argument could be shown as in the diagram below. The single arrow shows that it is the *combination* of R1 and R2 that leads to the conclusion.

For contrast, look at the next argument:

[2] Stormy conditions are likely to develop. Satellite pictures show a belt of very low pressure moving in from the Indian Ocean, and weather stations report huge clouds gathering in the north-west.

Activity

Analyse example [2] by identifying the reasons and conclusion. Try showing how its structure is different from argument [1].

Once we have listed the reasons and conclusion we get something very like we did in [1]:

R1 Satellite pictures show a belt of very low pressure moving in from the Indian Ocean.

R2 Weather stations report huge clouds gathering in the north-west.

Therefore

C   Stormy conditions are likely to develop.

But there the similarity ends, for either R1 or R2 on its own could be used to support the conclusion. Adding R2 strengthens the argument by giving additional evidence, but the argument doesn't fail without R2. Similarly, R2 could by itself support the conclusion, since huge clouds, like belts of low pressure, are signs of bad weather approaching.

To show the structure, we need a diagram in which both the reasons point separately to the conclusion.

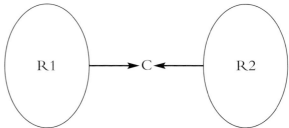

Arguments with more than two reasons

In arguments with more than two reasons (or premises) the picture can quickly get more complicated. There may be a mixture of reasons that work in combination and reasons that work independently.

Activity

Try unpacking this argument, by identifying the reasons and conclusion and showing the structure.

[3] It is obvious that Rajinder cannot be trusted to keep a secret. He was the only person apart from me who knew about Jed and Jill getting engaged. I haven't said a word to anyone, yet now the news is all round the college. Also, he's spread a story about Daniel Li that I told him in confidence.

Once again the first sentence is the conclusion, but this time it is supported by four or five reasons (depending on how you chose to unpack them).

R1 Rajinder was the only person, apart from me, who knew about Jed and Jill getting engaged.

R2 I haven't said a word to anyone.

R3 Now the news is all round the college.

R4 Rajinder spread a story about Daniel Li that I told him in confidence.

Therefore

C It is obvious that Rajinder cannot be trusted to keep a secret.

The first three reasons work together. Obviously, if I had told several people, or if others had known besides Rajinder, it might not have been Rajinder who was to blame; and if the news hadn't spread there would be no reason to suggest Rajinder had told anyone the secret. R4, on the other hand, does not have to be true for the conclusion to follow from the other three. Therefore, although R4 adds strength to the argument, it is separate from the other reasons: an additional reason for concluding that Rajinder can't be trusted.

You could show this in a diagram.

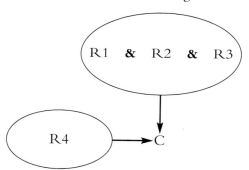

Don't worry if you have unpacked the sentences a little differently. For example, some people might prefer to treat R4 as two reasons: Rajinder spread the story; and, R5, I told it to him in confidence. These two reasons would of course be dependent on each other, so the alternative analysis would be as shown in the diagram opposite.

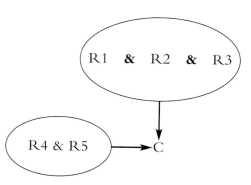

You will find, as you work on more complex arguments, there can be some minor differences in the way an argument is analysed. If yours is not exactly the same as the one suggested in the book, this won't necessarily mean that yours is wrong. What is important is that you recognise the conclusion and the main reasons, and that you are satisfied that you understand the argument and can explain it clearly.

Summary

In this unit we have looked at how an argument works by unpacking or analysing it, identifying the reason(s) and the conclusion and showing the structure.

Reasons (premises) can work together, or independently of each other, in support of a conclusion.

End-of-unit assignments

Analyse the following arguments using the methods discussed in this unit.

1 People should not be so ready to spend their money on bottled mineral water. On a number of occasions there have been health alerts about the chemicals found in bottled water. It is absurdly expensive. And tap water is improving in quality all the time.

2 There will always be some athletes who will give way to the temptation of taking performance-enhancing drugs. At the highest levels of sport, drugs can make the difference between winning gold and winning nothing. At the same time the rewards are so huge for those who reach the top that the risk will seem worth taking.

3 No sport should be allowed in which the prime object is to injure an opponent. Nor should any sport be allowed in which the spectators enjoy seeing competitors inflict physical harm on each other. Boxing should consequently be one of the first sports to be outlawed. What boxers have to do, in order to win matches, is to batter their opponents senseless in front of large, enthusiastic crowds.

Answers and comments are on pages 255–6.

5 More complex arguments

In the last chapter we saw how reasons – independently or in combination – support a conclusion. In every case there was just one conclusion.

But in some arguments there may be more than one conclusion. One or more of the reasons may lead to an *intermediate* conclusion, which then leads on to a main conclusion.

Here is an example:

> [1] In a number of countries, including Malaysia, South Africa and the UK, cars drive on the left. This can result in accidents involving drivers and pedestrians from other countries who are used to traffic being on the right. Roads would be safer, therefore, if in all countries the rule were the same. Countries where cars keep to the left are in a very small minority. So those countries should change over to the right.

Activity

Give an analysis of this argument that identifies the two conclusions, and shows which is the main one.

 In this argument four reasons can be found, leading to the conclusion that left-of-the-road countries should change to the right:

R1 In a number of countries cars drive on the left.

R2 This can result in accidents involving drivers and pedestrians from other countries who are used to traffic being on the right.

R3 Roads would be safer (therefore) if in all countries the rule was the same.

R4 Countries where cars keep to the left are in a very small minority.

Therefore

C Those countries should change to the right.

But, as you may have noticed, not all these reasons point directly to the conclusion. If you look carefully at R1 you will see that it is not really a reason for concluding C, at least not a *direct* one. Nor is R2 a direct reason for concluding that left-of-the-road countries should change to the right. The direct reasons are R3 and R4. R1 and R2 are there to support R3, so they only indirectly support the final conclusion.

So what we have here is a *preliminary* argument: (R1 & R2) ➔ R3, linking into a second argument (R3 & R4) ➔ C. This means that R3 is both a conclusion (of one argument) and a reason (in the other). We can therefore call it an intermediate conclusion – IC for short.

Put into words, the fact that in some countries cars drive on the left, *and* the claim that this can cause accidents, together lead to the conclusion that roads would be safer if all countries did the same. This, together with the fact that there are many more right-hand countries than left, *then* leads to a final, or main, conclusion that the left-of-the-road countries should change to the right.

Full analysis:

> R1 In a number of countries cars drive on the left.
>
> R2 This can result in accidents involving drivers and pedestrians from other countries who are used to traffic being on the right.
>
> *(therefore)*
>
> IC: R3 Roads would be safer if in all countries the rule was the same.
>
> R4 Countries where cars keep to the left are in a very small minority.
>
> *Therefore*
>
> C Those countries should change to the right.

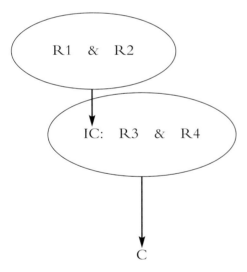

We call a complex argument like this, where one argument links into another, a chain of reasoning. The diagram shows clearly why it is called a 'chain'.

Study this argument carefully and make sure you follow the steps in it. It is important to understand how the conclusion of one argument can also be a reason given in support of a further argument. It is also very important to be able to distinguish between the main conclusion in an argument and any intermediate conclusions reached on the way, especially since this pattern of reasoning is very widely used.

Here is another argument that consists of a chain of reasoning. Analyse it using some of the techniques discussed in the last example. Then look at the suggested analysis that follows.

> [2] We should not rush headlong into large-scale recycling projects without carefully weighing the gains and the losses. Recycling used materials may in the long run prove uneconomical. The cost of collecting up and sorting rubbish, plus the cost of the recycling process itself, often makes the end-product more expensive than manufacturing the same product from raw materials. This extra cost has to be paid by someone: if it is not the consumer, then it is the taxpayer in the form of subsidies. Nor is recycling always the best solution environmentally. The high levels of energy required for processing waste can cause pollution. This can also add to global warming.

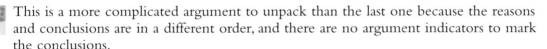

This is a more complicated argument to unpack than the last one because the reasons and conclusions are in a different order, and there are no argument indicators to mark the conclusions.

The main conclusion is the first sentence: 'We should not rush headlong …'. There are two direct reasons for reaching this conclusion. The first is that recycling may be uneconomical. The second is that it may harm the environment. Each of these has its own supporting premises, making each one an intermediate conclusion leading to the main conclusion.

Exactly how you list and label the reasons does not matter, provided that you correctly identify the main conclusion, and observe that there are *two* chains of reasoning leading to it. For example:

> R1 The cost of recycling often makes the end-product more expensive than manufacturing the same product from raw materials.
>
> R2 This extra cost has to be paid by someone: if it is not the consumer, then it is the taxpayer in the form of subsidies.

(therefore)

IC: R3 Recycling used materials may in the long run prove uneconomical.

> R4 The high levels of energy required for processing waste can cause pollution.
>
> R5 This can also add to global warming.

(therefore)

IC: R6 Recycling is not always the best solution environmentally.

Therefore

> C We should not rush headlong into large-scale recycling projects without carefully weighing the gains and the losses.

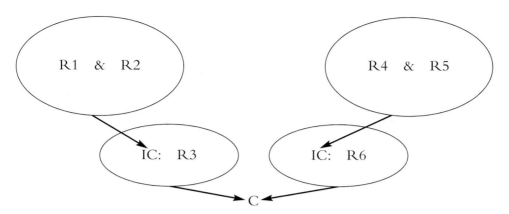

This argument is illustrated in the above diagram. There are two separate lines of reasoning and therefore two arrows leading to the conclusion. If you took away one of the lines, say R4, R5 and R6, you would still have an argument for C. It would not be as strong, because it would present only the economic reasons for not rushing into recycling, not the economic *and* environmental reasons. Similarly, if you took away or disproved the argument leading to R3, you would still have an environmental argument to fall back on.

A useful strategy

You saw in both [1] and [2] that there were direct and indirect reasons. A good strategy for unpacking difficult arguments is this: first select what you think is the main conclusion, then look for the direct reasons that support it. Then look for reasons (if any) that support the *direct* reasons. In other words, work backwards from what you think is the main conclusion. Find:

(first) conclusion ⬅ *(then)* direct reasons ⬅ *(then)* reasons for the reasons

Put them together to see if they make sense as an argument. If not, try again.

Spare parts

Sometimes when you unpack an argument you find there are parts of the text that don't seem to be reasons or conclusions. In fact they don't seem to belong to the argument at all. In some cases there are parts that even appear to oppose it. Here is an example:

> [3] Top women tennis players are unhappy that their prize money is significantly less than that paid to top male players in the same competition. They feel they are being unequally treated. But the difference in prize money is entirely fair. Male players have to win three out of five sets to take the match whereas women only have to win two sets out of three. Also, the men's game is faster and more powerful. They therefore expend far more energy on court than the women. Besides, if the winners of the men's and women's finals were to play each other, the man would always win.

How would you analyse this argument? In particular, what do you make of the first two sentences? Where do they fit in?

The short answer is that the first two sentences *don't* fit in – not to the main argument. In fact they seem to belong more to a *counter-argument* (see Unit 2) than to the argument itself, because they are about the women's case for equal prizes, not the author's case for keeping the men's prize money higher.

Yet, having said that, the argument needs these two sentences in order to make sense. Try reading it without them and you will see this for yourself. What the opening sentences provide is the target for the argument. The whole point and purpose of the argument is to respond to the women's claim of unfairness and inequality. Another way to say this is that the first two sentences put the argument into context. Or you could say that they introduce it, or give the background information for it. Any of these labels would do. So a full analysis would be something like this:

> *Context*
>
> Top women tennis players are unhappy that their prize money is significantly less than that paid to top male players in the same competition.
>
> They feel they are being unfairly treated.
>
> *But ... (main argument)*
>
> R1 Male players have to win three out of five sets to take the match whereas women only have to win two sets out of three.
>
> R2 The men's game is faster and more powerful.
>
> *(therefore)*
>
> IC: R3 The men expend far more energy on court than the women.
>
> R4 If the winners of the men's and women's finals were to play each other, the man would always win.
>
> *Therefore*
>
> C The difference is entirely fair.

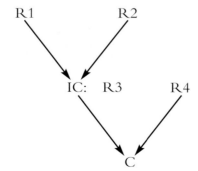

The value of analysis

Thoroughly unpacking an argument is the surest way to get a thorough understanding of it. It also gives you the best chance of responding to it appropriately. When you see its parts laid out for inspection, and the links between them, you can quickly spot strengths, weaknesses, gaps etc., which may not be at all obvious when the argument is wrapped up in ordinary, everyday language.

The kind of detailed analysis you have practised in the last few pages will not always be necessary. Once you become more skilled at it, you will be able to recognise the main conclusion of an argument and see the lines of reasoning which lead to it without listing and labelling all the parts.

Summary

Some arguments have intermediate conclusions that lead on to a main conclusion.

An intermediate conclusion has its own supporting reason(s). It is both a conclusion and a reason for a further conclusion.

Some sections of a text may not be reasons or conclusions: they may just introduce or provide a target for the argument.

End-of-unit assignments

Analyse the following arguments to show their reasons and conclusions, including any intermediate conclusions. Also separate and label any background information, or opposing views which are there as a target for the argument.

1 Recently the operators of a cruise liner were fined $18m for dumping oil and other hazardous waste at sea. This may seem substantial, but in the same year the ship earned profits of $340m. The company could well afford the fine, and dumping saved them the considerable expense of storing and legally disposing of the waste. So emptying their tanks into the ocean was probably a risk worth taking. Nor was it much of a risk. In the last decade only a handful of companies have been fined and every year there are unsuccessful attempts to prosecute. We must give the authorities greater powers and demand that they use them. Otherwise the oceans of the world are in danger of becoming open sewers.

2 The South Pole must once have been much warmer than it is today. Scientists have recently discovered some three-million-year-old leaves preserved there in the ice. Despite their age, they are so undamaged, and preserved in such fine detail, that they could not have been carried there by wind or sea. Therefore, they can only be from trees that once grew there. The leaves belong to a species of beech tree that grows only in warm or temperate regions; and beeches do not evolve quickly enough to adapt to changes in climate.

OCR, Teachers' Support Pack, Critical Thinking, September 2002 (adapted)

Answers and comments are on pages 256–7.

6 Claims

A claim is a sentence that is *supposedly true*. We say 'supposedly true' because it may not be true, but it has to be the kind of sentence that could arguably be true. In other words it must be a sentence about which it makes *sense* to say: 'That's true', or 'I agree with that.'

Therefore, grammatically, claims usually take the form of statements:

(a) Memphis is south of Cairo.
(b) Dinosaurs were cold-blooded.
(c) Top footballers are paid obscenely high wages.

You cannot call a question or command or exclamation 'true' or 'false': it wouldn't make sense. Although other sentence-types are sometimes used to make claims, they succeed only if they are understood as statements.

For example, imagine a couple of tourists driving out of Cairo on their way (they hope) to Memphis. One says:

> [1] That sign read 'North'. Memphis is south. So how can this be the right road?

Grammatically the conclusion of [1] is a question. But it is clear in the context that the speaker is not seeking an answer – which is the usual purpose of a question – but making a statement. She could just as well have said: 'So we must be on the wrong road.' We call questions like this, that do not require an answer, rhetorical questions.

Alternatively, the speaker might have said:

> [2] That sign read 'North'. Memphis is south. So turn round!

Again, although the conclusion is grammatically a command, it implies a statement, a statement *that* the driver should be going the other way. In order to describe [2] as an argument, the conclusion has to be understood this way. Therefore, when you analyse an argument like [1] or [2], it is best to express all the parts, reasons and conclusion, in the form of statements, for example:

That sign read 'North'.

Memphis is south.

Therefore

You should turn round.

Fact or opinion

Claims can be divided roughly into those that state facts and those that express opinions. This is a useful distinction, but it needs some clarification.

A fact is a true statement. Of the three examples given at the start of the unit, the first claim, (a), is clearly a fact. What is more, it is a *known* or an *established* fact. You can check its truth in an atlas. Some people may not be aware of the fact, or even mistakenly think something different; but that doesn't in any way alter the fact. If they say, 'No, it's north', they are wrong, and that's all there is to it.

Activity

But what about the other two claims, (b) and (c)? How would you describe them in terms of truth or falsity?

The statement, that dinosaurs were cold-blooded, *may* be a fact, though if it is it is not a known fact. On the other hand it could just as easily be false. Scientific opinion on the subject is divided, with good reasons for claiming either that the dinosaurs were cold-blooded (like modern reptiles), or that they were warm-blooded (like birds and mammals). The best we can therefore say of this claim is that it is a belief (or judgement or opinion); and unless or until there is more factual evidence available, it will remain so.

This does not mean, however, that this sentence is neither true nor false. For either the dinosaurs were cold-blooded or they weren't. Scientists may never know the truth, but the truth exists and is there to be discovered – even if it has to wait for the invention of a time machine!

The third claim, (c), is *purely* an opinion. Two people can disagree as to whether it is true or not, and neither of them is necessarily wrong. It comes down to what they think or believe to be a reasonable wage, and/or what they think of as 'obscene'. To say that the sentence is true, just means that you agree with it. It can be 'true' in your opinion at the same time as being 'false' in someone else's.

Another way to distinguish this claim from the other two claims is to say that it is purely subjective. That means that its truth is decided by each individual person – or *subject* – who thinks about it. This is in contrast to the first two, which are objective: true or false regardless of what anyone thinks or knows.

Value judgements

Claims, like example (c), that something or someone is good, bad, better, best, nice, nasty, wicked, etc., are also called value judgements, for the obvious reason that they are opinions about the value or worth of things. It is *not* a value judgement to claim that dinosaurs had cold blood. Nor would it be a value judgement to claim that the world's top-ranking footballers are amongst the highest wage-earners in the world (leaving out the word 'obscene'); or that they earn more in a week than some people earn in a lifetime, for this is a matter of fact which can be checked by comparing the earnings of actual people.

It becomes a value judgement when you claim that there is something 'wrong' or 'excessive' or 'obscene' about a top footballer's earnings; or alternatively if you say that it is 'right' for such skilful athletes to get huge rewards. It might be *difficult* to support a claim that such huge pay differentials are 'right'; but in the end it remains a matter of opinion: there are no completely objective grounds for saying that it is 'wrong'.

Predictions

A prediction is a special kind of judgement, made about something that may or may not be true because it is still in the future. For example, someone might claim, at a certain time and place:

> (d) There's going to be a storm in the next 24 hours.

If there is a storm within one day of the sentence being spoken, then you can say, looking back, that the prediction (or forecast) was correct. But you cannot, even with hindsight, say it was a fact when it was made, because at the time of making it, it *was* not yet true or false.

All predictions have some level of uncertainty about them, or else they would be facts and not predictions. However, some predictions are based on such strong scientific or other evidence that it is *beyond reasonable doubt* that they are correct. For example, if an egg is dropped from a considerable height onto a concrete floor, I can say without any fear of being wrong that it will break. Similarly if the above claim, (d), was made by an expert meteorologist, on the basis of weather patterns that had *always* meant storms in the past, then we would have no hesitation in accepting it, even though it is not a *fact*.

Predictions are often found as the conclusions of arguments, when the other claims are facts or pieces of evidence. This is very common in scientific arguments. For example:

If they are dropped from a height, a dart and an empty can will fall at different velocities. One is more aerodynamic than the other.

However, a prediction is not always a conclusion. Sometimes predictions are made in support of other judgements or recommendations.

Recommendations

Look again at the argument on page 28 of the last unit. Its conclusion was:

> Those countries (where cars keep to the left) should change over to the right.

This is an example of a very common form of argument in which reasons are given for suggesting, advising or recommending something, in this case changing from driving on the left to driving on the right. You can ususally recognise the conclusion of such arguments by expressions such as 'should', 'ought to', 'must', and so on.

Look again at the argument on page 28 of the last unit.

Activity

Read the following short argument. What kind of claims are the first sentence and the last sentence; and which is the conclusion?

> All forward-looking governments should resist the urge to cling to traditional farming methods and instead welcome the benefits of genetic modification (GM). No scientific evidence has been found to suggest that GM in any way threatens either the consumer or the environment, whilst on the positive side, it promises to improve food quality, increases yield, and protects harvests from the ravages of pests. It is the technology of the future, and countries that do not take advantage of it will be left far behind.

 The conclusion is the first sentence. It is a recommendation to welcome GM, and it is supported by the three claims that follow: namely that there is no evidence of any threat; that there are positive advantages; and that countries that don't take those advantages will be left behind. *If* these claims are true they obviously make a strong case for the author's conclusion. (Most of the GM debate is about whether the first premise is true or not.)

You may have been tempted to say that the conclusion was the last sentence, but careful analysis will show that this wouldn't make sense. As you should have noticed, the last sentence is a *prediction*. If it is correct, then it is a reason for the recommendation to welcome GM. But the recommendation is not a reason for making or accepting the prediction. If you are in any doubt about this, go back and apply the 'therefore test' between the first and the last sentence. It only works in one direction.

Summary

Claims can be true or false, or they can be judgements.

A fact is a claim that is true.

A prediction is a claim about what will happen.

A recommendation is a judgement about what should or must be done.

A value judgement is a claim about the worth of something – whether it is good, bad, desirable, etc.

End-of-unit assignments

1 What kind of claim is each of the sentences in the three short arguments below? In each one, which sentence is the conclusion?

  (a) Many universities have insufficient income to meet their expenses. The government should introduce a graduate tax to raise more money.

  (b) These shrubs grow best in alkaline soil. Growth rate will increase if you add lime to the soil.

  (c) The election is going to be very close. Polls show both the main parties on equal terms. Everyone who cares about the outcome should turn out and cast their vote.

2 The introduction of postal voting in some parts of the country has been found to increase the number of votes cast, and has therefore been welcomed by politicians worried about poor turn-outs at elections. However, the opportunities for electoral fraud with postal voting are greater than they are under the traditional ballot-box procedure, and fraud does serious damage to public confidence in the democratic process.

  Think of a recommendation and a prediction that might be made on the strength of the above passage.

3 Search in a newspaper or magazine for an example of each of the following:

  (a) a fact

  (b) an opinion

  (c) a value judgement

  (d) a recommendation

  (e) a prediction.

Answers and comments are on page 257.

7 Conclusions

In Units 4 and 5 you learnt a very thorough method for unpacking arguments. In this unit you will be applying this experience to one of the most important skills in critical thinking: identifying conclusions.

Sometimes, if an argument is short and straightforward, the conclusion stares you in the face. With longer and more involved arguments, it can be very easy – as the saying goes – 'to get the wrong end of the stick': to mistake a reason for a conclusion, or an intermediate conclusion for the main one; or to misunderstand the direction of the argument altogether.

We'll start with a very short and simple example:

[1] **You must pack warm clothes. It is cold in Beijing at this time of year.**

Activity

Which is the conclusion of argument [1] – and why?
A You must pack warm clothes.
B It is cold in Beijing at this time of year.

As we said, this is a simple argument, making just two claims. It therefore gives a very clear picture of the relationship between a premise and its conclusion. The conclusion is A, of course. Even though A comes before B in the argument, logically it *follows from* B. It makes no difference which order the sentences are in. If you said, 'It is cold in Beijing at this time of year. You must pack warm clothes', the conclusion would still be A.

When we say that A follows from B we mean that B gives a reason for saying, or accepting, A. The converse does not make sense: A is *not* a reason for saying or accepting B. It makes no sense to say: 'You must pack warm clothes; *therefore* it's cold in Beijing'; but it does make sense to say: 'It is cold in Beijing, *therefore* you must pack warm clothes.'

Longer arguments

The procedure is the same for longer, more complicated arguments. To distinguish reasons from conclusions, or main conclusions from intermediate ones, you still just ask yourself: 'Which follows from which?' or: 'Which makes sense with *therefore* in front of it?'

Look at the next example and answer the multiple-choice question that follows it:

> [2] Parents naturally tend to think that, because they are older and more experienced, they know better than their children. They therefore assume that their judgements and decisions are the right ones. But in many ways children are much wiser than their parents give them credit for. They frequently display problem-solving skills that their parents do not possess; and they are more adventurous in their thinking, if only because they are less afraid of making mistakes. Parents should pay closer attention to what their children have to say, and allow them to make decisions for themselves. Apart from anything else, this would help to relieve many unnecessary family tensions.

Which one of the following best expresses the main conclusion of the argument? (As well as making your selection, give a brief reason why you think it is right, and why you thought the others are wrong.)

A Children are wiser than their parents think and often possess higher problem-solving skills.

B Parents naturally assume that their judgements and decisions are the right ones.

C Children don't mind making mistakes to the extent that their parents generally do.

D Parents should take their children's views more seriously, and allow them to make more of their own decisions.

E A reduction in family tensions would result if parents listened more to what their children think.

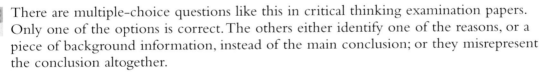 There are multiple-choice questions like this in critical thinking examination papers. Only one of the options is correct. The others either identify one of the reasons, or a piece of background information, instead of the main conclusion; or they misrepresent the conclusion altogether.

Even though you may not have to state your reasons in an exam, you need to *have* reasons for the selection you make: otherwise you are just guessing. So how did you go about answering the question? Did you read the passage, then immediately look through A–E to find the most promising response? If so, you were asking for trouble. This is not a good strategy. Although the incorrect responses are not designed to trick you, they are designed to make you think. They are called *distractors*, and with good reason, for it is very easy to be tempted by an answer because it echoes something in the passage, or simply because it 'sounds right'.

A much safer approach is to ignore the responses initially while you unpack the argument and identify its conclusion yourself; *then* to look for the response that best matches your analysis. That way you are not so much looking for the answer as looking for confirmation of your own answer. If you find a response that matches yours, you will have two good reasons for choosing it, not one.

So, what's the argument here? It starts by claiming that parents tend to think they know best and therefore assume their decisions etc. are the right ones. This is in itself a mini-argument, but it is clearly not the main one. For, like the tennis argument in Unit 5, the opening sentences are followed by the word 'But', signalling the counter-claim or counter-argument to come. What parents think is therefore just the introduction or target for the main argument.

The main argument begins with the claim that children are often wiser than parents think, supported by observations about their problem-solving skills, etc. Then comes the recommendation that parents should pay children more attention and allow them to make more decisions. This also looks a likely conclusion, but does it *follow from* the claim that children are wiser than their parents think, or *support* it?

Clearly it does follow: the passage is not saying (nor would it make much sense to say), 'Parents should pay closer attention to their children. Therefore children are wiser than they give them credit for.'

A full analysis would be:

> *Target*
>
> Parents think they know better than their children … etc. But
>
> > R1 Children often display problem-solving skills their parents don't possess.
> >
> > R2 They are more adventurous in their thinking since they don't mind making mistakes.
> >
> IC: R3 They are wiser than their parents think (from R1 and R2).
> >
> > R4 Paying children more attention etc. would relieve family tension.
>
> *Therefore*
>
> > C Parents should pay children closer attention and let them make more decisions.

Now look at the responses A–E. Which of them, if any, strongly resembles the final conclusion? Obviously it is D: 'Parents should take their children's views more seriously, and allow them to make more of their own decisions.' So we can safely select that one.

What about the other options, the 'distractors'? Even though you may feel confident in your choice, it is sound practice to reassure yourself that none of the others is as good or better – and why.

A is not the main conclusion: it is a combination of two of the reasons, R1 and R3. B looks like a conclusion partly because in the original text, this claim begins with the word 'therefore'. However, on a proper reading of the whole passage it becomes clear that it is only a target for the main argument that follows: this shows how the 'therefore' test is not by itself an infallible one; it can be a useful clue, but it has to be combined with an understanding of the argument as a whole. C is a reason for drawing the intermediate conclusion. It is not supported by any other claims and is not therefore a conclusion. E comes at the end of the argument, which is a natural place for a conclusion. However, it should be clear that it is there to give extra support to the argument, and is not its conclusion.

Eliminating A, B, C and E in this way is a worthwhile exercise to reassure yourself that you have made the right choice. But beware of using it as the *only* way of selecting the correct response. You need to have positive reasons for making your selection as well as negative reasons for rejecting the others.

Summarising the conclusion

Sometimes the conclusion of an argument is repeated, or stated in more than one way, at different points in the argument. For example, look at the next argument:

[3] We are taught from an early age that we should always tell the truth, the whole truth and nothing but the truth. But clearly it is not always wrong to lie and it is not always right to tell the truth. Some people may tell the truth just to cause trouble; others may decide *not* to tell the truth just to save someone else from distress or to protect them from danger. It is the motive a person has for what they say that makes it right or wrong. The simple act of saying what is so, or what is not so, is neither right *nor* wrong.

Activity

Which would you say was the main conclusion here?

A It is a person's motive for what they say that makes it right or wrong, not just whether or not it is true.

B Some people tell the truth for a good reason and others tell an untruth for a bad reason.

C As we grow up we are conditioned to be truthful, not to tell lies.

What makes this a tricky argument to analyse is that the conclusion seems to be spread out, rather than stated in a single sentence or phrase. It is clear enough that the first sentence is the target and the rest of the passage an argument against it.

It contains two reasons for contesting the idea that we should always tell the truth:

R1 Some people tell the truth to cause trouble.

R2 Some people do not tell the truth to save others from distress etc.

But from these reasons follow three closely related claims, out of which it is difficult to decide which is *the* conclusion. Instead of one giving support to another, they all seem to be making roughly the same point, only in slightly different ways.

- It's not always wrong to lie and not always right to tell the truth.
- It's the motive a person has that makes what they say right or wrong.
- The act of saying what is so or what is not so is neither right nor wrong.

In such circumstances you can do one of two things. You can either choose the sentence which you think is the clearest expression of the conclusion. Or you can *summarise* the conclusion that the argument is making. That is what A does so that is the correct answer here. B is a combination of the two reasons. C is the introductory part of the argument that sets up the target.

You might feel that the problem with the last question was that [3] was a badly written argument, because its conclusion was not clearly stated in one straightforward sentence. However, writers do this all the time, as a way of emphasising the point they are making. In analysing such arguments, therefore, you must be ready to summarise conclusions; or, in questions like the last one, to recognise a summary of the conclusion.

Besides, not all arguments are as clearly written as they might be, and part of the skill of critical analysis is recognising the point the author is making, even when the way it is expressed is vague or repetitive.

Summary

Arguments consist of reasons leading to a conclusion.

Sometimes the conclusion is contained in more than one part of the argument, in which case it needs to be summarised in the analysis.

End-of-unit assignments

Consider each of the following arguments, then answer the multiple-choice question which follows. There is only one correct answer to each question.

As well as answering the question, justify your selection by saying why you think it is the right one, and why the others are wrong. This will greatly help you to improve your scores in multiple-choice tests.

1 When cities become congested with traffic, the usual solution is to make a charge for bringing a car into the centre. This works, but it is wrong to do it, because it discriminates in favour of those who can easily afford to pay. The less well-off in society are penalised so that the rich can enjoy the luxury of clear streets. Therefore congestion charges everywhere should be abolished. A system of rationing car use should be introduced instead, allowing each driver into the city just once or twice per week. Then everyone benefits equally.

Which of the following expresses the main conclusion of the argument?

A The usual solution to congestion is charging to drive cars into the city centre.

B It is wrong to charge drivers because it discriminates in favour of the rich.

C Rationing car use should be brought in to replace congestion charges.

D Everyone would benefit from an abolition of congestion charges.

2 Train fares differ enormously, with the most expensive always applying when people have to commute to and from work, and when the trains are most crowded. Some call this a cynical and unfair policy because it exploits the fact that commuters have to travel then and will pay whatever is charged and put up with the over-crowding, because there is no alternative. But it is perfectly fair and necessary to do this. For one thing it is simply market forces at work. For another it is the only way the system can work. During off-peak periods people are travelling from choice and would not travel at all if there were no cheap fares. But the cheap fares would not be economical for the transport companies unless they can be subsidised by high fares at peak times.

Which of the following best expresses the conclusion of the above argument?

A It is fair and necessary to charge commuters the highest fares.

B Charging commuters peak rates is the only system that will work.

C It is cynical and unfair to charge commuters more than other travellers.

D Train companies exploit commuters because they have to travel at peak times.

E Cheap fares would not be economical without the subsidy of peak-time fares.

3 Meat eaters, in defence of their eating habits, often give the excuse that they (and we) do not have the teeth or the stomachs of natural herbivores, and therefore we must be carnivores. This is nonsense. We may not have the digestive equipment to eat raw grasses but nor do we have the teeth and digestion of predators: we are as far removed from the wolf as we are from the horse. Seeds, nuts, berries, leaves and roots are the natural diet of our closest relatives in the animal kingdom.

Which of the following best expresses the main conclusion of this argument?

A It is nonsense to say that we must be carnivores.

B Seeds, nuts, berries, leaves and roots are our natural diet.

C We do not have the teeth or stomachs of predatory animals.

D We are no more like wolves than we are like horses.

E Eating meat is a disgusting habit.

Ucles, October/November 2002, AS Level Thinking skills, Syllabus 8435/1, Q.37 (adapted)

Answers and comments are on pages 257–8.

8 Drawing conclusions: inference

The examples you worked on in the last unit were whole arguments in which conclusions were stated. In the next example there is no conclusion *given*, but there is a fairly obvious conclusion – or inference – that can be drawn from it. An inference is a claim that can be made on the strength of some information or evidence. To infer something means to draw it as a conclusion.

[1] Doctors investigating an outbreak of food poisoning discovered that all the people who were affected had eaten at the Bayside fish restaurant the day before reporting sick. There is a legal obligation on any establishment that may be linked to cases of food-related sickness to close while it is being investigated, and not to open again until it has been given a certificate of fitness from hygiene inspectors.

Activity

Can any of the following claims safely be inferred from the passage above?

A The source of the outbreak of food poisoning was the Bayside fish restaurant.

B Fish was the cause of the outbreak of food poisoning.

C To comply with the law the Bayside must close during the investigation.

 According to the passage we have two facts:

1 All the people who reported sick had recently eaten at the Bayside.
2 Any establishment that may be linked to a case of food poisoning is legally obliged to close until it has passed an inspection.

Fact (1) establishes that there may be a link between the Bayside restaurant and the outbreak. If (2) is correct, it has to follow that by law the Bayside (or any other restaurant that may be linked) must close.

What about the first claim? Can that be inferred, too? No. Though there are reasons for saying that the restaurant must close by law, it cannot be inferred that it had caused the outbreak. If still in doubt, read it again. Note, for example, that we are not told anything about the people who became sick except that they ate at the Bayside. It is possible that there were other links between them: they may have all been one big party or family who had shared other food and drink besides the meal at the restaurant, and *that* had made them sick.

Nor are we told anything about numbers involved. 'All' could mean three or four people, which would not provide a large enough sample to point the finger definitely at the Bayside. What is more, the statistics refer only to those who *reported* sick. There may well have been others who did not report their illness. If there were others, we do not know whether they had eaten at the Bayside or not. So all we really have is suspicion. Suspicion is enough to mean that legally the restaurant has to close during the investigation. It is certainly not enough to infer that it was the source of the outbreak.

Can it be inferred that *fish* was the cause? Again, no. Fish restaurants serve other things besides fish. There is no guarantee that the people who were sick even ate fish. And there are plenty of other possible causes that would need to be ruled out, such as contaminated water or lack of hygiene in the kitchen. Blame cannot safely be laid on fish – or on any other particular type of food or drink – without a lot more information and evidence.

Jumping to conclusions

Often when people read of incidents like the one in this scenario, they 'go too far' in what they infer, given what they know – or rather what they don't know. For example, if it was announced on the news that there had been an outbreak of food poisoning and that the Bayside had to close while there was an investigation, it would be very tempting to conclude that the restaurant was guilty.

It is particularly easy to jump to a conclusion if you carry some prejudice on the matter. Suppose, for example, you had eaten a couple of times at the Bayside, and had not enjoyed the meal. Perhaps one of the waiters had been rude, or the service had been slow. In other words, you had reasons to be critical of the restaurant, but none that had anything to do with sickness. Alternatively, you may hate fish, but your friends all love it, and are always wanting to eat at seafood restaurants. You hear about a few cases of sickness and some link to a well-known fish restaurant. The opportunity is too good to miss, so you 'put two and two together and make five'.

It is very easy to let our own feelings and opinions influence what we conclude, instead of looking coldly at the evidence. With this warning in mind, look now at the next example, and at the multiple-choice question following it:

[2] There is a huge and fast-growing industry arising from compensation claims following even the most minor accidents. With millions of dollars often going to successful claimants, there is an obvious temptation to exaggerate, if not invent, the harm that has been done. There has also been a dramatic increase in law firms advertising for accident victims, and lawyers offering their services on a no-win-no-fee basis, which allows people on low or moderate incomes to go to court with no risk of running up expenses they couldn't otherwise afford. Lawyers earn nothing for unsuccessful claims but take a big percentage when damages are awarded.

Activity

Which of the following is a conclusion that can reliably be drawn from the above?

A Without the no-win-no-fee option, and advertising by law firms, there probably would be fewer accident claims.

B Lawyers encourage clients to exaggerate or invent injuries.

C The no-win-no-fee system benefits the lawyer much more than it does the claimant.

D It is the greed of lawyers, not of their clients, which is responsible for the huge growth in compensation claims.

Although the passage makes some fairly negative noises about the compensation 'industry', it is careful in what it actually claims. And we have to be careful what we infer from what is claimed. It would be easy to be led by feelings rather than by critical analysis.

You cannot, for example, infer from [2] that lawyers are all bad. For example, there are no grounds for saying, as D suggests, that lawyers are any greedier than their clients. And you certainly can't conclude that they encourage their clients to exaggerate or invent, as B does. They may benefit from the increase in claims, but that does not mean that they have necessarily encouraged false claims. It cannot even be inferred that lawyers benefit more than claimants from the no-win-no-fee system (i.e. C). A genuine claimant who could not afford to risk huge legal costs if she loses, is much better off with a no-win-no-fee arrangement.

That leaves A. A would not be a *safe* conclusion if it simply said that advertising and no-win-no-fee had caused the growth in the number of claims. It is the word 'probably' that allows us to infer A. Law firms would not be very likely to advertise if it did *not* bring in more clients. And no-win-no-fee makes it less of a risk for many people to make claims. Therefore it does seem very probable that without these two factors there would be fewer claimants.

So A is the answer. Of the four responses it is the only one that does not claim too much or jump to a conclusion.

Other sources

Printed texts are not the only sources of information from which we can draw conclusions or inferences. Exact figures vary from country to country, but typical figures for a prosperous nation we shall call Bolandia can be seen here, presented in the form of a bar chart and line graph.

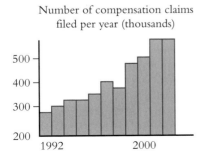

Number of compensation claims filed per year (thousands)

% of law-firms offering 'no-win-no-fee' services

Can either of the following be inferred on the basis of the above data?

X The growth in no-win-no-fee legal services has increased the number of compensation claims.

Y The rising number of compensation claims has encouraged lawyers to offer their services on a no-win-no-fee basis.

We will start with X. X looks like a conclusion you could draw, because it seems very likely that no-win-no-fee arrangements would encourage more people, especially those on lower incomes, to make claims. But we don't know this just from the data given in the bar chart or the graph. It could be that the number of claims was rising *anyway*, and would have risen even with lawyers charging ordinary up-front fees. In fact, it could be the other way around: that the increase in claims has encouraged lawyers to compete for clients by offering risk-free representation. This is what Y suggests, but in fact there is no more reason to infer Y than there was for inferring X. Neither is a reliable conclusion. What they offer are two different ways of explaining the data, but we simply don't know enough to choose between them.

What can be concluded? Only what is actually supported by the data, for example:

Z Compensation claims following accidents have risen in line with the increasing percentage of Bolandian law firms offering no-win-no-fee services.

Cause and correlation

The last example raises a very important point, and it is this. The bar chart and the graph between them show what is called a correlation. All that means is that a pattern can be seen in the data, namely that during the time when one figure was rising the other was rising too. Thus we can say that there is a correlation between the number of compensation claims and the increase in no-win-no-fee cases. But that is *all* we can safely say. In particular we cannot say that one of these is the cause of the other. Just because both are rising doesn't mean there is any causal connection.

Z simply notes the correlation and does not jump to any further, unsupported conclusions. X and Y both infer too much from too little.

This does not mean you can never draw reliable conclusions about causes. Suppose, as well as the bar chart and the graph, you had been given the following data, based on a questionnaire given to a large number of accident victims.

Question	Yes	No	Not sure
Would you seek compensation following your accident if you thought that losing could cost you money in legal fees?	22%	64%	14%
Would you seek compensation following your accident if you knew that losing would cost nothing in legal fees?	59%	18%	23%

Given this *additional* data, could you now draw either X or Y as a safe conclusion?

It should be fairly clear that X can now be inferred with reasonable confidence. What was missing from the bar chart and the graph was any evidence that the rise in claims was *due to* the rise in no-win-no-fee arrangements. But with the questionnaire indicating how prospective claimants feel about legal fees, there is a strong reason to conclude that no-win-no-fee representation has caused the number of claims to rise. There is no similar support for concluding Y.

Summary

It is important to distinguish between drawing a reliable conclusion (or inference) that is supported by the available evidence or information, and *jumping* to a conclusion, which may have insufficient support.

A correlation does not necessarily indicate any causal connection – so beware of inferring one without good reason.

End-of-unit assignments

1 Study the following information and then answer the question that follows:

Measurements were taken showing the growth of 16 fir trees planted at the same time but at different altitudes on a hillside. The results were recorded as shown in the graph.

Which of the following can reliably be concluded from the results shown?

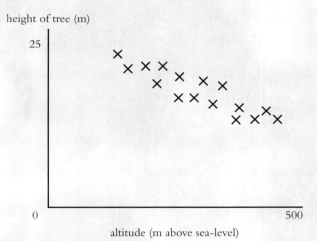

A The higher a tree is planted, the poorer its growth.

B The growth rate of a tree can be accurately predicted from the height at which it is planted.

C The higher up a hillside you go, the poorer the soil.

D The fir trees planted at higher altitudes tended to be shorter.

E Air temperature decreases with altitude, which accounts for the poorer growth rate of trees.

2 In October 333 BC Alexander's Macedonian force confronted the Persian king, Darius III, and his army at Issus. The Macedonians, though more disciplined than the Persians, were hugely outnumbered. Yet, surprisingly, in the desperate encounter that followed, it was Darius's massive force that fled in defeat, leaving Alexander victorious.

Which of the following can reliably be concluded from the above passage?

A   In ancient warfare it was better to have a small, disciplined army than a very large one.

B   Being so heavily outnumbered inspired Alexander's army to fight more fiercely than the Persians.

C   Having such superiority in numbers made the Persian commanders at Issus over-confident.

D   The weapons and tactics used by Alexander's army were more successful than those of the Persians.

E   Having numerical superiority on a battlefield need not always be a decisive advantage.

3 What reliable conclusions can be drawn from a careful examination of the photograph? Discuss not only what can be inferred but also what cannot, and say why.

Answers and comments are on page 258.

9 Assumptions

So far, when we have talked about reasons, they have been explicit reasons, meaning that they are stated in the text. But in many, if not most arguments, there are some claims that are implicit – which means they are not stated. Some of these are as important for the argument as the stated reasons are. We call them assumptions.

Remember the four prisoners who were buried up to their necks in sand and had to work out the colour of their hat–bands? You can remind yourself of the story by turning back to the Introduction.

Sancho's reasoning was as follows:

[1] There are two hat-bands of each colour. Pedro's hat-band is black. If mine was black too, Carlos would have known straight away that his was white and called out by now, but he hasn't said a word. Therefore, my hat-band must be white.

This is not just a good argument, it is a brilliant argument. And it is a lifesaver. Given the facts, and provided Sancho is not mistaken about what he sees and hears (or doesn't hear), the conclusion is almost inescapable. Here is an analysis of the argument:

R1 There are two hat-bands of each colour.

R2 Pedro's hat-band is black.

IC: R3 If mine were black too, Carlos would have known straight away that his was white and called out by now.

R4 Carlos hasn't said a word.

Therefore

C My hat-band must be white.

If [1] is such a good argument, why do we say the conclusion is *almost* inescapable, and not completely so?

The answer is because Sancho is still relying on a number of assumptions. He *knows* that Pedro's hat-band is black because he has the evidence in front of him, and can see it with his own eyes. But he can only *assume* that Carlos can see too. Carlos could have sand in his eyes, or his hat could have slipped forward over his face. In fact, any number of things *could* have happened to stop him seeing, and Sancho just has to trust that they haven't.

Even if he is satisfied that he can see, Sancho also has to assume Carlos is not stupid, or that he hasn't lost his voice (as people sometimes do when they are frightened). These are only *possibilities*, but the fact that they are possible means that certain assumptions have to be made – including the assumptions that Carlos can see, hear and think straight. If any of these is not true, our otherwise brilliant argument is in trouble.

Assumptions that have to be made for an argument to work are sometimes called underlying assumptions, because the argument rests on them just as heavily as it does on its stated reasons. (You could also call them necessary assumptions, or key assumptions.)

With this in mind, look at the next example. It is much shorter than the first:

> [2] I paid for your ticket, so now you owe me $500.

To accept this argument is it necessary to assume that the ticket cost $500?

The answer is 'no'. Not only does it not have to be assumed, it *should* not be assumed (even though it may be true). It is perfectly possible, for instance, that you already owe me $250 and that the ticket cost $250, making a total debt of $500.
It is equally possible that the ticket cost $700, but that *I* had previously owed *you* $200. In either of these circumstances, and in many others besides, the conclusion could logically follow from the reason without assuming that the ticket cost $500.

In these two short arguments you have seen an example of what *has to be* assumed, and another of what *should not* be assumed. We turn now to a longer and more involved argument, of the type you are likely to meet in thinking skills exams.

> [3] In the days before the arrival of the Internet, publishers and booksellers effectively controlled what people read, since very few would-be authors could afford the high financial risks of publishing themselves. The Internet has changed all that. Now anyone can express views publicly, or distribute information, at little or no cost. Those who are fearful of the Internet should therefore stop dwelling on its faults, and acknowledge that its continued growth is, on balance, in the public interest, not against it. For, almost at a stroke, it has given us freedom of information on a scale that could never previously have been imagined.

Quickly analyse the argument so that you are clear about its reasons and conclusion. Then decide which of the following is an underlying assumption:

A There is no reason for anyone to be fearful of the Internet.

B Freedom of information is in the public interest.

C In the past publishers and booksellers told authors what to write.

D The Internet will continue to grow.

E Everyone has the right to express any opinion.

 The first two sentences of the argument are background information: 'In the days before … changed all that.' Then comes the argument which, slightly simplified, is as follows:

> R1 Now anyone can express views publicly or distribute information, at little or no cost.

(therefore)

> IC: R2 The Internet has given us freedom of information on a scale that could never previously have been imagined.

Therefore

> C Those who are fearful of the Internet should … acknowledge that its continued growth is in the public interest.

The step from the intermediate conclusion to the main conclusion works only if we assume that freedom of information is itself in the public interest, since that is the sole reason given for saying that the Internet benefits the public. If it could be shown that on balance freedom of information was *not* in the public interest – i.e. that it did more harm than good – then the argument would be fatally damaged.

Does one of the five options A–E express this assumption? Yes, B does. It states it plainly: 'Freedom of information is in the public interest.' None of the other claims is required for the argument to succeed:

A doesn't have to be assumed: there could be reasons to be wary of the Internet whilst still concluding that *on balance* it was a good thing.

C is not necessary for the argument. We are told that publishers, booksellers etc. may have controlled what was read by deciding to print this or sell that; but that is not the same as telling authors what to write.

D does not have to be assumed either. The argument is about whether the Internet is good for people, not how long it will last. It doesn't really even imply that it will last, though it is plainly the author's *hope* that it will.

E cannot be assumed. It is beyond the scope of the argument, which claims only that the Internet gives people the *ability* to express their own opinions. This does not imply that they have a *right* to express any opinion, as E claims.

Missing premises

Another way to think of an underlying assumption is as a missing premise. It is a premise because it is needed to support the argument. It is missing because, in the author's mind at least, it does not need to be stated.

This does not mean an assumption cannot be questioned. It can be challenged just like any other premise. Not everyone thinks that completely unchecked freedom of information is a good thing, because it permits *anything* to be published, however obscene or subversive it may be. Consider how different the next argument is, and ask yourself what makes it so different:

> [4] The Internet has brought many advantages. It is a wonderful source of knowledge and, used intelligently, it provides for a healthy exchange of views. But history will prove that the Internet is a far greater force for harm than for good. Its great flaw is that the information on it is not, and indeed *cannot* be, regulated. Anyone can access it and anything can be published on it, freely and at little or no cost.

Activity

What is a key assumption underlying this argument?

You were on your own with this question: no multiple-choice prompts to help you. However, it should have been obvious that arguments [3] and [4] rest on completely opposite assumptions. In [3] the author takes it for granted that unregulated freedom of information is a good thing. The author of [4] argues that the Internet will prove more harmful than beneficial, giving as the reason that it cannot be regulated. For the conclusion to follow it *has to be assumed* that unregulated exchange of information is bad.

In some arguments, such as [3] and [4], what is assumed is a matter of opinion. You could easily imagine someone who thought freedom of information was a good thing changing her mind after seeing websites that encourage violence, racism or gross indecency. You could also imagine someone moving the other way and deciding that freedom of information is a basic right that should be protected even if some minority groups abuse it.

But in other cases the assumptions we make are more deep-rooted. Many arguments make assumptions based on strong beliefs, strict laws or shared cultural attitudes that we grow up with and keep for a lifetime. Realising when an argument rests on assumptions we take very much for granted, and do not question, is an important part of critical thinking and intelligent debate.

Read the following passage and identify one or more major assumptions underlying the argument. How might someone oppose this argument?

> [5] After a much-publicised legal battle, Hanne Albrecht watched with satisfaction as a family of travellers was forcibly escorted off the corner of her 1200-hectare estate where they had been living in a caravan for eighteen months. Not before time. It had taken four appeals and cost Hanne $700,000 in legal fees, but justice had prevailed in the end. The travellers claimed they were following a nomadic way of life going back thousands of years, but their way of life shows no respect for private property or the rule of law. They did not seek the landowner's permission, and they did not pay rent. Ms Albrecht therefore has nothing to be ashamed of in prosecuting the trespassers, and the court was right to order their eviction.

The key assumptions in this passage are about property rights. The author clearly assumes that a property owner, like Hanne Albrecht, has right completely on her side to choose who can and cannot stay on her land; and just as clearly assumes that travellers have no comparable rights to live the life they choose if it means infringing property laws. There is also an assumption that trespassing is not only illegal (which in this case is a fact), but wrong (which is a value judgement). Without this assumption it would not follow that Hanne has 'nothing to be ashamed of', or that the court was 'right' to order the eviction.

The fact that the author assumes all this rather than stating it, or offering any argument for it, indicates that he or she simply takes it for granted, and no doubt expects that many if not all readers will do the same. In the culture to which the author belongs there are laws that protect property and punish trespass, and the majority accept such laws because it is in their interests to do so. Laws that prevent travellers from setting up home wherever they like also prevent them from moving into *your* house or setting up camp in your front garden. Consequently, people who own or rent homes of their own tend to accept such laws, even if at times they seem harsh. The author does not see any need to spell all this out or argue for it. It 'goes without saying'.

But that doesn't mean the argument or its assumptions cannot be challenged. Not every social group adopts the same attitudes to private property as the author. There are people who choose to live, or would prefer to live, nomadic lifestyles without permanent homes, who might start from the entirely opposite assumption that *no one* has the right to own a piece of land and keep others from using it, especially a large estate like Hanne Albrecht's. Many people seriously question the assumption that trespass is morally (and not just legally) wrong, or that trespass laws are just laws, or that anyone needs 'permission' to go where they choose. They might say that Hanne showed a complete lack of compassion in prosecuting the family: that she used her money and her power to evict underprivileged people for no obviously good reason other than exercising her legal right. They might say that she has *everything* to be ashamed of, and certainly much more to be ashamed of than the travellers.

How you evaluate and respond to an argument like this depends very much on your own political and cultural viewpoint. But whichever side you take on the issues, you will not have dealt critically with the argument unless you have recognised and questioned the assumptions on which it rests.

Summary

Many arguments depend upon underlying assumptions or missing premises, which are not stated in the text.

Some assumptions reveal deep-rooted beliefs or attitudes.

End-of-unit assignments

1 Class or group activity: take part in a discussion or debate on the question of whether laws on trespass and private property are just or unjust;

or

Write a short argument of your own for or against trespass laws that could be used in such a debate.

2 Raisa will hate this book. For a start it's a documentary, not a novel. But worse still it's about mountain climbing.

Say whether any, or all, of these are assumptions that are needed for the above argument:

A   Raisa hates documentaries.

B   Raisa hates books about mountain climbing.

C   Raisa likes novels.

3 Study the following argument and answer the question.

> Nashida is claiming compensation from her former employers on the grounds that she was forced to leave her job. The employers are saying that they did not actually dismiss Nashida. However, they do admit that they altered the terms and conditions of her job without her agreement. The law allows that, if employees are forced to accept changes in their working conditions that mean they would suffer as a result, and for that reason they choose to leave, then their entitlement to compensation is the same as if they had been dismissed. Therefore Nashida's claim should be upheld.

Which of the following is an underlying assumption of the above argument?

A   Nashida would have suffered as a result of the changes to her job.

B   Nashida had done nothing to deserve dismissal.

C   There was no good reason for the employers to change Nashida's job.

D   Employees must be consulted before changes are made to their job.

E   The employers were probably trying to force Nashida to leave.

OCR, Teachers' Support Pack, Critical Thinking, September 2002 (adapted)

4 'Alcopop' is the name given to a range of drinks that contain alcohol but taste like fruit drinks. Their recent arrival in the shops has been blamed for a recorded rise in alcohol consumption by children and young people, and with good reason. It is common sense that if you make alcohol sweet and fruit-flavoured you are encouraging children to drink it. Therefore its sale should be banned.

Which of the following is a missing premise of the above argument?

A   Alcopops were manufactured specially to appeal to children.

B   Children of an early age do not like the taste of alcohol.

C   Children like the taste of sweet, fruit-flavoured drinks.

D   Alcopops are the only alcoholic drinks that children can afford.

E   Sweet drinks do not appeal as much to adults as to children.

OCR, Teachers' Support Pack, Critical Thinking, September 2002

Answers and comments are on page 258.

10 Sound or unsound?

In this unit we consider what it is to say that an argument is 'sound', or that it is 'unsound'.

Interestingly we use the same language about things like boats or buildings; and about more abstract objects such as ideas, plans or theories. When you describe something as sound what you are saying is that it is safe, reliable and free of faults. You would not call a boat sound if it was full of holes and sank ten minutes after setting off from the shore. You would not call a plan sound if it led to a disaster. And you don't call an argument sound if it leads to a false or dubious conclusion. (A bad argument is often said to be 'full of holes'.)

The soundness of an argument depends on two key factors:

- firstly, the truth or acceptability of the reasons (premises);
- secondly, whether or not the reasons support the conclusion.

Obviously, if we don't accept the reasons that are given, then we cannot trust the conclusion that is drawn from them. But even if we do accept all the reasons as true, we may still find, on careful inspection, that what is inferred from those reasons – the conclusion – simply does not follow.

Here is a very short example to illustrate what is involved in judging the soundness of an argument.

> [1] Many insects have wings and those that do can fly. Birds also have wings, and parrots are birds, so they can fly too.

Activity

Decide for yourself whether this argument is sound or unsound, giving reasons for your evaluation. Take some time over this. It is not as simple as it looks.

We'll begin by analysing the argument. It presents three reasons, followed by the conclusion:

R1 Many insects have wings and those that do can fly.

R2 Birds also have wings.

R3 Parrots are birds.

Therefore

C   Parrots can fly too.

Firstly, there is no problem with the reasons: they are all true. What is more the conclusion is also true – parrots *can* fly – which may have fooled you into thinking that the argument was sound. It isn't. Although the conclusion is true it is not *made true* by the reasons. The fact (R2) that birds have wings doesn't mean all of them can fly, and therefore the fact (R3) that parrots are birds doesn't establish that they can fly either. R1 really adds nothing to the argument, because what is true for insects has no bearing on what is true for birds.

We can see how unsound [1] is if we substitute penguins for parrots, because penguins are birds that cannot fly:

> [2] **Many insects have wings and those that do can fly. Birds also have wings, and penguins are birds, so they can fly too.**

Validity

In [2] the premises are still all true, and the reasoning is the same as in [1], but now the conclusion they lead to is false. Reasoning which sometimes gives us a true conclusion and sometimes a false one, even when the reasons are true, cannot be relied upon. It is like a boat that sometimes floats and sometimes sinks.

We describe such an argument as invalid. A valid argument, by contrast, would be one that *guarantees* that if all the reasons are true the conclusion will *never* be false. In fact, an argument can be valid even if the reasons are false, on the grounds that if they were true then the conclusion would be true as well.

Compare [1] and [2] with the following, even shorter argument:

> [3] **All birds can fly. A penguin is a bird, so of course it can fly.**

Activity

Is this argument sound? Is it valid?

 No, it is not sound, but yes, it is valid. It is valid because *if* all birds could fly then penguins *would* be able to fly because they are birds. It is not a fault with the reasoning that makes this argument unsound, it is simply the fact that the first premise is untrue.

The point to remember is that validity is to do with the form of the argument, not the subject-matter. This is easier to understand if you take out the details and look at the bare argument using letters instead of particular animals. [3] then becomes:

> R1 All As can do B.
>
> R2 *x* is an A.
>
> *Therefore*
>
> C *x* can do B.

You should now be able to see that this argument will *never* give a false conclusion if R1 and R2 are true. That is why we say it is valid.

You can test its validity by substituting different words for A, B and *x*: for example:

R1 All fish can swim.

R2 A shark is a fish.

Therefore

C A shark can swim.

Try some other substitutions yourself. Provided you don't substitute words that make either R1 or R2 untrue, you will always get a true conclusion.

Activity

Here is one more bird-argument to consider. Ask yourself the same two questions: Is it valid? Is it sound?

[4] To fly by itself an animal must have wings. A tortoise has no wings and therefore you will never see a flying tortoise.

 It is both valid and sound. The argument is that wings are necessary for an animal to fly, and therefore without wings no animal can fly. That *has* to mean that you will never see a flying tortoise.

Deductive arguments

Examples [3] and [4] are valid arguments and [4], as you saw, is sound as well. To be more precise we ought to say that these are deductively valid arguments. That is because the idea of validity really just applies to certain types of reasoning called deduction, or deductive argument. Deductive arguments, so long as they are valid, are very strict, rigorous arguments in which the conclusion follows *inescapably* from the reasons. But by the same token, an attempted deduction that is invalid fails completely, so that regardless of the truth of its premises it is unsound. You cannot have a deductive argument that is 'a bit valid' or 'very nearly valid': it's all or nothing.

Here is a centuries-old example that logicians have used to illustrate deductive argument:

[5] All men are mortal. Socrates is a man. Therefore Socrates is mortal.

You may have noticed that it is very similar in form to example [3] above, and it is valid for the same reasons. It is often contrasted with the next argument, which makes all the same claims but is certainly *not* valid:

[6] All men are mortal. Socrates is mortal. Therefore Socrates is a man.

Activity

Why is [6] not valid? What is wrong with it, and how is it different from [5]?

In [5] we are told Socrates is a man and that all men are mortals. That tells us that Socrates is also mortal. In [6] we are again told that all men are mortals but not that all mortals are men. In fact, they are not: women, children, wolves, parrots and so on are also mortal. Therefore the premises in [6] do not themselves establish that the Socrates referred to in the argument is a man. 'Socrates' could just be the name of a parrot.

Here is a more up-to-date example. Suppose someone has inherited a ring with a large stone in it that she correctly believes to be a diamond. A friend – some friend! – offers to have it valued for her. He returns with the surprising news that it is worth only five dollars and he spins her the following argument:

> [7] 'If a stone that large was a real diamond it would be worth several thousand dollars. Yours is only worth five dollars. So it is not a real diamond. Sorry!'

He volunteers to buy it from her for his daughter and, accepting his argument that the stone is not a diamond, she also accepts the offer.

Activity

Is the argument deductively valid? Is it sound?

This argument is valid. Make no mistake about this. What makes it valid is that if its premises *had* both been true, there would have been no escaping the truth of the conclusion. For no large, genuine diamond would have a value of only five dollars, and this ring, according to the friend, has. *If* both claims had been true, then the stone could not have been a diamond.

Of course *we* know that the conclusion is also false. But that doesn't make the argument invalid either. For, as we have seen, the conclusion would have been true – and could not have been false – if all the premises had been true.

What *practical* use is validity in assessing an argument, if we already know the premises are false? Not a lot. We would reject this argument as unsound because it is based on a lie, so it hardly seems to matter whether its conclusion would have been true under other circumstances.

But validity becomes very useful if we don't know the truth or falsity of the premises. To see this, look at the next example. It, too, is about a ring.

Activity

Read the following carefully and decide if you think it is sound or unsound.

[8] No ring with a diamond that size would sell for less than ten thousand dollars. Miranda Marchi's ring fetched fifteen thousand, so it has to be a diamond.

This time we are not told whether the reasons are true or not, but let's suppose they are, for the sake of argument. So we accept that the stone in the ring is big enough to be worth over ten thousand dollars, if it's a diamond; and that the ring really did fetch fifteen thousand dollars. Could these two premises be true and still lead to a false conclusion?

Yes, they could. There are all kinds of circumstances under which the ring could have sold for such a high price without being a diamond. The buyer could have been a fool. Alternatively Miranda Marchi could have been a celebrated film-star, and have worn the ring (with a fake diamond in it) in her best-known film. No one had ever pretended it was real: it just had high value as a collector's piece.

There are numerous plausible scenarios in which the premises could be true and the conclusion false. So the argument is *not* reliable. Unlike the ring in [7], which could *not* have been a real diamond and fetched only five dollars, this stone *could* have been a fake and still sold for thousands. That possibility makes the argument invalid.

A fair assessment of this argument would therefore be: we don't know if the premises are true or not, but we can say that the argument is unsound anyway, because the reasons do not support the conclusion. Even if we later found out that the conclusion was in fact true, and the ring did contain a genuine diamond, the argument would still remain a fraud!

Different standards

The arguments we have been considering in this unit so far have been deductive in character. The standard of validity required for a deductive argument is very strict and unbending, and rightly so because deductive arguments are intended to draw conclusions with absolute certainty. The kind of proofs that logicians and mathematicians use depend on rigid deductive arguments, and nothing less will do.

But by no means all arguments are deductive in character. Nor can they be, and nor do they need to be. Many of the most important conclusions that we reach in our everyday lives require less demanding standards than deductive validity. Yet they can still be very good arguments.

Take the method by which scientists frequently draw conclusions. They observe results that occur repeatedly under certain circumstances and they infer from these that, under similar circumstances, the same result will recur. This is a perfectly rational way to proceed and the conclusions scientists draw on this basis are extremely reliable. But it does not amount to deduction. In fact, to distinguish it from deduction it is technically referred to as *in*ductive reasoning, or *in*duction.

Consider the following weather forecast and the reasons that are used to support it:

[9] Satellite pictures show a cold front moving eastwards across the Canadian coastline with a trough of low pressure along its leading edge. As this heads out to sea it will meet up with a large mass of rotating wind moving in across the Atlantic and strong north-easterly winds sweeping down from the Arctic. Consequently violent storms can be expected to develop in the north Atlantic in the next 24 hours.

Activity

How would you assess the inference made in the last sentence of the above passage? Is this a sound argument?

[9] is an example of inductive reasoning. It takes the weather conditions as they exist at the time and predicts that they will cause violent storms in the north Atlantic. But it is not just guesswork. Weather experts can do this because past experience shows that when conditions like these have occurred previously, violent storms have been the result, and they *assume* that they will have the same result in the future. But of course they don't *know* that the result will be the same this time: there is just a possibility that some *un*predictable development will change everything, however unlikely that may be. That small uncertainty is enough to mean that [9] does not have deductive validity.

So is [9] still a good argument? Yes. In fact it is as good as an argument for a future outcome can be. Also its author recognises that the conclusion is less than certain by adding the small phrase, 'can be expected'. With this addition the conclusion is softened just enough so that it does follow from the available facts. For even if some freak of nature were to occur and prevent the storm, it would still have been right to *expect* it, given the conditions. We can therefore say that this is a sound inductive argument despite its not being deductively valid.

'Beyond reasonable doubt'

An expression that is often used to describe a conclusion that has less than deductive validity, but is still highly probable, is that its truth is beyond reasonable doubt. This is a term that is regularly used in criminal trials to instruct the jury how to reach their verdict. If juries had to be sure beyond any *possible* doubt that a defendant had committed a crime, no criminal would ever be convicted, because in real life there is always some room for doubt, however remote. The standard of proof that is usually required for a conviction is that the defendant's guilt is so likely that it would be unreasonable to doubt it. It is not enough to believe that the defendant is 'probably' guilty, or guilty 'on the balance of probability'. Those are different and less demanding standards.

Nevertheless, these different levels of probability have their place in reasoned argument, and an argument need not be unsound just because its conclusion is less than certain. The important thing to recognise when you are evaluating an argument is what kind of argument you are dealing with, what kind of inference it is making. If it is claiming that a conclusion follows from the reasons with absolute certainty, then you will need to apply the standard of deductive validity. If the claim is only that it is beyond reasonable doubt, or simply very likely, then a less strict test is required.

The topics of reasonable doubt and balance of probability are dealt with in more detail in later units.

A matter of opinion

We will finish this unit with an argument of a different kind again. Read it now and then answer the questions that follow:

[10] More and more countries are passing laws that ban smoking, on health grounds, in public places such as bars and restaurants. Many people object that this contravenes an individual's liberty, because smoking harms only the smoker. Now, however, doctors are increasingly certain that the danger to non-smokers from so-called 'passive smoking' (inhaling other people's smoke) is much greater than once thought, possibly causing thousands of deaths a year. Since a non-smoker's right not to have their health put at risk far outweighs a smoker's right to freedom of choice, a ban on smoking in enclosed public places should be introduced at once.

Activity

How is this argument different from examples [1]–[9]?

Do you think it is a sound argument, or not?

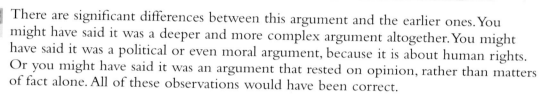

There are significant differences between this argument and the earlier ones. You might have said it was a deeper and more complex argument altogether. You might have said it was a political or even moral argument, because it is about human rights. Or you might have said it was an argument that rested on opinion, rather than matters of fact alone. All of these observations would have been correct.

The last of these differences is probably the one that most affects the way we judge the soundness of the argument. Since one of the claims is an opinion, or value judgement, we cannot say objectively whether it is true or not. It comes down to a question of whether we agree or disagree with it.

But even if we do accept or agree with the reasons, we still have to answer the second question: does the conclusion follow from them? To do this, we first need to unpack the argument so we can see how it reaches its conclusion.

The actual argument is a simple one and is contained in the last two sentences, the first two sentences being the target.

Target

Many object that a smoking ban contravenes personal liberty, because smoking harms only the smoker.

However …

R1 Doctors are increasingly certain of dangers from 'passive smoking'.

R2 The non-smoker's right not to have their health put at risk far outweighs the smoker's right to freedom of choice.

Therefore

C The banning of smoking in enclosed public places should be introduced at once.

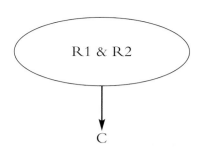

R1 & R2

C

Note that the reasons work together, and depend on each other, to support the conclusion.
Therefore both are needed to secure the conclusion.

With the argument laid bare like this it should be fairly clear that if we do accept the reasons it would be strange not to accept the conclusion. If there is enough medical concern to suggest there is a serious health risk, as R1 claims, *and* the danger does outweigh the right to free choice, then the ban should surely be introduced. You simply could not agree with R1 and R2 and sensibly reject C. To put it another way, accepting R1 and R2 virtually *commits* you to the conclusion.

But of course you are not obliged to accept either R1 or R2. And since they are both needed for the conclusion to stand, you would only have to reject one of them to reject the argument. So let's return to them.

R1 is a factual statement. In order to decide whether or not it is true you could talk to doctors or run a questionnaire to find out if it is true that they are becoming more and more sure that passive smoking is a serious health risk. R2, however, is not the same kind of claim and there is no similar way to establish whether it is 'true' or not. It is an opinion, a value judgement. If someone said: 'I believe there is *nothing* more important than my right of freedom to choose what I do, not even the health of other people', there is not much you could do but disagree. You could call his attitude selfish or inconsiderate, which he could hardly deny. But you couldn't *prove* his claim 'false', as you could if he had given incorrect evidence.

Critical consideration of the argument in [10] should therefore lead you to this evaluation: It is a sound and effective argument *if* we accept the judgement it makes about people's conflicting rights.

Summary

The soundness of an argument depends on two factors: (1) the truth of the reasons and (2) whether or not they adequately support the conclusion.

There are different standards for judging (2), depending on the type of inference being made.

The highest standard for judging (2) is that of deductive validity. But there are other standards of soundness ranging from 'beyond reasonable doubt' down to 'on the balance of probability'. Choosing the right standard is a large part of the skill of evaluation.

1 Are either, neither, or both of these two arguments sound – and why?

    (a) Citrus fruits have a sharp, acidic taste. Lemons taste sharp and acidic. Therefore lemons are citrus fruits.

    (b) Citrus fruits have a sharp, acidic taste. Lemons are citrus fruits. So lemons have a sharp, acidic taste.

2 Comment on the following argument.

A real diamond is so hard it will scratch glass. But when we drew a line on the glass with the stone in your ring it didn't leave any mark at all. Therefore it is not a real diamond.

3 What can you say about the soundness of this argument?

If the president were guilty of corruption, as you say he is, he would be in prison, not on an official state visit to South America. He is not in prison. In fact he is in Chile and is flying on to Argentina tomorrow, and he will not be back until next week. Therefore he is not corrupt.

4 Take part in a group discussion on the issue of a smoking ban in public places, arguing either for or against it.

Answers and comments are on page 259.

11 Finding flaws

As you saw in the last unit, you can find fault with an argument in two different ways. (1) You can disagree with one or more of the reasons. (2) You can show that, whether the reasons are true or not, the conclusion doesn't follow from them anyway. This is particularly useful when we can't decide whether the reasons are true.

Arguments that are unsound for this second reason are said to contain 'reasoning errors', or 'flaws in the reasoning'.

Activity

The following argument is unsound. In what way?

[1] The outstanding success of Amulk's company, which was launched against the advice and without the support of bankers, business consultants and financiers, just goes to show that one person's vision can prove all the experts in the world wrong. Anyone thinking of setting up in business should therefore trust their own judgement, and not be influenced by the advice of others.

 Let's unpack the argument first. The second sentence is the conclusion. The first, much longer sentence is the reasoning given in support of it. However, this long sentence really contains three claims rolled into one, so a full analysis of it would be:

R1 Amulk's company is/was an outstanding success.

R2 It was launched against the advice of bankers ... etc.

(This goes to show that ...)

IC One person's vision can prove all the experts in the world wrong.

Therefore

C Anyone thinking of setting up in business should trust their own judgement, and not be influenced by the advice of others.

Are the reasons true? We'll start with R1 and R2, which are by nature factual, and we'll assume they are true. If they are true then it does seem that the IC is also true, for if Amulk's company really *was* such a success, and the bankers and others all thought it would *not* be, then it seems fair to say one man's success (Amulk's) can prove the experts wrong. It means assuming that the bankers and others are 'experts', but we can let that pass. So we can accept that the first stage of the argument is sound.

But does the main conclusion follow from the intermediate one? This time the answer is, No. Even if everything we are told is true, we cannot conclude from this one single example of success, or from this one misjudgement by the 'experts', that anyone setting up in business should ignore advice. It would be a crazy conclusion to draw, a reckless thing to do. It would be like arguing as follows:

> [2] Beata passed all her exams without doing any work, so anyone taking an exam should stop studying!

Not studying may have worked for Beata, just as ignoring advice worked for Amulk, but that doesn't mean it will work for anyone else – let alone everyone.

Generalising from the particular

It is easy enough to see that [1] and [2] contain a serious flaw in the reasoning, one that makes the conclusion unreliable. It is also easy to see that it is the same kind of flaw in each case, even though the contexts are different. But what exactly is the flaw? How do we identify it?

[1] and [2] are both examples of generalising from a particular case. The particular case in [1] is the success of one company. In [2] it is a single person's exam results. Neither of these is a strong enough reason to support a sweeping generalisation.

Another criticism you could make of both these arguments is that they rely on anecdotal evidence. (An anecdote is a story; so a piece of anecdotal evidence is just one story, and usually just one among many.)

Anecdotal evidence itself can be very useful, as in the next example:

> [3] Three people fell through the ice last winter when they were walking across the lake. You should think twice before you try to cross it.

This is a sound argument, and its conclusion is sound advice. There is nothing wrong with the evidence in this example, even though it is purely anecdotal. The fact of three people falling through the ice last year is a very good reason for *thinking twice* about walking on it now, and it would be irrational not to think twice about it if you value your safety. But compare [3] with the following argument, which uses exactly the same evidence:

> [4] Three people fell through the ice last winter when they were walking across the lake. You should never walk on frozen lakes.

Activity

What is the difference between [3] and [4]?

The difference is that [3] is a sound argument and [4] is not. [4] is flawed, like [1] and [2], and in the same way: its conclusion is too general to draw from one particular piece of (anecdotal) evidence. In the right conditions it is perfectly safe to walk on frozen lakes, and people do it all the time. What happened to the three unfortunate people who fell through the ice was no doubt caused by the conditions being unsafe at that time. But it doesn't mean, as [4] concludes, that they are never safe.

Is it sufficient?

Another way to say what is wrong with [1], [2] and [4] is that in each argument the reason is not sufficient – i.e. *not strong enough* – to support the conclusion. In all three cases the argument goes too far, or claims too much. In [3], by contrast, the conclusion is much more limited in what it claims: it just suggests a bit of caution.

In the next example the story is a bit different. Now we have four separate observations being used as reasons to support the conclusion, not that it is dangerous, but that it is safe to cross the ice.

> [5] People cross this lake every year from November through to March. The ice can be anything up to a metre thick. People drive cars across it. I've even seen bonfires on the ice at New Year and folk sitting round having a party. So there is no risk of anyone ever falling through in the middle of February.

Activity

Assuming the reasons are true, is this argument sound, or does it have a flaw?

This is a classic example of anecdotal evidence being used carelessly. The reasons are insufficient for the conclusion they are being used to support, even if you add all four of the reasons together. The fact that people have done various things on the ice in the past, and come to no harm, does not mean there is never going to be a risk in the future. In fact, if some scientists are right about global warming, what has been observed about frozen lakes up until now will not be very reliable evidence in years to come. On many lakes the ice in February may become thinner and much less safe – just like the reasoning in [5]!

Reasons

Conclusion

A useful analogy for an argument is that of a see-saw, or balance arm, with reasons on one side and the conclusion on the other. If the conclusion is too strong, or claims too much, the reasons may not have sufficient 'weight' to support it. For an argument to be sound the reasons must at least balance the conclusion. In [5] they don't. They are insufficient.

Identifying flaws

It is one thing being able to see that an argument is flawed. It is another being able to say what the flaw is. It is not enough just to say: 'The reasons don't support the conclusion', because that is only the same as saying the argument is flawed.

In this unit you have seen two very common reasoning flaws. One was taking a particular point (e.g. about one person's business experience) and drawing a general conclusion from it (e.g. about how to start up *any* business). Another was using past experience to draw an unwarranted conclusion about the future.

Thus, if you were asked to describe the flaw in [5] you could answer:

A   It assumes that what has been true in the past remains true now, or in the future.

Or, if you wanted to be more specific:

B   It assumes that because people have walked on the ice safely in February in the past, it will always be safe to do so.

Either A or B would be a correct answer if they were options in a multiple-choice question.

But there is another way of identifying an error of reasoning which does not explicitly describe the flaw. Instead it shows it up, or 'exposes' it.

Activity

Which one of the following most effectively exposes the flaw in argument [1] on page 67?

X   Many people may have been put off starting their own businesses because they paid too much attention to the advice of so-called experts.

Y   Business consultants and financiers know far more about setting up in business than the man in the street knows.

Z   Amulk may have been lucky, or the 'experts' who advised him may have had poor judgement on this occasion.

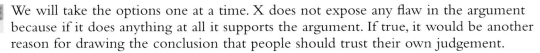

We will take the options one at a time. X does not expose any flaw in the argument because if it does anything at all it supports the argument. If true, it would be another reason for drawing the conclusion that people should trust their own judgement.

Y looks much more of a challenge than X did. But challenging an argument is not the same as showing up its actual flaws. Even if we accept that Y is true, you could still argue that Amulk's experience proved them wrong on this occasion. The flaw is not that Amulk *knew less* than the experts because nowhere in the argument is it claimed that he knew anything at all – only that he was successful. The mistake is in drawing a conclusion about other people's chances of success from Amulk's success alone. So Y does not point to the flaw.

So, it must be Z. But why? The answer is that Z shows why Amulk's success is not a sufficient reason to recommend ignoring expert advice in general. Amulk, Z suggests, may have just been lucky, in which case it was not ignoring the advice that made him successful: it was luck. Alternatively, in Amulk's case, the particular individuals who advised him may have given bad advice, on this particular occasion. But it doesn't follow from that that expert advice would always, or even often, be wrong; or that it should, in general, be ignored. By showing other equally likely explanations for Amulk's success, Z exposes a serious flaw in the reasoning.

Confusing cause with correlation

This is another dangerous error that you have already met up with in Unit 8. Just because two things are both observed to happen, it doesn't mean they are connected. In particular, it doesn't mean that one *caused* the other.

Suppose we learned that our friend, Amulk, was the member of a very exclusive and expensive country club; and that many of the other members of the club were also successful business-people. We could not assume that joining the club had been the cause of Amulk's success, even though it *could* have been a contributory factor (for example by providing useful business contacts). Nor could we assume that he had joined the club *because* he had become successful (for example because all successful business-people in the town were expected to join the club). The mere coincidence of club membership and business success does not mean they are causally related.

Arguments that assume causal connections, without any basis, are very often flawed.

Recognising and avoiding flaws

There are many other common reasoning errors besides those you have seen in this unit. Some have names such as 'slippery slope' or 'restricting the options'. These and other well-known flaws will feature in the coming units and you will learn to recognise them, so that you can reject unsound arguments and avoid making similar errors in your own reasoning.

It is a good idea to keep a notebook of common flaws that you come across. There is a suggestion in end-of-unit assignment 3 on how to start and organise such a notebook.

Summary

An argument is flawed if the reason/s given are not sufficient to support the conclusion.

Some common flaws are:

- arguing from a particular case to a general conclusion;
- relying too heavily on anecdotal evidence, or past experience;
- mistaking a correlation for a cause.

End-of-unit assignments

1 Recent research suggests that, contrary to popular belief, the firms that are making the most money tend to have the least happy workers. Therefore firms that deliberately make their workers unhappy can expect a rise in profits.

   (a) Which of the following, if true, identifies the flaw in the argument above?

A   It assumes workers are unhappy because of their work.

B   It assumes that unhappiness causes a rise in profits.

C   It assumes that workers do not get a share of the high profits.

D   It assumes that successful managers have to be hard on their staff.

Ucles, October/November 2002, AS Level Thinking Skills, Syllabus 8435/1, Q.44 (adapted)

(b) Which of the following circumstances would show that the argument was flawed? (There may be more than one.)

A   It has been found that workers in rich and successful companies become resentful and disgruntled.

B   It has been found that the owners and managers of highly profitable companies stop caring about the welfare of employees.

C   It has been found that companies that try to make their employees happy are not always financially rewarded for their efforts.

2   The famous author, Farrah Lavallier, died at the age of 98, just before finishing the 35th book of her distinguished literary career. Critics were in almost unanimous agreement that it was as sharp and witty as any she had written. Clearly she had all her faculties right up to her last days. She also left a diary that revealed, amongst other things, that she had never done a stroke of physical exercise in her entire life. She was fond of joking that if she walked once round her study, she needed to sit down for a rest. So, if a long and productive life is what you want, you should forget about jogging or pounding round the gym. Save your energy.

Which of the following, if true, *exposes* the flaw in the above argument?

A   Women didn't go to gyms when Farrah was young.

B   Farrah's grandfather lived to 104, and her mother to 106.

C   According to her diaries Farrah had never been seriously ill.

D   Few people are still working in their late nineties.

E   Many writers live physically inactive lives.

3   Start a file, or database, of common reasoning errors by listing the ones you have met in this unit. You could use three headings, or fields:

Name (or brief description): e.g., *Relying on anecdotal evidence*

Explanation: *Using a single occurrence of something and drawing a general conclusion from it.*

Example: *I know someone who fell through the ice at this spot. Therefore it is never safe to cross this lake.*

Whenever you encounter flawed or suspect arguments, add them to the file.

Answers and comments are on page 259.

12 Challenging an argument

Even if an argument does not have an error in its reasoning, you may still want to challenge it, for example with a counter-argument, or by producing some evidence which undermines it. We'll start with an example from the last unit. Here it is again, with a small but important change.

> [1] People cross this lake every year from November through to March. The ice can be anything up to a metre thick. People drive cars across it. I've even seen bonfires on the ice at New Year and folk sitting round having a party. So there shouldn't be much of a risk of falling through the ice today because it is still only February.

Activity

Compare this with the original, flawed argument on page 69. What effect do the changes have? Do you think the argument is still flawed and, if so, why? If not, is there anything you can think of which would challenge or weaken the argument?

The change to the argument may not seem very big, but its effect is considerable. What it has done is to reduce the strength of the claim made in the conclusion. The new conclusion is no longer a sweeping generalisation that there will never be a risk, but a specific claim about risk on a particular day. Also it is a more cautious statement, claiming not that there is *no* risk but that there isn't *much* of a risk, which, arguably, the reasons do support. To use the see-saw analogy again, [1] looks more like the picture here – very different from the picture on page 69.

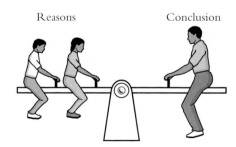

Reasons   Conclusion

[1] is an example of what is called a 'risk assessment'. Because it acknowledges that there is some risk, it is not a fatally flawed argument any more. However, you may still feel that it is questionable whether there is sufficient evidence for concluding that the level of risk is low enough to justify taking it – given the possible consequences.

How would you go about challenging [1] in a way that would weaken it? You can't just say 'There *is* a risk', because that is simply a contradiction of the conclusion, not an argument. What you need is some reason, or reasons, of your own which, if true, would upset the balance.

Suppose for example you knew that the winter in question had been an unusually mild one; or that winters were steadily becoming warmer year by year, as some scientists claim they are. If such evidence could be produced and verified it would certainly cast some doubt on the conclusion. Alternatively, suppose you found records showing that the last New Year party on the ice was thirty years ago; or that there had been one or two cases of people falling through the ice over the years … and so on. Armed with these, or similar counter-claims, you would have good reasons to challenge the conclusion, especially if you knew people were going to act on the advice and walk out on to the lake.

Evaluation

So, what would be your final assessment of [1]? Is it a good, sound argument, or does it have serious weaknesses that can be challenged? Let's begin by analysing it:

R1   People cross this lake every year from November to March.

R2   The ice can be anything up to a metre thick.

R3   People drive cars across it.

R4   Parties and bonfires have been seen on the ice at New Year.

R5   It is still only February.

Therefore

C   There shouldn't be much of a risk of falling through the ice today.

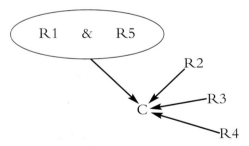

On the face of it the argument looks quite strong, with four separate lines of reasoning all pointing to the conclusion. However, if you look carefully at the reasons you can see that they leave a lot of questions unanswered. Take R1 and R3: 'People cross this lake …' and 'People drive cars across it'. *Which* people? Were they sensible people, daredevil people, local people (with local knowledge)? And how *many* each year? (If only one or two it would not tell us much.) Have any ever fallen through? The mere assertion that 'people do' something doesn't make it safe or sensible.

Then there is R2: 'The ice can be anything up to a metre thick.' But what does that mean? 'Up to a metre' can mean any thickness less than a metre. And even if we knew the actual thickness of the ice, we would still need to know how thick it needs to be in order to be *safe*. Lastly we have R4: 'Parties and bonfires have been seen on the ice at New Year.' Parties and bonfires have been seen on the River Thames in London – once or twice a century. No one in their right mind would take that as a sufficient reason to walk across the Thames if it happened to freeze over tomorrow.

What thorough, critical *evaluation* shows is that the argument is hopelessly vague and imprecise. Even the conclusion itself is vague. It says there is 'not much of a risk'. What does 'not much' mean? One chance in a hundred? One in a million? We would certainly need to know what level of risk the author considers to be 'not much' before we could trust his argument – or the ice.

Though not flawed in the strictest sense, it is safe to say this is a weak and vulnerable argument.

The impact of further evidence or information

A typical question in critical thinking examinations is this: 'Which of the following – if true – would *weaken* such-and-such an argument?' It can be a very penetrating question. It makes us look beyond the stated reasons, and not simply take the argument at face value.

An example of such a question follows the next passage:

> [2] The quest for alternative, renewable sources of energy has led to the development of wind turbines to generate electricity. Many people living close to these turbines complain about the noise they make and see them as spoiling the landscape. But the most obvious objection to them is that in periods of calm weather, they don't generate sufficient electricity. Demand for electricity is so high that we cannot possibly rely on a source of energy that will fluctuate in its production. We need to generate power every day of the week, which is why the construction of wind turbines is a fairly pointless exercise.

Activity

Which of the following, if true, most weakens the argument in the passage above?

A Power generated by wind turbines on a windy day cannot be stored for future use.

B Turbines are sensitive to air movement and are built in exposed places.

C The best solution to energy problems is to reduce demand.

D Wind turbines are a valuable complement to other sources of energy.

 Setting aside the first two sentences as introductory, the bare bones of the argument are as follows:

R1   In periods of calm weather, wind turbines cannot generate sufficient electricity.

R2   We cannot rely on a source of energy that fluctuates.

R3   We need to generate power every day of the week.

Therefore

C   The construction of wind turbines is a fairly pointless exercise.

The chief weakness of this argument is that it assumes wind turbines have to produce a constant supply of energy to be of any use. It overlooks the contribution they can (and evidently do) make by complementing other sources that do not rely on the weather. If D is true, and wind turbines are a valuable addition to the total source of electrical energy, then the conclusion that constructing them is pointless is thrown into serious doubt. D therefore weakens the argument.

What is interesting about this question is that there is nothing obviously wrong with the reasons themselves. They are all self-evidently true: we *do* need power all the time; we *cannot* rely on a source that fluctuates; and wind cannot therefore generate sufficient electricity when there is no wind. It is the gap between these reasons and the conclusion that is the weak point, because of the assumption it forces us into. And the assumption is open to the challenge of D: that wind turbines are a valuable complement to other sources of energy.

What about the other options, A, B and C? It should be obvious that A *strengthens* the argument, because if electricity cannot be stored, the turbines make no contribution during calm weather. B implies that wind turbines make the most of what wind there is, but this doesn't alter the fact that when the weather is calm there is little or no supply. C goes off into another argument altogether. Very probably C is true, but the argument here is about *meeting* the existing high demand for energy, not about reducing it. Therefore B and C neither weaken nor strengthen the argument.

Bringing skills together

You may have noticed that in the last exercise you needed to use two of the skills introduced earlier in the course before you could exercise the new skill of recognising what will weaken an argument. Firstly you needed to establish what the conclusion and supporting reasons were (Units 4–7). But then you also had to see that the argument rested on an assumption (Unit 9), because it was the assumption that option D challenged.

This shows why good analysis is such an essential skill in critical thinking. If you have not properly grasped the structure of an argument you can't really expect to evaluate or respond to it intelligently.

Summary

Even if an argument is sound it can have weaknesses that are open to challenge from new evidence, counter-examples, etc.

The weakness of an argument may be in what it *states*, or in what it *assumes*.

1 Here is an argument you analysed in Unit 5. Re-read it and then answer the question that follows:

> Top women tennis players are unhappy that their prize money is significantly less than that paid to top male players in the same competition. They feel they are being unequally treated. But the difference in prize money is entirely fair. Male players have to win three out of five sets to take the match whereas women only have to win two sets out of three. Also the men's game is faster and more powerful. They therefore expend far more energy on court than the women. Besides, if the winners of the men's and women's finals were to play each other, the man would win.

Which of the following, if true, would most weaken the above argument?

A   Tennis players can earn far more from sponsorship and advertising than they do from prize money.

B   There is no legal obligation to reward male and female players equally.

C   Because of the dominance of power-play in men's tennis, spectators find the women's game more entertaining.

D   If payment to female players were increased, male players would also seek an increase.

E   Paying more to the top players would leave less money for developing the sport at lower levels.

State briefly why you think your selection is the right one.

Ucles, May/June 2001, AS Level Thinking Skills, Syllabus 8435/1, Q.44 (adapted)

2 Although it happens all the time, there is no justification for rejecting a job applicant on the grounds that they are 'over-qualified'. Job shortages and competition often force people to apply for positions for which they have more than the required ability or training. If they need and want such jobs they should not be penalised because they have worked harder and passed more exams than other applicants. Besides, companies are bound to benefit if they fill their vacancies with the most highly trained people available.

Which of the following, if true, most strongly challenges this argument?

A   People should apply for jobs that make the most of their talents and qualifications.

B   Employees who are over-qualified will probably move on as soon as a better opportunity occurs.

C   All applicants have a right to be judged on their ability to do the job.

D   A person who accepts a job for which she is over-qualified will not earn as much as she could by working elsewhere.

State briefly why you think your selection is the right one.

3 It is an extraordinary fact that 200 years ago, when public executions were commonplace across Europe, pickpockets operated amongst the crowds who came to watch. They were evidently undeterred by the horrifying spectacle of the death penalty being carried out for crimes no more serious than their own. Obviously, severe punishment is not an effective deterrent against petty crime.

To what extent, if any, do you think the following comment weakens the above argument?

Pickpockets knew that it was easy to escape detection in dense crowds, especially if there was something very absorbing going on.

Answers and comments are on page 259–60.

13 Lending support

Just as an argument can be challenged and weakened – for example by bringing in new evidence – it can sometimes be strengthened by making supportive claims.

We will return once more to the example about the frozen lake that appeared at the start of the previous unit. Look back to page 74 and remind yourself of the reasons that were given for the conclusion. Although there were four of these, they were not altogether convincing as an argument for taking the risk involved.

Activity

Would any of the following claims, if true, give you any more confidence in the conclusion? In other words would any of them *strengthen* the argument, and if so by how much?

A Last night was the coldest night of the year.

B There is no scientific proof that global warming is taking place.

C Local temperatures have not risen above –10 °C since mid–December.

D No one has fallen through the ice this year.

 Clearly none of these weaken the case. All of them *go along with* the argument; but how much do they actually strengthen the reasoning?

A would be more supportive if we knew that 'the year' in question had been no warmer than other years; but on its own, and without any such background information, this claim does not really add much to the argument. Nor does B. To be told that there is no proof of global warming does not mean that there is **dis**proof either; nor that the current temperature is normal for the time of year. The fourth claim, that no one has fallen through the ice, similarly leaves too many questions unanswered. It may be true only because no one has ventured out on to the ice this year; or because when they did it was colder then than it is now.

The third statement, however, is a different matter. As everyone should know, lake water freezes and stays frozen at temperatures well above –10 °C. So, if it has not been warmer than that for the best part of two months, it is likely that the ice will be thick enough to walk on safely. Provided it is true this claim, along with some very basic general knowledge, really does strengthen the argument.

Choosing the strongest

Look next at the following argument and consider what kind of additional evidence might be used to strengthen the conclusion.

> [1] Many cyclists use masks to protect them from city air pollution. The filters in the masks are effective against most pollutants, but only for approximately 30 days. Therefore all users of such masks, who wish to maintain their health, should replace them regularly.

OCR, Teachers' Support Pack, Critical Thinking, September 2002

Activity

Which of the following, if true, would *most* strengthen the above argument?

A The masks and filters can be produced very cheaply.

B After 30 days' use, chemicals absorbed by the mask result in more inhalation of pollutants than not using a mask at all.

C One of the commonest air pollutants is carbon monoxide, against which a mask is no protection.

D City cyclists are especially at risk from pollution because they inhale deeply in heavy traffic.

The argument in [1] is very straightforward. The recommendation to regularly change masks follows simply from the fact that the masks remain effective for only about 30 days. Loss of effectiveness after 30 days is a good enough reason even by itself. But if after 30 days the masks become positively *harmful*, as B claims they do, then there would obviously be an even more compelling argument.

None of the other three claims adds any serious weight to the argument. A points out that the filters in the masks can be produced very cheaply; but that does not mean they are necessarily cheap to buy. Besides, the argument in [1] really rests on health grounds, not on cost, so even if the cheapness were passed on to the customer, A would not support the conclusion as strongly as B. C gives no support. It might be given as a reason for not bothering with a mask at all, but the argument is not about whether a mask should be used: it is about changing the mask frequently if you do wear one. D *is* a reason for city cyclists, in particular, to use a mask. But, as with C, this is not central to what is being argued. So B is the right answer.

Assessing a response

Sometimes a claim will strongly and decisively support an argument, as with option B in the example above. In fact, if B is true, there would really be no further argument. Changing the mask at least once a month would not only be sensible, but *necessary* – if, as the argument assumes, the user wants to maintain good health.

But supporting claims are not always so conclusive. Look at the next passage and the statement printed below it.

[2] The principal reasons for placing traffic lights at road junctions are to prevent collisions between vehicles approaching the junction from different directions, and to relieve traffic congestion by allowing cars from side roads to cross or turn onto major roads. But it has been discovered that when, for some reason, the lights fail, drivers show more caution and consideration than they do when the signals are working. Surprisingly, there are often fewer collisions during these times. Therefore traffic signals should be removed permanently.

OCR Teachers' Suppport Pack, Critical Thinking, September 2002

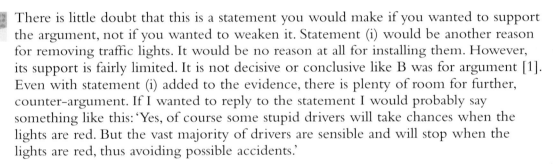

Activity

Statement (i): Drivers often take chances at traffic signals by crossing after the lights have changed to red.

Do you think statement (i) strengthens argument [2], weakens it, or neither? If you think it supports the argument, how strongly would you say it does so?

There is little doubt that this is a statement you would make if you wanted to support the argument, not if you wanted to weaken it. Statement (i) would be another reason for removing traffic lights. It would be no reason at all for installing them. However, its support is fairly limited. It is not decisive or conclusive like B was for argument [1]. Even with statement (i) added to the evidence, there is plenty of room for further, counter-argument. If I wanted to reply to the statement I would probably say something like this: 'Yes, of course some stupid drivers will take chances when the lights are red. But the vast majority of drivers are sensible and will stop when the lights are red, thus avoiding possible accidents.'

Therefore the most you can say about statement (i) is that it gives *some* support. You could not say it wins the argument, or even that it boosts it by very much. To use the see-saw analogy, it tips the balance a little bit, but not enough to outweigh all the possible arguments on the other side.

Activity

Here is another statement made in response to the same argument.

Statement (ii): Traffic signals have, in most cases, been found to cause long queues rather than reduce them.

Where would you place this response on the following scale of assessments?

A Statement (ii) gives strong and effective support to the argument.

B Statement (ii) gives some support to the argument.

C Statement (ii) neither strengthens nor weakens the argument.

D Statement (ii) weakens the argument.

Again there is no doubt which side the statement is on. It is a further reason for drawing the conclusion, not for opposing it. But this time the support is much more effective. In the passage we are told that there are two main reasons for having traffic lights at road junctions: to prevent accidents and to relieve congestion. The argument itself deals with the first of these by claiming that taking lights away would reduce collisions. It doesn't say anything about the congestion issue. But statement (ii) does: it offers evidence that traffic lights cause long queues. If true, it decisively supports the argument. It may not fend off all challenges, but it is certainly strong and effective. So A would be the best answer here.

Before leaving the traffic-light debate, here are three more statements to consider:

> **Statement (iii):** On freeways, with their fast-moving vehicles, there are no traffic signals at all.

> **Statement (iv):** The caution and consideration drivers show during temporary signal failure is not evident at junctions where there are no traffic signals at all.

> **Statement (v):** No signalling system can completely control today's huge and unmanageable volumes of traffic.

Activity

Assess each of these three statements using the same scale A–D.

Statement (iii) may look as though it supports the argument, by implying that the lack of traffic lights is what allows the vehicles to move fast. But freeways are a special case because they don't have crossroads, and therefore traffic lights are not necessary or appropriate. Therefore (iii) is more or less irrelevant to the argument and C is the right answer.

Statement (iv) *weakens* the argument. It does so by challenging the relevance of the main premise, which uses evidence of traffic-light *failure* to support the recommendation to remove the signals altogether. Statement (iv) points out that what is evident during temporary failure is not so evident when there are no lights at all. This does not mean the evidence is untrue: it just means that it does not support the conclusion. The correct answer is D.

Statement (v) neither weakens nor strengthens the argument. The fact that traffic lights, or any other signalling system, are not perfect does not mean that having no lights would be any better – or any worse. So the answer is C.

Summary

Bringing in additional evidence can support an argument as well as weaken it.

1 Wanda is claiming compensation from her former employers on the grounds that she was forced to leave her job. The employers are saying that they did not actually dismiss Wanda, but that she chose to go. However, they do admit that they made 'necessary changes' to her working conditions and moved her to a new branch. The law allows that, if employees are forced to accept changes in their working conditions that make the job significantly less attractive, and that for that reason they leave, then their entitlement to compensation is the same as if they had been dismissed. Therefore Wanda's claim for compensation should be upheld.

Which of the following, if true, would strengthen the above argument?

A   Wanda had, to date, given her employers good service.

B   The new branch is on the opposite side of the city from where Wanda lives.

C   Employees must be consulted before changes are made to their conditions of employment.

D   The employers had no intention of making Wanda leave her job.

2 Read the following argument and the comment that follows:

> General elections will never produce leaders who will make the world a better place. Why? Because in order to succeed in the cut-throat world of electioneering, a candidate must be ruthless and single-minded. These are the very last qualities that the world needs for its rulers and law-makers. Those who have the right qualities, such as humility, thoughtfulness and a willingness to listen, don't get a look in, because vote-winning is so fiercely competitive. A momentary hesitation, generosity to a rival, or a second thought is seized upon as weakness by opponents, and the race is lost.

Statement: Even before the electorate come to vote, the less ambitious candidates have all been eliminated.

If true, does the statement:

A   give strong support to the argument?

B   give some support to the argument (but not much)?

C   neither support nor weaken the argument?

D   slightly weaken the argument?

E   seriously weaken the argument?

Answers and comments are on page 260.

14 Explanation

In this unit you will be turning your attention to a particularly important branch of reasoning: explanation. Begin by looking at these two statements, which, although they are expressed differently, say substantially the same thing.

[1] Seawater is salty. This is because the river water that drains into the oceans flows over rocks and soil. Some of the minerals in the rocks, including salt, dissolve in the water and are carried down to the sea.

[2] The river water that drains into the oceans flows over rocks and soil. Some of the minerals in the rocks, including salt, dissolve in the water and are carried down to the sea. Consequently seawater is salty.

Activity

[1] and [2] are synonymous: they say the same thing. Are they arguments and, if so, what is their conclusion? If you don't think they are arguments, say why not.

They are not arguments. They are explanations, or to be more precise they are the same explanation. Typically, explanations tell us *why* something is as it is, or *how* it has come about. The explanation here consists of two reasons: (R1) that rivers flow over rocks and soil; and (R2) that the rocks and soil contain minerals that dissolve in the water. These two reasons, between them, explain a fact, the saltiness of seawater.

Explanations are similar in appearance to arguments. Like arguments, they involve reasons. They also use similar language, in particular connectives like 'because', 'consequently', 'therefore', 'so'. They even have a similar grammatical structure. But 'seawater is salty' is not a conclusion, and the reasons, R1 and R2, do not support it in the way that premises support a conclusion in an argument. Anyway, no support is needed. The saltiness of water is not an uncertain or disputed claim: it is an accepted *fact*. The reasons are there to tell us *why* it is so, not *that* it is so.

Explanation and cause

By discovering why something happens you are also saying what *causes* it to happen. It is the minerals dissolving in river water, and the rivers running into the sea, that cause the sea to be salty.

Explaining away

Explanations are particularly useful when there is something surprising or puzzling that needs to be 'explained away'; or where there is a discrepancy – i.e. two facts or observations which seem to be at odds with each other.

Here is an observation that may seem to be at odds with the fact that oceans are salty and that the salt is carried there by rivers:

> Rivers *don't* taste salty.

We are told by the scientists that seawater gets its saltiness from the rivers that flow into it. So why can we not detect the salt in the river water? Unless you know the explanation, there appears to be a discrepancy here: if one tastes so strongly of salt, why does the other taste fresh? By analogy, if you poured some water from one cup, A, into another cup B, and you were told B tasted salty as a result, you would expect the water in A to be just as salty, or more so; and you would be puzzled if it wasn't. You would probably infer that the salt hadn't come from the water in A after all.

But the salt in the oceans *does* come from the rivers. Fortunately there is a perfectly good scientific explanation.

Activity

Try giving an explanation for this discrepancy. You may know the scientific reason; or you may have to go and find it out from a reference book or from the Internet. Or you might like to just try guessing.

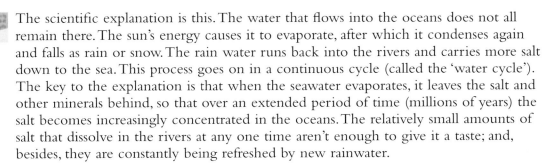

The scientific explanation is this. The water that flows into the oceans does not all remain there. The sun's energy causes it to evaporate, after which it condenses again and falls as rain or snow. The rain water runs back into the rivers and carries more salt down to the sea. This process goes on in a continuous cycle (called the 'water cycle'). The key to the explanation is that when the seawater evaporates, it leaves the salt and other minerals behind, so that over an extended period of time (millions of years) the salt becomes increasingly concentrated in the oceans. The relatively small amounts of salt that dissolve in the rivers at any one time aren't enough to give it a taste; and, besides, they are constantly being refreshed by new rainwater.

The analogy of the two cups is therefore a bad one. It misses out the key factors of evaporation and the large time-scale. To explain why seas are salty and rivers are fresh, you have to include the fact that the process takes a very long time.

Suggesting explanations

So far we have dealt with explanations or causes for which there is good scientific evidence. Scientists can measure the minerals that are dissolved in rivers; they can test rainwater and confirm that it is pure, and so on. But not all facts or happenings can be explained with the same confidence.

Historians, for example, do not just list the things that have happened in the past. Like scientists, they try to work out why they happened, what their *causes* were. For example, you may remember the following passage from the end-of-unit assignment in Unit 8:

In October 333 BC Alexander's Macedonian force confronted the Persian king, Darius III, and his army at Issus. The Macedonians, though more disciplined than the Persians, were hugely outnumbered. Yet, surprisingly, in the desperate encounter that followed, it was Darius's massive force that fled in defeat, leaving Alexander victorious.

This is neither an argument nor an explanation: it is simply a statement of historical fact. However, it is a fact in need of an explanation because it is – as the text says – a surprising fact. Normally, if one side in a battle hugely outnumbers the other, the larger army wins, unless there is some other reason for the outcome. If the larger army does win no one is very surprised, and no explanation is needed. It is only when the result is *unexpected* that we want to know *why*.

With this case, as with many other historical events, we don't know what the explanation was, and probably never will. But we can look at various suggestions and judge whether or not they would provide an adequate and/or a plausible explanation.

Activity

Think of two or three statements that would, if true, adequately explain the outcome of the Battle of Issus.

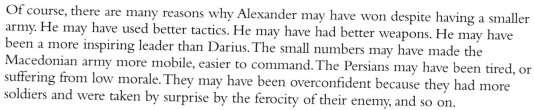

Of course, there are many reasons why Alexander may have won despite having a smaller army. He may have used better tactics. He may have had better weapons. He may have been a more inspiring leader than Darius. The small numbers may have made the Macedonian army more mobile, easier to command. The Persians may have been tired, or suffering from low morale. They may have been overconfident because they had more soldiers and were taken by surprise by the ferocity of their enemy, and so on.

One or more of these could have been sufficient to change the course of the battle from the foregone conclusion most people would have predicted (on the basis of numerical superiority alone). We cannot say which, if any, really was a factor on the day. All we can say is that they are competing hypotheses. But we can say that they are all *plausible*; and that if they were true, they would have explained why the battle went Alexander's way.

Equally, we can say that certain statements would *not* adequately explain the outcome. The fact that Alexander's soldiers were Macedonian is not an adequate reason. It might be adequate if we also knew that Macedonians were particularly skilled or dedicated fighters, but on its own the fact of being Macedonian does not explain their victory. Similarly, if we were told that Alexander became known as 'Alexander the Great', that would not explain his success – though his success might well explain why he was called 'the Great'. Nor would the fact that Darius's soldiers fled when they realised they were beaten be an explanation: it would just be another way of saying that they were defeated, not a reason why.

Don't jump to conclusions

You saw in previous units that some of the worst reasoning errors come from jumping to conclusions, including conclusions about causes. Just because an explanation is plausible it doesn't follow that it is the actual or only cause. If it were a fact that Darius had a huge but poorly trained army, that *might* explain Persian defeat at Issus, but so might any number of other factors. If the same army had met a different enemy, Darius might have won, which would suggest that the cause was as much to do with Macedonian excellence as Persian failings.

Indeed, it might be neither of these: the outcome of the battle may have been determined by a magic spell that Alexander's mother had cast! Although this is not a very serious suggestion, it helps to make the point that plausibility is not the only consideration. We can say that a plausible explanation is more *likely* to be the cause of some event than an implausible one. But that is as much as we can say.

Summary

Arguments should not be confused with explanations.

There may be many possible explanations for an outcome or event, though some are more plausible than others.

End-of-unit assignments

1 The first part of the assignment is based on an unusual scientific experiment involving floating and sinking. Two unopened drink cans, R and D, were placed in a bucket of cold water. Can R contained regular cola, Can D diet cola. Both were expected to sink.

The outcome of the experiment, and some of the relevant data, are given in the following table. (With some well-known brands of cola this actually happens: you can test it yourself.)

Study the information, then answer the questions that follow.

Item	R	D
Description	aluminium can (red), sealed	aluminium can (silver), sealed
Contents	regular cola: 330 ml	diet cola: 330 ml
Ingredients	carbonated water, sugar, colour (caramel), phosphoric acid, flavourings, caffeine	carbonated water, sweeteners (aspartame, acesulfame K), colour (caramel), phosphoric acid, flavourings, caffeine
Outcome	sank	floated

Control: the cans were then emptied and flattened and replaced in the water. Both cans sank.

(a) Summarise the outcome of the experiment, in your own words.

(b) Suggest a plausible explanation for the outcome you described in (a).

(c) Which of the following, if any, can reliably be drawn as a conclusion from the above information?

A   Diet cola is less dense, i.e. lighter by volume, than regular cola.

B   Sugar is heavier by volume than aspartame and acesulfame K.

C   There is more air inside a diet cola can than there is inside a regular cola can.

D   The red paint used on can R makes it heavier than the plain aluminium diet cola can.

(d) Which of the same four statements, if true, could be an explanation for can R sinking and can D floating?

2 Which of the following short passages are arguments, and which are explanations?

A   Icebergs are formed from glaciers breaking off into huge chunks when they reach the sea. The process is known as 'calving'. The glacier is formed from snow, so it consists of fresh-water ice. The oceans consist of brine (salt water), which has a significantly lower freezing point than fresh water. Therefore the sea around icebergs remains in a liquid state.

B   Ice is less dense than liquid water. Consequently, ice forms on the surface of lakes and ponds, instead of sinking to the bottom.

C   In our ordinary everyday lives we use the word 'weight' as if it meant the same as 'mass'. For example, we weigh cooking ingredients in the kitchen to tell us how much to use, not to measure how much downward force they exert on the scales. But in science you have to preserve the distinction. A bag of flour on the surface of the earth has a different weight from the same bag on the moon: here it is approximately six times heavier. And in an orbiting spacecraft we would say it was weight**less**. But in all three locations the amount of matter remains the same, and this constant amount is what is meant by its mass.

Answers and comments are on pages 260.

15 Looking at evidence

When you make a decision, or draw a conclusion, you don't just pull it out of the air. You base it on evidence – or at least that is what you should do if you want it to be a sound conclusion. You collect evidence; you analyse it; you critically evaluate it. *Then* you decide. The stronger the evidence, the more confidence you can have in the conclusion.

The next four units of the book deal with making decisions and drawing conclusions on the strength of evidence.

Weight of evidence

Sometimes the evidence for a conclusion is so overwhelming that no room is left for doubt. The evidence we saw in Unit 1, for claiming that the Earth is round, is so strong that it is regarded by most people as proof. In other words, the evidence is conclusive. It settles the matter, especially now that there is the 'hard' evidence in the form of eye-witness observations and photographs from space showing the Earth's true shape.

Conclusive proof, however, is not always available. As often as not the evidence *for* a decision or conclusion has to be 'weighed' alongside the evidence *against* it; and the conclusion is based not on certainty but on a balance of probabilities. Take the evidence that black holes exist in our galaxy and elsewhere in the universe. It is not as overwhelming as the evidence that the Earth is round. For one thing, cameras cannot photograph a black hole, since it does not send out any light. But plenty of evidence exists from which astronomers *infer* that there are black holes. Gravitational effects have been observed, for example, near to where black holes are thought to exist. This makes for a strong and persuasive argument for the *probable* existence of these invisible but massive objects, even if doesn't amount to proof.

Another question for which there is no conclusive answer is whether the dinosaurs were warm-blooded or cold-blooded. It is not that there is no evidence: the problem is that there is evidence for both sides. For example, both birds and lizards are thought to have evolved from dinosaurs; but birds are warm-blooded and lizards cold-blooded. It is the same with the evidence gleaned from dinosaur fossils: some of it points to characteristics consistent with warm-blooded animals, some with cold-blooded animals. There is a balance, leaving even the experts divided on the issue.

Judging the balance

When we evaluate evidence in order to reach a verdict we have to ask ourselves: 'Does the evidence for a conclusion outweigh the evidence against it? And, if it does, is the imbalance sufficient to convince us one way or the other?' This is the same whether we are evaluating scientific evidence, historical evidence, legal evidence, or just making everyday decisions on the basis of what we know or believe to be true, though obviously the consequences of some decisions are more serious than others.

Activity

What decision would you come to if you were investigating the following incident?

A young woman, Ms Peralta (Ms P), is walking out of a newspaper shop one day carrying a bag, when a store detective, accompanied by a police officer, catches up with her and accuses her of shoplifting. The detective says, 'I was standing behind Ms P and saw her take something from a shelf and slip it quickly into her bag, then later leave the shop without paying.' The policeman takes the bag and opens it. He confirms that inside are some groceries and a glossy magazine, which the store detective claims is the stolen item. The shopper denies the charge. She says she bought the magazine earlier, in the general store where she got the groceries, and it was already in the bag when she went into the newspaper shop.

What *evidence* is there, in this short account, for concluding either that the shopper stole the magazine or that she did not? Look at it critically and draw what conclusions you can.

The main facts of the case are the magazine found in the bag and the fact that Ms Peralta left the shop without paying. Other than that we have only the statements of the two witnesses, Ms P and the store detective; and of these one is the accused, the other is the accuser. It's one person's word against another's. (Note that we call a person a 'witness' even if he or she is directly involved in the case or dispute.)

Circumstantial evidence

It is useful when handling evidence to distinguish between circumstantial evidence, and evidence in the form of statements made by witnesses. Circumstantial evidence consists of facts, or circumstances. Here, as we have seen, the main piece of circumstantial evidence is the fact that there is a magazine in Ms P's bag and the fact that she had been in the shop and left without paying for anything. We can call these factual matters because they are not in dispute.

But what do they tell us? Nothing much beyond the facts themselves. They give Ms P some explaining to do, but they do not come close to proving that she stole the magazine. For a start, Ms P has a perfectly natural explanation for how the magazine came to be in her bag, and there is no more reason to accept her explanation than there is to reject it.

On its own the circumstantial evidence in this scenario is weak. What is missing is hard, or concrete, factual evidence to back up the detective's claim that Ms P committed a theft. If, for example, the newspaper shop had been equipped with a surveillance camera that had recorded the incident, or if the magazine had had an electronic tag on it that had activated an alarm, Ms P's position would look a lot less comfortable. On the other side, if she, Ms P, had been able to produce a receipt from the general store showing that she had bought goods there, including a magazine, that would have been hard evidence to support her story. But unfortunately no such hard evidence exists.

Credibility

What about the witnesses' statements? Is one any more credible than the other, given that the facts on their own don't really get us very far?

Credibility comes down to a number of issues. There is the credibility of the witness herself: for example, how trustworthy she is, or how likely it is that she is telling the truth. And there is the credibility of the actual statement: how likely or plausible it is; how well it fits in with the circumstances, or with other witnesses' statements.

Activity

If you have not already done so, consider (or better still discuss) how credible you think the two opposing witnesses and their statements are.

We have already noted that Ms P's defence is perfectly believable. People do buy things in one shop and then go into another that sells the same item; and they do look round shops and leave without buying anything. There is nothing unusual or implausible about Ms P's story, though that in itself does not make it true. But nor is there anything implausible about the detective's accusation. Sadly, people do steal from shops, for one reason or another, and it is because of that that many shops employ store detectives. The detective would not be there if no one ever took things from the shelves and left without paying for them.

So what about the witnesses themselves? How reliable are they? We'll start with the detective. It is reasonable to assume that a store detective would normally be a reliable witness. You also have to ask why a person in her position would bother to make up the story if it wasn't true. There would be nothing obvious to gain from lying; and arguably a lot to lose. As a professional security officer it would reflect badly on her if she were found to have falsified evidence.

Of course, there is no such puzzle about Ms P's story, since she is accused of shoplifting. If she did steal the magazine, she has a very obvious motive to lie. The natural reaction to her story is: 'She would say that, wouldn't she!' But we cannot infer that someone is lying simply because she *may* have a motive to do so. And we can't assume she did steal the magazine, because that is what we are trying to find out. In the end there is no more reason to suppose Ms P is lying than that she is innocent and telling the truth.

The other possibility, of course, is that one or other of them is mistaken. This time it is more unlikely to be Ms P. She would hardly have failed to notice whether she put something in her own bag or not! But in the case of the detective there are any number of factors that could have affected her ability to see exactly what went on. The shop may have been crowded; the view may have been obstructed. We know, from the detective's own statement, that she was *behind* the shopper. This alone would have made it hard for her to see exactly what she was doing, because presumably her movements and her facial expressions were hidden.

This leads us to the most dubious part of the detective's evidence: her use of the words 'slip' and 'quickly'. Could the witness really be so precise, not just about the fact that Ms P put the magazine in the bag, but the manner in which she did it, when, as stated, Ms P had her back to her? If correct, it is a very important part of the evidence, because it would imply that the suspect was doing something underhand. But is it not also very judgemental on the store detective's part? Can we be sure she is really presenting facts here, or is she making an assumption?

Possibly the detective saw very little, but acted purely on suspicion. We cannot even be sure that she knew what was in the bag before the police officer opened it and the magazine was discovered. She merely said in her statement that Ms P took 'something'. The very fact that she is so definite about the incriminating way the shopper 'slipped' something off the shelf, yet so unspecific about what it was, has to throw some doubt on the reliability of the account. How much did she really see, and how much did she *think* she saw?

Reasonable doubt

Because of the lack of 'hard' evidence, the case against Ms P would be very unlikely to convince a judge or jury that she was guilty beyond reasonable doubt. That is the usual standard of proof required to find someone guilty in a criminal court. But the fact that there are insufficient grounds to prove Ms P guilty does not mean she did *not* steal the magazine. Nor does it even mean that on the balance of probabilities, Ms P did not steal the magazine. On the balance of probabilities we can't say whether she stole it or not.

What we can say is that it is possible that Ms P bought the magazine elsewhere. We can also say that it is possible that the detective was mistaken. We can even say that it is possible, though less likely, that the detective was deliberately lying. It is because of these possibilities that there is reasonable doubt about Ms P's guilt.

But in raising doubts like this, you have to be satisfied that they are reasonable. Ms P would escape conviction in this case because her own story is a plausible one. Had she protested instead that she didn't know how the magazine got into her bag, but that someone must have put it there when she had her back turned, her defence would have been a lot less credible, because things like that don't normally happen. Why *would* they?

Corroboration

Corroboration means agreement. It plays an extremely important part in evaluating evidence. If two pieces of evidence both point to the same conclusion, their weight can be added together. This can greatly strengthen an argument. For example, if two or more witnesses both tell the same story, or stories that point to the same conclusion, the likelihood of the story being true is greatly increased.

Had Ms P been backed up by a shop assistant in the store where she claimed she had bought the magazine, this would have corroborated her story. So would a witness who claimed to have seen her reading the magazine in a café before going to the second shop.

Obviously, when taking corroboration into account it is important to be sure that the witnesses concerned are neutral. If one turns out to be a close friend of the other, this casts doubt on their evidence. They may just be acting out of loyalty. It is also important that a witness can be seen to have come up with the story independently, without, for instance, having heard it from someone else.

Summary

In this unit we have run through some of the main issues surrounding evidence. We have compared circumstantial evidence with witness statements, discussed credibility, plausibility and reasonable doubt; and the strengthening effect of corroboration.

End-of-unit assignment

Imagine an investigation that turns on whether a certain person, whom we'll call Mr White, visited another person, Mr Green, one Saturday afternoon. Mr Green is accusing Mr White of coming to his house and assaulting him. A witness, Mrs Short, who lives in the flat below Mr Green, says that she saw a man answering White's description arriving by car at the house on that Saturday. Later, when she went out to the shop, she noticed the car again, and thought she saw a parking ticket on the windscreen.

White says he was nowhere near Green's house, and produces a second witness – a restaurant owner – who testifies that White was in his restaurant on the Saturday in question, and that he stayed there all afternoon; and that his car – a white Peugeot – was in the restaurant car park the whole time. White and the restaurant owner are old friends and business partners.

On the Sunday evening a third witness, Mr Long, who lives opposite Green but doesn't know him or White or the restaurant owner, comes forward and states that he had seen a white Peugeot parked outside his (Long's) house the previous day. He couldn't be sure of the time. The Sunday papers had printed the story of White's arrest, with a recent photograph of him getting out of the same white car at a friend's wedding.

1 How strong is the evidence provided by Mrs Short? Does it count as corroboration for Mr Green's accusation?

2 How reliable is the restaurant owner as a witness?

3 What problems are there with Mr Long's evidence?

4 Where would you look for further evidence if you were investigating this case?

Answers and comments are on page 261.

16 More about evidence

We continue our exploration of the topic of evidence by considering the following scenario:

A visiting politician was greeted by a large student demonstration. As the politician was stepping out of his car a raw egg thrown from the midst of the crowd struck him on the side of the head and broke, followed by a second egg, which landed on the car. A 20-year-old sociology student, Arun Vithlani, was arrested soon afterwards. He had been standing in the part of the crowd from which the eggs were thrown.

He was carrying a shopping bag containing, amongst other provisions, an egg box with four eggs in it. The box was of the kind that has six compartments. Two of the compartments were empty. The police photographed the eggs in the carton and the egg fragments on the car. After examining the broken shells by the politician's car it was found that they were the same size and colour as the four in the carton. They even had the same trademark stencilled on the shells. The student was arrested and taken into custody for questioning.

Activity

What kind of evidence is the above? How strong is this evidence and what conclusion, if any, can be drawn from it?

Would you say Arun was:

A Guilty – beyond reasonable doubt?

B Guilty – on the balance of probability?

C Not guilty?

This evidence is entirely of the kind we call circumstantial. However, as circumstantial evidence goes, it looks fairly damaging for Arun. Like Ms Peralta in the previous unit, he has some explaining to do, but in his case the evidence is more heavily stacked against him.

What makes the evidence stronger in Arun's case is that there is an accumulation of evidence. There are several different pieces of evidence, and they corroborate each other: the number of eggs thrown, the colour of the shells, the matching trademarks, Arun's position in the crowd. They all add up, and they all point towards the same obvious conclusion.

Even so, circumstantial evidence is rarely completely conclusive. It may shift the balance of probabilities very much in one direction, but not enough to remove all reasonable doubt, even in this seemingly convincing scenario. There is still no cast-iron *proof* that the eggs that were thrown were from the box found in Arun's bag. Nor is there any proof that he threw them. All that can be said is that two eggs were thrown and that there were two empty compartments in the egg box, and that the shells matched. These are circumstances that are highly consistent with the accusation that Arun threw the eggs, but they are far from being sufficient for anything approaching certainty.

B is the safest answer.

Arun's defence

When he was questioned, Arun stated that he lived in lodgings with three other students and it was his turn to shop. He had bought four eggs so they could have one each. He had bought the eggs loose in the nearby market and taken his own carton to put them in, because that was the cheapest way to do it.

Activity

Is this a plausible story (or is it far-fetched)? Does it clear Arun? Where would you go for further evidence to help settle the case?

It is a *plausible* story. There should be little disagreement about that. Anyone who has been a student or knows students would confirm that they are always looking for ways to make their money go a bit further, and if eggs can be got more cheaply by taking a container and buying them loose, then students will do it. What is more, if there are only four students in the lodgings, then it makes perfect sense to buy four eggs instead of a full box of six: otherwise there would be two left over between four.

This does not prove Arun not guilty, but it goes some way towards tipping the balance back in his favour. However, there is still the problem for him that the eggs he had in his bag matched the broken ones photographed at the scene. So, if you were investigating this case, especially if you were hoping to defend Arun, where would you turn next for further evidence?

There are many routes that could be taken. Perhaps the most obvious would be to ask Arun where the eggs came from. It might also be worth checking if there really were four students in the flat. Let us suppose these lines of enquiry were followed up, and that they uncovered the following two new items of evidence:

Item C: Statement from a stall-holder in the market: 'Most of the students buy their eggs loose, and they always want the cheapest. I give them a discount if they bring their own containers, because it saves me the trouble. I've sold hundreds of eggs that way today.'

On her stall the cheapest eggs were the ones with the brand-name found on Arun's eggs; and it was the same on many of the other market stalls.

Item D: Responses from two of the students from Arun's lodgings, questioned separately whilst Arun was still in custody:

Question: Whose turn was it to cook today? Answer: Arun's.
Question: Do you know where Arun is? Answer: Gone to the market.

Activity

What impact does the above evidence have on the argument that Arun is guilty of throwing eggs at the politician?

Does it alter the conclusion you drew earlier?

All of a sudden, the circumstantial evidence looks very weak. It fits just as well with Arun's statement as it does with the charge made against him. What always has to be remembered with circumstantial evidence is that if it can be explained away, and the explanation is not far-fetched, no safe conclusion can be drawn from it. An evaluation of the evidence in this case would not be nearly strong enough to justify a conviction because any number of students, or others, could have bought the same brand of eggs. Arun is no longer in a special position, but is one of many potential suspects. All we are really left with is the claim that Arun was standing near to where the eggs came from; but that, on its own, is not strong evidence.

Postscript

Given the evidence available at the time, Arun Vithlani was released without any charge being made.

Unfortunately for him, he was also filmed by a television crew. The film, on which he could be seen hurling the first of two eggs at the car and shouting insults at the top of his voice, was watched by millions on the 9 o'clock news. Vithlani was immediately rearrested.

First- or second-hand

You should have noticed that the stall-holder's statement in the last example was printed in speech marks. This is to denote that these were her actual words, and that we are getting them 'first-hand', rather than reported and/or interpreted by someone else. If a witness's evidence is not first-hand, there is always the possibility that it has been exaggerated, or bits have been added or left out. For that reason second- or third-hand evidence is generally less trustworthy than first-hand accounts; and often in courts of law only first-hand evidence from witnesses is admissible.

In this next scenario the principal of a college is investigating allegations that one of the students, Corinne Blake, has been cheating. Several claims have been made; all are denied by Corinne:

A Corinne copied an essay straight off the Internet.
B She took notes with her into an exam.
C She asked a postgraduate student to do a piece of coursework for her in return for payment.

The evidence in front of the principal also consists of three items, all of them letters:

(a) a letter posted to the principal from another student. In it she says that she heard Corinne telling a friend that she had taken an article off the Internet and handed it in to her tutor; and that Corinne and the friend were having a good laugh about it.

(b) a letter from a different student saying that she sat behind Corinne in an exam and watched her unfold a page of notes and read it under the desk before answering each of the questions.

(c) a note intercepted by a tutor, saying: 'Dear Corinne – I can't believe you are asking me to write your essay for you for money. It shows what kind of friend you are. As far as I am concerned, our friendship is over. Don't bother to reply.' The signature and handwriting are those of the postgraduate student named in the third allegation.

Activity

Rank these three items according to the weight you would give them, and give reasons for your evaluations.

The first of the items should be ranked as the weakest. It is a form of evidence often referred to as *hearsay*. Had the student who wrote the letter said she had *seen* Corinne download the article, that would have been a different matter. It would have been a first-hand, eye-witness account. However, the report of an overheard conversation, even if it faithfully repeated what was said, would not be reliable evidence that Corinne had actually copied the article or handed it in. She could have been joking or showing off, both of which might make her look silly, but they are not the same as cheating. Besides, who is to say that such a report *does* give an accurate account of what was said?

The second and third items are obviously more reliable. The letter about the exam counts as a direct eye-witness account. If it is true, it gives considerable weight to allegation B. However, we know nothing about the student who made the allegation: what relationship, if any, she may have had with Corinne. If it turns out she had a motive to get Corinne into trouble, her evidence could not be taken very seriously. If, on the other hand, she barely knew Corinne, and had rarely come into contact with her, then the evidence would count for more because there would be no plausible reason for it to be untrue.

The note sent to Corinne is perhaps the most serious evidence against her, because it is written and signed by the person whom Corinne allegedly asked to do her coursework for her. Weight is added by the fact that the note was intercepted, presumably by accident, and was therefore not meant to be an accusation. It is possible that the postgraduate student allowed it to fall into the tutor's hands out of malice, perhaps because she had had an argument with Corinne; but this is beginning to sound a bit far-fetched. Nevertheless it would be relevant to know the circumstances under which the tutor came by the letter before ruling out the possibility that it was an act of spite.

None of the evidence is entirely conclusive by itself, though together the three items add up to a strong case against Corinne, especially if it were known that the witnesses had not been in contact with each other. It would be an unlikely coincidence if she were *wrongly* accused of three such acts of dishonesty, unless there were some kind of conspiracy against her.

Credentials

Rightly or wrongly, we sometimes take a witness's status, qualifications, respectability, etc. into account when evaluating evidence. Had the witness who reported seeing Corinne use notes in the exam been the official invigilator instead of another student, we would probably be inclined to place more weight on the evidence. This is not because invigilators are necessarily more honest than students, or any more accurate in their observations. It is because they hold responsible positions and are expected to be trustworthy and reliable. In general, too, an invigilator would be expected to be *neutral*, whereas another student may have some personal involvement that could influence her one way or the other.

Expertise, too, is often a factor when assessing evidence. To illustrate this point, we will look at one more piece of evidence (d) that could have been presented in the investigation of Corinne Blake's alleged dishonesty. Imagine that because of the complaints made against Corinne an educational psychologist was brought in to talk to her after the exam. The psychologist's report included the following statement:

> (d) 'Miss Blake seemed agitated and anxious. Her mannerisms and body language were consistent with the behaviour of someone who has something to hide. When asked to repeat the answers she had given to some of the questions in the exam she gave a number of incoherent responses which suggested to me that she had less knowledge of the subject-matter than her written answers might have indicated. I do not believe she could have given those answers without external help of some sort.'

How much weight should be placed on this statement? How damaging is it to Corinne's case?

There is no doubt that if the educational psychologist is right in her assessment, then it looks bad for Corinne. Firstly it is said that she appears nervous, etc.; secondly that she seems to have something to hide; thirdly that she seems unable to provide the answers that she gave in the exam, lending support to the claim that she had cheated. This is persuasive evidence, and anyone reading it would be bound to be influenced by it, particularly because it is offered by a qualified person who presumably has experience of similar cases.

But if we look critically at the extract *itself* it is hard to find anything more than impressions and opinions. Look at the second sentence: 'Her mannerisms and body language were consistent with the behaviour of someone who has something to hide.' Although the language sounds impersonal and objective, all it is really saying is that Corinne seemed, to the psychologist, to have something to hide. Similarly, the crucial claim about her responses to the questions merely 'suggested to me that she had less knowledge of the subject-matter than her written answers might have indicated'. The passage is heavy on opinion, and light on fact. Yet because it is the opinion of an acknowledged expert, it looks very convincing.

So a witness's credentials – their titles, jobs, interests, qualifications etc. – are often presented as a form of evidence, or used to imply that a judgement should be taken more seriously than it would be if it had been made by someone with no such credentials. Similarly, people's status and/or respectability are sometimes offered as evidence that they are more reliable as witnesses.

Such claims are not always unjustified. Experts *do* tend to know more about their specialist subjects than the general public, and this must be taken into consideration. People in responsible jobs *do* tend to be more reliable than criminals or drop-outs, even if the only reason for this is that they value their reputations and don't want to damage them by being accused of dishonesty.

However, we cannot place too much weight on these factors. The truth is that people in all positions are capable of making mistakes, or of lying if they have reason to. And people in lesser positions can have high standards of honesty and good judgement.

Summary

Circumstantial evidence is rarely conclusive by itself.

The most reliable evidence from witnesses is a first-hand or eye-witness account. Hearsay evidence is not as reliable.

A witness's qualification or reputation are important, but do not guarantee that their evidence is reliable.

1 Read the following and then answer the question below:

Three young tourists have been accused of deliberately smashing the glass door of a café, during a sudden thunderstorm, after an argument with a waiter. One of the tourists claims that he ran into the door because it was hidden by a bead curtain, and he couldn't see that it was closed. He blames the café for his injuries.

The owner of the café, Emilio, gave a statement to the police. In his statement, he said that he had been upstairs at the time and had run down when he heard the noise. He stated that his waiter had told him there had been 'a big argument' over the bill. Emilio said: 'They appeared at the door, kicking it and punching it until it smashed.' Asked if the door was shut, Emilio said: 'Yes, there was a storm.' Asked if the curtain had been taken down, he replied: 'Of course.' The waiter was not available for questioning. Emilio is demanding payment from the tourists for the damage to his door.

How much weight can be given to Emilio's statement?

2 *Either:* Search through a newspaper or magazine and find an article that presents evidence of something that is *alleged* to have happened. It doesn't have to be a crime: it could be anything that someone is reputed to have done – good or bad – but about which there may be some doubt.

List the evidence and decide for yourself whether it establishes the truth about the matter being reported.

Or: Invent a scenario of your own. Give an outline only of the known facts and describe some of the evidence an investigator might find useful in deciding what had really happened.

Answers and comments are on page 262.

17 Case study: who's telling the truth?

The diagram is a plan of the Management Suite on the first floor of a firm's premises. Some money, in a brown envelope, has gone missing from the safe, and an investigation is under way.

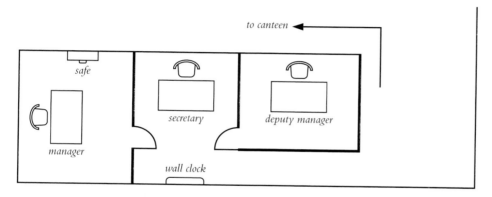

General facts

Three people are employed in the Management Suite:

- the manager (Mrs Mann)
- the deputy manager (Mr Depp)
- the secretary (Rita)

Only the manager knows the safe combination.

Secretary's evidence

'I took the manager her morning coffee at 9.30. I noticed the safe was open and the brown package was visible inside it. I took her the mail at 10.00 and it was still open.

Immediately after that the manager left her office and went straight along the corridor. She was away about 20 minutes. Mr Depp, the deputy manager, came out of his own office and visited the manager's office twice that morning: once at about 9.45 and again while the manager was away − I couldn't say the exact time.'

Manager's evidence

'I was away from the office for about twenty minutes. I didn't lock the safe. I quite often don't lock it in the daytime, and nothing has ever gone missing before. I am fairly certain the deputy manager's door was open and his office was empty when I left, and it was still empty when I returned. It was when I got back that I realised the money was missing.'

Deputy manager's evidence

'I went into the manager's office only once, and she was there at her desk. At around 10 o'clock I went to the canteen because there was a driver who had a problem to discuss – an argument he had had with another worker. It took over half an hour to sort out.'

Driver's evidence

'I was with Mr Depp in the canteen from around ten. We talked for quite a long time. I didn't notice how long. We were sorting out a personal problem.'

> ### Activity
>
> Following on from the discussions in the last two units, assess the evidence given above. Use it to ask yourself who, if anyone, is not telling the truth.

 What we have here is two conflicting stories. The secretary, Rita, claims that the deputy manager went into the manager's office twice, once while she was in there and once after she had left. The deputy manager, Mr Depp, confirms that he went into her office the first time, but denies the second. He claims that during the time he was alleged to have entered the manager's office, he was in the canteen talking to a driver. At some time during all this, some money went missing from the wall safe. The secretary's statement, if true, casts considerable suspicion on Depp.

We will start by considering the witnesses themselves. The three occupants of the Management Suite are the manager, the deputy manager and a secretary. The driver is also a witness. Their ranking in the company is probably in that order. So does this mean we should rank the reliability of their evidence in the same way: the manager's more than the deputy's, the deputy's more than the secretary's, the driver's least of all?

In a word, no. In some cases there may be more reason to trust a manager's judgement more highly than a junior employee's, on the grounds of their respective qualifications and experience. But we are not talking about *judgement* here, only about honesty and accuracy. You may argue that a manager has more to lose than a secretary. But it would be quite unjustified to assume that *therefore* the secretary is more likely to be dishonest. It would be even more unjustified to assume that the secretary was less likely to be *accurate* in her statement. If you looked carefully at the evidence you will have seen that it is the secretary who is the most exact in the information she gives, the manager the most vague and imprecise. And it should not be overlooked that the manager left the safe unlocked, suggesting some absent-mindedness or carelessness on her part.

What about the statements themselves: are they equally *plausible*? On the face of it, yes. There is nothing improbable about Depp going into the manager's office, or about him going to talk to the driver. They are both normal, unsurprising events in a typical office day, and there is no obvious reason to believe one rather than the other. It is only because they conflict that we would question them at all. But since they do conflict, we have to question them.

Corroboration

Where Depp's statement scores over Rita's is that it gets some measure of corroboration both from the driver and from the manager herself. Rita has no witnesses or circumstances to corroborate her counter-claim. However, the corroborating evidence is not 100% solid. The manager says that she is 'fairly certain' the deputy manager's door was open and his office was empty when she left.

The driver, too, gives rather vague estimates: 'I was with Mr Depp … around ten. We talked for quite a long time.' Conceivably, by this reckoning, the meeting could have ended in time for Depp to go back to his offices before Mrs Mann returned. So, although the corroboration of two other witnesses adds to the probability that Depp is telling the truth, it does not by any means remove all doubt about his version of events.

Suppositional reasoning: 'What if … ?'

So far it looks very much like a case of one person's word against another's, much like that of Ms Peralta and the store detective. But there is a way forward. It involves a very useful technique known as suppositional reasoning. Suppositional reasoning typically starts with phrases such as 'Supposing …' or 'What if … ?'.

For example, suppose that the secretary is right: that Depp did go into the manager's office while she was away, which was also during the period when the money went missing. What would follow from this? It would mean, of course, that Depp had an opportunity to take the money. It would also mean that he was lying when he said he was away from the offices throughout the manager's absence, unless he had mysteriously forgotten where he had been that morning. And it is hard to understand why he would lie unless he had something to hide. But would he really have walked into the manager's office, taken the money and walked out again with the secretary sitting at her desk, then simply denied it in the hope that he would be believed and not her?

If the secretary is right it also means that the manager wrongly thought the deputy's office was empty when she passed it on two occasions; and that the driver's statement is questionable. In other words, we would have to disbelieve *three* people's statements, in order to believe the secretary's statement. For them all to be wrong would be quite a coincidence. For them all to be lying would require some mysterious explanation.

So although the secretary's story seems credible enough in itself, when we subject it to this kind of critical examination, it turns out to have some unlikely consequences. A consequence is something that follows from something else. If we find that a certain claim, or version of events, would have puzzling consequences, that must throw some doubt on the claim.

What if we accept the deputy manager's account? First of all it is consistent with what two other witnesses are saying, and that has to be in Depp's favour, even if their statements are a bit vague and uncertain. But, of course, it means that Rita is lying. It also means that Rita was alone in the Management Suite for about twenty minutes when the money went missing. She therefore would have had a much better opportunity than Depp to steal and hide the money with no one around to see her. If she did steal the money, she also had a motive for trying to pin the blame on someone else.

If you compare the two suppositions, Depp's story has much more believable consequences than Rita's. This does not put it beyond reasonable doubt that the secretary is a thief and a liar, but it does make her story harder to swallow.

Suppose the deputy manager planned the theft with the driver. He waited for the manager to leave her office, walked in there as the secretary reported, took the money and later slipped out to give it to the driver and tell him to say they had been in the canteen all the time. So that the manager would think he was not in his office he left the door open and hid behind it as she passed. Is this all *possible*? Yes, it's possible. But it is unlikely. For a start, how would Depp know when the manager was going to leave? This, added to the fact that the secretary would see him, makes such a possibility too remote to take very seriously.

On balance of probabilities, it seems that the secretary's version of events is altogether less credible than Depp's. And that is the most rational conclusion.

Summary

If two accounts conflict, it is often a good strategy to consider what consequences each one has. If the consequences are hard to believe, or don't sit well with other facts, then there has to be doubt about the account itself.

End-of-unit assignment

Write a short, reasoned argument for charging one or more of the following with theft:

- the manager
- the deputy manager
- the secretary
- the driver.

18 Case study: collision course

Two drivers – Ed Farr and Ray Crowe – collided and spun off the track in heavy rain in the last race of the Supa-Cars season earlier today. Neither driver was injured, but the incident put both cars out of the race, leaving Crowe as the World Champion for the second year running. Before the race there was just one point between the two drivers. If Farr had finished the race ahead of Crowe, he would have moved into first place and taken the title.

Farr's team manager reacted furiously by claiming that Crowe had deliberately swerved and forced their driver off the track as he tried to overtake on a notorious S-bend known as The Slide. 'It was no surprise, either,' she added. 'With Ed out of the race, Crowe knew he had won the championship. Of course he meant to do it.'

A television camera team filmed Crowe walking away from his wrecked car. He appears to be smiling as he removes his helmet. He says to reporters: 'I hope you're not all going to blame this on me. I just "held my line", and that is completely within the rules.' Later he added: 'It was all Ed's fault. He could have killed us both. It was a crazy place to try to overtake. He has only himself to blame.'

Ed Farr, not surprisingly, told a different story: 'There was plenty of room to get past if Crowe had held his line. He waited till I came level, then drove into me.' Today's race winner Waleed Akram, who was just behind the two cars at the time, commented: 'That's motor racing. Ray had earned his one point lead, and he was just defending it. If it had been the other way round, Ed would probably have done the same. Everyone was expecting something like this to happen.' Asked if he had seen Crowe swerve, he said: 'Maybe not a "swerve" exactly, but he could have avoided the crash. Anyway, it stands to reason that he would take Ed out of the race if he got the chance. It's not the first time he's done something like that.'

Overhead cameras recorded the positions of the cars just before, and just as, they made contact. This is shown in the pictures.

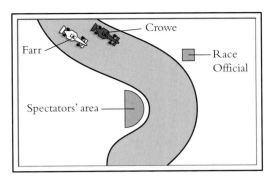

- 'Holding your line' means staying on your chosen course, not swerving or cutting across another driver.
- The rules of the sport state that the driver who is in front is allowed to choose his line and hold it, but not intentionally to cause a collision.
- S-bend: a double bend in a road or track, shaped like the letter S.

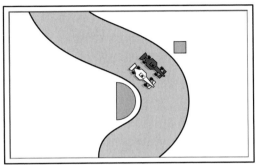

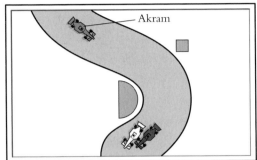

A race official, stationed on the bend, reported: 'There was a lot of spray as the cars rounded the bend. Farr tried to cut through on the inside. He was almost past when the two cars touched. They both spun and ended up on the verge opposite. It is hard to tell, but to me it just looked like an accident.'

Journalist Gudrun Brecht added to the controversy by reporting that she had been at a party two days before the race and that she had heard Crowe openly boasting that he would 'do anything necessary to win the championship'. She wrote: 'I know Crowe well, and he makes no secret of his determination to win, whatever it takes.'

Crowe was involved in two similar controversies last season, but on both occasions he was cleared of any blame.

After the race an inquiry was called for into allegations that Ray Crowe had *intentionally* collided with his opponent's car.

Activity

What is the team manager's argument for blaming Crowe for the incident?
How strong is her statement as evidence against Crowe?

The manager's argument is based on what she sees as Crowe's motive. She is pointing out a *fact* when she says that with Ed out of the race Crowe would win the championship. But she infers too much from it. Besides, she is probably biased and sounds angry. As Ed Farr's manager she has a vested interest in the outcome of the race. We say someone has a vested interest in an outcome if they are likely to benefit, financially or otherwise, if the decision goes one way rather than the other. Crowe, Farr and the manager all have an obvious vested interest in the outcome of this case. The other witnesses may or may not; but there is no reason to think they have.

We don't know if the manager actually witnessed the incident first-hand, but even if she did, it would be very hard to say that one of the drivers had acted intentionally. She uses the tell-tale phrase 'of course' to show that she is *assuming* there was intention on Crowe's part because it would be to his advantage.

On its own this is not strong evidence. The fact that someone stands to gain from some act or other does not mean he or she will commit that act. However, taken together with other evidence, motive does add *some* weight to the argument. Let's put it this way: if he didn't have a motive, there would be much less reason to think Crowe caused the crash deliberately.

Activity

How reliable is Akram as a witness? Consider what he has to say in the light of other information and evidence available. What impact should his statement have on the outcome of the inquiry?

Akram claims to be an eye-witness. However, given what the race official says, and taking into account his (Akram's) position on the track when the collision occurred, it is doubtful whether he could have seen very much. Like Farr's manager, Akram bases his assessment of what happened partly on Crowe's motives, but also on his past record. He says, 'It stands to reason' that Crowe did it on purpose.

Unfortunately, it doesn't really stand to reason at all. Akram is unable to say that Crowe actively 'swerved', yet he is prepared to say he allowed the crash to happen. As a professional racing driver, we can give Akram credit for having the expertise to make such a claim: he would know better than most people if an accident could have been avoided or not. But that is not to say that Crowe let it happen *intentionally*. It could just have been carelessness that caused it, or poor visibility. Akram is not really in a position to make such a judgement objectively.

Activity

How seriously can you take the evidence provided by Gudrun Brecht?

This evidence cannot be taken very seriously at all. It is a classic case of *hearsay* evidence: she 'heard him' boasting that he would do anything necessary to win. We don't have any means of knowing if these were his exact words, or if they were a journalist's colourful way of presenting them. Besides, even if they were his exact words, they don't really tell us how far Crowe was prepared to go. Maybe he meant he would try as hard as he could, but would draw the line at risking his life and the lives of others just to get the title.

Also, Gudrun claims, 'I know Crowe well.' She doesn't say whether she likes or dislikes him, but from the statement she makes it is more likely that it is **dis**like. If she were fond of him, she would hardly imply so strongly that he was prepared to cheat. This makes her a less reliable witness, since she may have a biased view. As sports-page gossip, what she says is of some interest, but it ought not to count for much as evidence of guilt in an official inquiry.

Can you draw any conclusions from Ray Crowe's behaviour, and his comments, as the camera team filmed him walking away from the crash site?

Crowe's actual denial counts for very little, for obvious reasons. If he had collided with Farr in order to win the championship, naturally he would deny that it was intentional. It could also be said that he was very quick to deny it, doing so even before he had been asked about it. On the other hand he may have expected a hostile reaction from the media, whether he was guilty or not, especially given his apparent reputation.

The smile he appears to have as he takes off his helmet may be a smile of satisfaction, or of relief. It may even be a sarcastic smile, at seeing the cameras and the television crew appear so quickly. Smiles and other facial expressions are often seized on by the media, and conclusions drawn, but it would be wrong to interpret Crowe's apparent smile as a sign of guilt.

As for his own defence, which takes the form of a pre-emptive attack on Farr, there may be some justification for what he says. We do not have a great deal to go on other than the three aerial shots of the incident. These are the focus of the next question.

Activity

What evidence can be found in the aerial pictures to support either of the two sides involved in the dispute?

Unlike almost all the evidence supplied by witnesses, the photographs at least constitute facts. The saying 'the camera never lies' is often challenged because nowadays almost anyone can fake or 'doctor' a photograph. But it is still true that the camera *itself* doesn't lie: it is what is done with the photographs afterwards that can create deception. Anyway, we will assume these pictures are genuine.

One way to approach this question is to draw on the picture the line you think Crowe would have chosen through the S-bend. Usually racing drivers like to steer straight through bends by the shortest route, but if other cars are in their way, they have to go wide to get round them. Remembering what the rules are, do you think Crowe does keep strictly to his natural line, or does he steer over into Farr as he comes level and cause the collision?

Read again what the two drivers had to say, and what the race official saw, and on the strength of the pictures, decide whose story is more believable. There is no right or wrong answer to this: you have to draw your own conclusions – and support them with the evidence as you find it.

Summary

Pictures, and actions, can often speak louder (or more reliably) than words. That is the main lesson of this unit. Most of the witnesses involved in the story were expressing no more than their opinions, and probably biased opinions at that.

End-of-unit assignment

On the basis of the evidence, can it be concluded that Ray Crowe intentionally collided with Farr? Give a short, reasoned argument to support your answer.

19 Introducing longer arguments

We return now to arguments, but to longer and more elaborate arguments than you have been working on so far. 'Real' arguments, that you find in newspapers, magazines, on the Internet, etc., are rarely as neat and tidy, or as short, as the examples presented in the earlier units. They may have several strands of reasoning, not just one; they may contain quite a lot of background information; they may come to the conclusion in a roundabout way rather than coming straight to the point. They may introduce counter-arguments in order to reply to them. And, of course, they may make assumptions, commit reasoning errors, and so on.

Learning to recognise and respond to these various features of argument, in a longer and more complex argument, is the objective for this unit.

Activity

Read the passage below and note its main conclusion. It is followed by a number of questions that bring you into close critical contact with the article.

Thrill of the chase

In crowded cities across the country there has been a growing number of crashes as a result of police officers pursuing stolen cars. Tragically, many of these high-speed chases end in death, not just of the car thieves but also of innocent bystanders or other road users. The police should be prohibited from carrying out these car chases. If someone dies as a result of police activity and the fatal weapon is a gun, there is rightly a huge outcry. But if it is a car, that seems to be accepted as an unavoidable accident.

The police say that they are not putting the public at unnecessary risk, because their policy is to stop the chase when the speed becomes too high for safety. This merely emphasises the stupidity of carrying out the chases. Either the policy is adhered to, and the car thieves escape, or the policy is ignored, and injuries or deaths result. Not only is it obvious that this policy is ineffective – otherwise the crashes would not have happened – but it is also easy to understand why.

The police officers will find the chase exciting, since it is a break from routine, and gives them the chance to feel that they really are hunting criminals. Once the adrenaline is flowing, their judgement as to whether their speed is safe will become unreliable. Car chases can be huge fun for all the participants.

Moreover, those police officers who are trusted to undertake car chases are the most experienced drivers who have had special training in driving safely at high speed. The car thieves, however, are almost all young men with very little driving experience. By the time the police driver judges that his speed is unsafe, he will have pushed the pursued driver well beyond his limit of competence.

The police may say that if they were not allowed to chase car thieves, this would encourage more people to commit more of these crimes. Would it be so terrible if this did happen? Surely saving lives is more important than preventing thefts of cars, and the police would be more profitably employed trying to catch serious criminals, rather than bored and disadvantaged young men who steal cars for excitement. In any case, there are other ways of stopping stolen cars. For example, a certain device has been developed which can be thrown onto the road surface in front of the stolen car in order to bring it safely to a halt. And sometimes the chases are unsuccessful – the car thief succeeds in evading the police, abandons the car, and escapes.

The conclusion is in the first paragraph, and you should have had no problem identifying it: 'The police should be prohibited from carrying out these car chases.' The two sentences before the conclusion are introductory and explanatory. The two sentences that follow it form the beginning of the argument, and we will return to them shortly.

Activity

Identify three or four of the main reasons which the passage offers to support the conclusion that car chases should be banned.

You could have chosen any or all of the following as the main reasons offered in support of the conclusion:

- Car chases have led to deaths of car thieves and innocent bystanders.
- The police drivers' judgements as to whether their speed is safe will become unreliable.
- By the time the police driver judges that his speed is unsafe, he will have pushed the pursued driver well beyond his limit of competence.
- Saving lives is more important than preventing thefts of cars.
- The police would be more profitably employed trying to catch serious criminals.
- There are other (safe) ways of stopping stolen cars.
- Sometimes the car chases are unsuccessful.

Note that these reasons have simply been extracted from the passage. A list like this doesn't show how the argument is structured, or how the reasons are grouped together to form sub-arguments within the whole argument.

Nor does the list show all the claims that are made in the passage. For example, it doesn't include the claim that car chases can be fun (paragraph 3). This is because it is not one of the *main* reasons. Yes, it contributes to the argument by helping to explain why police drivers may drive too fast for safety, namely because they enjoy it. But by itself it does not provide any grounds for believing that car chases should be banned. We would therefore classify the claim about car chases being fun as an *indirect* reason, leading to an intermediate conclusion, rather than directly to the main conclusion.

Similarly, the last half-sentence, after the dash, explains in what sense car chases are sometimes unsuccessful. And it is the claim that they are sometimes unsuccessful (as well as dangerous and time-wasting) which is a *main* premise here, and therefore makes it into the list.

Finally, of course, there are some claims that are not reasons at all, or conclusions, but have other functions in the passage. The first sentence of paragraph 2 is a good example. It offers no support at all for the conclusion, either directly or indirectly. Its role is to *set up* an objection that an opponent – in this case the police – might wish to make. The objection is that they, the police, have a policy, which is to stop the chase if it becomes too fast for safety, and that therefore they are not putting the public at unnecessary risk. The author claims that the policy is both ineffective and stupid, and devotes the middle three paragraphs of the passage to supporting these claims. The next pair of questions focuses on this section of the argument.

What grounds does the author have for saying that the police policy 'emphasises the stupidity' of car chases?

What two explanations does the passage offer as to why the policy is 'ineffective'?

The author uses quite an ingenious piece of reasoning to criticise the policy. She considers the possible outcomes. Firstly, she considers what will happen if the policy is observed ('adhered to') by the police. Then she considers what will happen if it is ignored. If it is observed, says the author, the thieves will get away, presumably because the police will have to give up before the thieves do. If it is ignored, then accidents will continue to happen, just as they have happened in the past. And since they have happened in the past, it is obvious that the policy does not work as it is claimed to.

The question asked you to identify the *explanations* that are offered for the policy's failure to work. There are two of these. The first is that police officers find the chase exciting, and that this affects their judgements about safety. The second is that whereas the police driver is likely to be competent to drive safely at high speed, the pursued driver has little driving experience, so that the officer will overestimate what is a safe speed for the car thief.

She concludes that the policy not only *is* ineffective, but that it is 'easy to understand why'.

How successful is this reasoning? (This was not part of the question you were asked, but it is part of the next one.) Like all arguments, its success depends not just on what is stated but also on what is assumed, and whether the assumptions that the argument rests on are warranted assumptions.

Activity

Are there any *assumptions* that are not stated in the passage but that the author appears to be making in connection with the claims made in paragraph 2?

Yes, there are. The most significant assumption is that it is not possible for the police officer to catch the thieves without driving too fast for safety. She claims that if the policy is adhered to, the thieves will get away; and if it isn't, accidents will result. In so doing she overlooks a third possibility: that some police drivers may be sufficiently skilled to remain within safety limits *and* to keep up with some of the thieves. She paints it as a so-called 'no-win situation', but is it? Without some statistical evidence it is hard to know what grounds the author has for predicting that the policy will inevitably fail one way or the other.

There is another assumption, too, although it is a lot less obvious. It is that if the stolen car were not being pursued, its driver would not drive unsafely anyway. The author wants to persuade the reader that there is no overall benefit to the public from chasing car thieves, only increased danger. That implies that the danger to the public comes only, or mainly, when car thieves are pursued. If they were left to drive around the streets unpursued, can we be sure there would not be just as many accidents – or even more, if would-be thieves get the idea they won't be chased and arrested? Again, the author is making a prediction on the basis of no hard evidence. Her prediction may be right: the policy may prove ineffective. But it doesn't follow from the reasons she gives unless she makes these two major, and questionable, assumptions.

'Restricting the options'

What we have exposed in the above discussion is a very common reasoning error. It is sometimes called 'restricting the options', because it consists in claiming or implying that there are fewer possibilities to consider than there really are. This is easier to understand by seeing an example of an argument that commits this error:

> [1] When you go into business you can either adopt ethical practices or you can make a profit. *Herbco* has declared itself to be an ethical company, so if you want to see good returns, you really need to invest your money somewhere else.

On the face of it this looks like sound advice, given the two premises. If it really is true that you have to choose between ethics and profit – and it often is – then surely it is not a very good plan to invest money in an ethical company if your aim is just to get a good return.

But, like the author of *Thrill of the chase*, the speaker here is restricting the options to just two, and assuming that there are no others. Yes, you *can* choose between ethics and making a profit, as the first premise says. But you don't *have* to choose between them unless they are the only choices. By drawing the conclusion that it does, argument [1] clearly makes the assumption that it is a straight choice between ethics and profit with no other options. But it is not a straight choice: Herbco could operate ethically *and* make a profit – for example, if it suddenly became very fashionable to buy goods produced by ethical companies.

The same sort of restriction is imposed in considering the police driver's options. Either the driver can obey the rules and let the thief escape, or drive dangerously and capture him. The possibility of obeying the rules *and* catching the thief is not even considered.

Of course, you may happen to agree with the author, even after recognising that she has restricted the options. Like her, you may feel that there really are only two possible outcomes of the policy because there is no way of *partly* observing the rules: either you do or you don't. And if you do you have to let thieves escape, which makes it pointless, and if you don't you put the public at risk. By saying that an argument rests on an assumption you are not necessarily saying that it is unsound. If you consider the assumption to be a fair one, then you can still accept the argument and the conclusion.

So in the end there is still room for agreement or disagreement, and scope for further argument. It is a piece of further argument that we turn to in the next question.

Activity

Here is a point someone might raise on reading *Thrill of the chase*: 'Some of those who steal cars are attempting to escape after committing serious crimes.'

Does this statement, if true, strengthen or weaken the argument (or neither). Give your reasons.

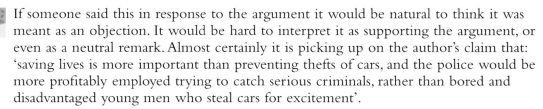

If someone said this in response to the argument it would be natural to think it was meant as an objection. It would be hard to interpret it as supporting the argument, or even as a neutral remark. Almost certainly it is picking up on the author's claim that: 'saving lives is more important than preventing thefts of cars, and the police would be more profitably employed trying to catch serious criminals, rather than bored and disadvantaged young men who steal cars for excitement'.

In fact, the comment suggests that there is a fault in the argument very similar to the one we were discussing in the last question. The author is assuming that there is a choice between using police time to catch 'serious' criminals (whatever that means) and chasing 'bored young men'. And there is a further assumption that the latter are not serious criminals. Again, we have to ask whether this is a straight choice. The objection implies that it is not, suggesting that there may be some circumstances in which the car thief *is* a serious criminal – for example an armed robber using a stolen car as a getaway vehicle.

As this possibility could be used to support a conclusion that car chases should not be banned altogether, it does to some extent undermine the argument. However, it is not a particularly difficult challenge to counter. There are several ways this could be approached. One is to say that the argument is mainly directed at the large number of cases in which the car theft itself is the only crime. Car theft in connection with more serious crimes such as murder or armed robbery is rare and a special case, and could be given special treatment without altering the author's general conclusion. Another, more robust, reply would be that it doesn't matter how serious a crime is, catching the criminal is never a good enough reason for endangering the lives of innocent bystanders. And finally the author can fall back on her last-but-one premise: that you don't have to chase stolen cars, because there are other, safer ways of stopping them.

Taken together, these responses to the statement take most of the sting out of it. The best assessment is therefore that if it weakens the argument at all, it does so only slightly.

Analogy

The last feature of this argument we are going to examine is found in the first paragraph. It is called *arguing from analogy*. Used well, it is a very powerful tool. However, it is often used badly or misleadingly, in which case it creates a flaw in the reasoning, not a strength.

An analogy is a comparison. For example, suppose you are arguing about what it is to be a good leader, and how a good leader should behave towards the people he or she has been chosen to lead. A well-trodden approach is to compare the nation-state to a family, so that being a ruler is analogous to being the head of a family. If we accept this broad analogy we can draw certain conclusions from it. An obvious conclusion is that a ruler does not merely have authority over the citizens but also a duty of care towards them, just as a parent has a duty of care towards his or her children. If you want to say that an authoritarian but uncaring parent is a bad parent (as most people would) you are also committed to saying that — by analogy — a purely authoritarian ruler is a bad ruler. This kind of reasoning is what is meant by argument from analogy. It stands or falls on whether the analogy is a *fair* one or an unfair one; and that is what you as the critic have to decide.

But what is a 'fair' analogy? Obviously the two things being compared are not exactly the same, or you wouldn't need to draw the comparison. What an analogy does is to say that two things are alike in certain relevant respects. In the analogy above, a ruler is being likened to the head of a family. There is a difference in that the citizens are not the ruler's own offspring or close relatives, and of course there is a difference in the size of the 'family'. But by using the analogy for the argument you are saying that these differences do not matter: the two are sufficiently alike for the same kind of duties and responsibilities to apply.

Most people would probably agree with the nation–family analogy, especially if disagreeing with it meant approving of a leader who treats people as slaves rather than citizens. However, agreeing broadly with the analogy does not mean accepting any conclusion someone might draw from it. If someone argued that a good ruler has to treat every citizen like his or her own children, that would be taking the analogy too far. In other words it would not be a fair analogy for that argument: the differences between being a parent and being a prime minister or president are too great for such an extreme conclusion.

So the fairness of an analogy depends not just on similarities and differences but on how the analogy is used.

Activity

An analogy is used in the first paragraph of *Thrill of the chase*. What two things is it comparing, and does the analogy successfully support the argument? Explain why you think it does, or does not, support the argument.

 The comparison is between deaths resulting from the police action of chasing stolen cars and deaths resulting from police action where a gun is the cause of death.

In order to give support to the argument, the analogy has to compare things that really are similar, and similar in ways that are relevant. It also has to be true that there *should* be an outcry if police action resulted in deaths from firing a gun. The author clearly assumes that there should by using the word 'rightly' when drawing the analogy.

The similarities are fairly obvious. Guns and car chases both kill. And if things go wrong, both of them kill innocent bystanders as well as criminals and suspects. It is often said that a car is potentially a lethal weapon and this is very much what the analogy is saying here. Is it a fair comparison? As far as the consequences go, yes, it seems very fair. Why should we disapprove of a shooting accident, but shrug our shoulders at a driving accident, just because the 'weapons' used are different?

But there are dissimilarities, too, and they cannot all be brushed aside. A gun is *designed* to be a weapon, whereas a car is not. Also, when a gun is fired by a police officer it is with the *intent* to kill or wound someone, whereas the driver of a pursuit vehicle only kills the person he or she is chasing by accident. Of course, this doesn't make an accidental death arising from police action any less painful for the bereaved relatives; nor does it make it any more acceptable by society. But it might explain the attitude that the author is complaining about: the attitude that 'if (the weapon) is a car, that seems to be accepted as an unavoidable accident'. It may even justify the attitude to some extent: they *are* different.

Does the analogy successfully support the argument? Not entirely. Although the similarities seem quite striking, they are undermined by significant differences. A gun *is* a weapon; a car only becomes a weapon indirectly. Also, if you place too much weight on this analogy, where do you draw the line? Do you want to say that any police action that results in tragic accidents should be banned, whatever the instrument − batons, riot-shields, water-hoses, tear-gas … ? If we completely disarm the police of all 'potentially lethal weapons', how can we ask them to protect the public from criminals who could also harm them? It is a genuine dilemma, and it cannot be solved by judging all actions by their sometimes-tragic consequences.

Summary

Thrill of the chase is not a bad argument. It tackles a difficult and controversial subject and draws a conclusion that many people will have sympathy with. But it does not have all the answers. In this unit we have looked at the strengths and some of the weak points in the reasoning, so that an informed and considered judgement as to whether its conclusions are acceptable or not can be made. Or you may decide that there is more to be investigated and more argument to be had.

1 In paragraph 3 it is observed that car chases can be fun for all the participants. In paragraph 5 it is implied that car thieves are predominantly bored young men looking for excitement. How could these claims be developed to counter the argument of some police officers that banning police pursuit would lead to an increase in car theft?

2 Find an example based on analogy – or write one yourself. Critically examine it, like we examined the example in the passage above, and decide whether it does its job successfully or not.

Answers and comments are on page 262.

LEARNING RESOURCE CENTRE
FILTON COLLEGE
FILTON AVENUE
BRISTOL
BS34 7AT

0117 9092228

20 Applying analysis skills

In the previous unit you looked at a longer piece of text and answered some searching critical questions. Some of them were about analysis, some about evaluation and some about objections and further argument.

In this and the next two units we will focus on another article, applying each of these skills in turn – starting with analysis. The article below is an argument about criminals who become celebrities. Read it through twice, once for general meaning, then again for more detail. Then answer the first of the questions that follow.

Time to get tough

It is an established legal principle, in almost all parts of the world, that convicted criminals should not profit from their crimes, even after serving their sentences. Obviously offenders such as drug dealers and armed robbers cannot be allowed to retire comfortably on the money they made selling drugs or robbing banks.

But the law does not go far enough. It should also apply to the growing number of notorious criminals who achieve celebrity status after their release from jail. Ex-convicts who become television presenters, film-stars or best-selling authors often make big money from their glitzy new careers. But they would never have had such careers if it weren't for their crooked past.

The producers, agents and publishers who sign the deals with celebrity criminals protest that the money does not come directly from a convict's previous crimes, but that it is a legitimate reward for their redirected talent, and for the audiences they attract. But this is an unacceptable argument. Firstly, the producers and others take a big cut of the profit, so obviously they would say something of that sort. Secondly, a notorious gangster needs no talent to attract an audience: their reputation is enough. Therefore, whether the income is direct or indirect, it is still profit from crime.

It is often objected that once a person has served a sentence, they should be entitled to start again with a clean sheet; that barring them from celebrity careers is unjust and infringes their rights. This is typical of the views expressed by woolly-minded liberals, who are endlessly ready to defend the rights of thugs and murderers without a thought for their victims. They forget that the victims of crime also have rights. One of those must surely be the right not to see the very person who has robbed or assaulted them, or murdered someone in their family, strutting about enjoying celebrity status and a mega-dollar income. Moreover, victims of crime do not get the chance to become chat-show hosts, or star in crime movies, because being a victim of crime is not seen as glamorous.

If the principle of not benefiting from crime means anything, all income, direct or otherwise, should be confiscated from anyone whose criminal past has helped them to get rich. After all, no one is forced to become a big-time crook. It is a choice the individual makes. Once they have made that choice the door to respectable wealth should be permanently closed. It's the price they pay. If would-be criminals know they can never profit in any way from their wickedness, they might think twice before turning to crime in the first place.

What is the main conclusion of the above passage?

Although arguments like this are longer and more involved than the ones you have been used to, the strategy for unpacking them is much the same: look for a likely candidate – perhaps some recommendation or prediction or verdict – and ask yourself if other parts of the argument are reasons for making such a claim, or not. If not, look for another candidate.

It should be fairly obvious what this passage, *Time to get tough*, is leading up to. It claims that the legal principle of no profit from crime should be extended to cover celebrity criminals. And it claims that, on principle, the income from criminal celebrity should be confiscated. These two claims between them summarise the author's main contention. If you had to pick one as the last word, it would be the second, the recommendation to confiscate income, since this follows from the more general claim that the law should be extended.

You might have been tempted by the last sentence of paragraph 3, which claims that there is no real difference between direct and indirect profit from crime. This certainly is a conclusion, as the word 'therefore' would suggest, and it follows from the reasoning in the third paragraph. But establishing this conclusion is only one step in the argument, and it is not the final step. It is therefore an intermediate conclusion, not the main one.

Best answer: 'If the principle of not benefiting from crime means anything, all income, direct or otherwise, should be confiscated from anyone whose criminal past has helped them to get rich.' (Or the same statement in your own words.)

Activity

Two objections, or counter-arguments, are raised in the passage. What are they? Why does the author raise them? How does she deal with them?

The counter-arguments are contained in the third and fourth paragraphs. They are recognisable from the use of the words 'protest' and 'object(ed)', but also from the obvious fact that they challenge the author's conclusions.

Why should an author challenge her own conclusions? Doesn't that weaken the argument? No, it strengthens it, because it shows that the author has an answer to the challenge. Imagine you were in a debate and it is your turn to speak. Even before the opposition have their chance to raise an objection, you have acknowledged it and responded to it. It is sometimes called anticipating an objection – dealing with it before it has been made.

Take the first 'protest' that producers and others allegedly make. The objection is that the money ex-convicts make from acting, writing, presenting, etc. is due to their talent and comes only *indirectly* from crime, not *directly* like the money from drugs or bank-raids. The reply, not surprisingly, is that this is unacceptable. Two reasons are given: firstly that the producers *'would* say something like that, *wouldn't* they', because they take a cut of the profits. Secondly, because gangsters have no talent: their criminal reputations are all they need. From this the author concludes that whether the income is direct or indirect, it is still profit from crime.

You may already have noticed that this paragraph is itself a complete argument: an argument within an argument. Here it is unpacked:

Target: the counter-argument

But …

R1 Producers would say something like that because they take some of the profit.

R2 Notorious gangsters have no talent; their reputation is enough.

(therefore)

IC Indirect income is still profit from crime.

Therefore

C This (counter-argument) is unacceptable.

The second objection is that ex-convicts have the right to start again. It is dismissed as a 'woolly-minded' argument, and as one that ignores victims, rights and feelings. It also points out an unfairness in that criminals gain from their crimes, whereas victims have no such opportunities.

These responses lead directly to the *main* conclusion that *all* income from crime should be confiscated.

Activity

As well as the responses to objections, what other reasons are given in support of the conclusion?

 The final paragraph adds a further set of reasons that directly support the conclusion. They are: (1) that criminals make a choice; (2) that if they make that choice, the door to respectable wealth should be closed; and (3) that if would-be criminals know they will never be able to cash in on their crime, they may think twice before choosing to be criminals.

What about the first paragraph: where does it fit in, and what is its function? It states that there is an established legal principle, namely that crime shouldn't pay, and provides two examples of unacceptable income that nobody could really argue with – profit from drugs and from bank robbery. So, should any of this have been included in the list of reasons; or are these just introductory sentences?

You may have interpreted this part of the argument as a premise (reason), on the grounds that without the principle, the argument wouldn't really make a lot of sense; and that, in a general sort of way, it does support the conclusion that profit from crime should be confiscated.

But on closer inspection this is not the best and clearest interpretation of what the author is aiming to achieve. For her argument is not really about crimes such as drug dealing and bank robbery. In fact, it is more or less taken for granted that the profits from these crimes should be forfeited if the criminal is convicted. No supporting reasons are given and none are needed. The *real* argument begins with the word 'But ...' at the start of paragraph 2. Reading it that way, the first paragraph can be seen more as an introduction than as part of the reasoning. The shape of the argument is:

Introduction

Criminals should not profit from crime.

the law doesn't go far enough.

all income from a criminal past should be confiscated.

Mapping the structure

The diagram above gives only the roughest outline of the argument. It is like a route map with just the main towns shown. It does not give any of the reasoning that leads from one to the next.

'Mapping' is a good word to use, because it suggests another very useful way of representing the steps in an argument. If you enquire how to get from one place to another, people will often give you a *string* of directions, for example: 'Go up to the traffic lights and turn right. Stay on that road through a couple of bends, past the big hotel on the left. Take the third exit from the roundabout and the immediate fork to the left ...' It can all be very confusing; and it is very easy to miss a turning or take the wrong one, after which you quickly lose any sense of where you are.

A simple map is much more helpful: it gives you an overall picture of how the journey looks, how the roads connect, how they relate to each other and the surroundings, etc.

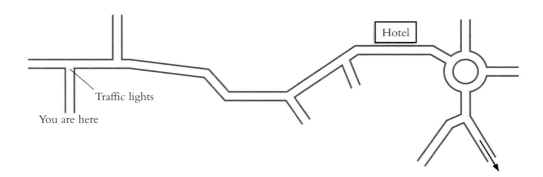

Try building up a more detailed map of the argument, *Time to get tough*, showing how, in your view, the different parts of the reasoning lead to the conclusion.

Notice that the task was to represent *your* view of the way the argument is structured. This does not mean that any analysis of the passage is as good as any other, but it does mean that there is some room for interpretation by the reader. Here is a *suggested* map of the argument. Don't worry if you have taken a slightly different route to the conclusion, or summarised the claims a bit differently. So long as you have correctly understood the direction of the argument and its final conclusion, then the exercise has served its purpose.

Introduction

Principle of no profit

But ...

Many criminals are becoming celebrities just because of their crooked past.

Law doesn't go far enough / should be extended.

No one forced into crime.

The producers' argument is wrong: all income is profit from crime.
(reply to counter-argument 1)

CONCLUSION
All income ... should be confiscated

Once criminal has made choice, door should be closed.

Victims also have rights / don't become celebrities.
(reply to counter-argument 2)

Would-be criminals might think twice.

Summary

Longer arguments can be analysed in broadly the same way as shorter ones.

Longer arguments may have sub-arguments as part of their reasoning.

A very common line of reasoning is to set up a counter-argument and then knock it down.

Using some of the methods discussed in the unit, map out the structure of the following argument.

SAY NO TO CHEATS

The governing bodies who control international sport are right to prohibit the use of performance-enhancing drugs and to operate their policy of zero tolerance against athletes who break the rules. There is more than enough medical evidence to establish that many of the substances that sports stars are tempted to use to increase their strength and stamina are extremely harmful to their health. Permitting their use, or turning a blind eye to it, can have tragic long-term consequences, as many former athletes have discovered to their cost.

Young people are natural risk-takers and are often reckless about their own futures. That, coupled with the huge rewards that can be won by reaching the top in their chosen sport, will often drive them to disregard medical advice and think only of the gold medal, or the big sponsorship deal, or the glory of competing for their country. Those who regulate the sports have a duty of care over these men and women. To stand by whilst they harm themselves would be grossly irresponsible.

But there is another reason why the use of drugs in sport cannot be tolerated. The purpose of sport is to discover who is the best. The only way to achieve that is to start with a level playing field and for every competitor to have an equal chance of winning. You can't say who is best if some competitors are cheating by stealing an advantage. Therefore, if drugs can be driven out of sport, we will once again know who the real champions are.

It is sometimes argued that drugs give no more of an advantage than other perfectly legitimate practices, such as following special diets and taking dietary supplements, which can also boost an athlete's performance. So can the latest hi-tech equipment and clothing, computerised training programmes, physio- and psychotherapies, and so on. Is that not cheating?

No. There is all the difference in the world between eating certain foods and taking drugs because drugs, unlike foods, are banned substances. Any athlete who wants to can take advantage of a special diet or the latest equipment and training techniques. But only those who are willing to break the rules can benefit from taking drugs. Anyway, if you start saying that drug-taking is fine because it is no different from energy-giving food you would end up having to allow athletes to run races with jet engines strapped to their backs.

One more thing: if the top athletes get away with taking drugs, the young people for whom they are role models are far more likely to do the same. For their sake too, the pressure on the cheats must never be relaxed.

Answers and comments are on pages 262–3.

21 Critical evaluation

In the last unit you worked on mapping out the structure of an argument. In this unit you will be looking at the same argument from the point of view of its strengths and weaknesses, its success or failure – in other words *critically evaluating* it.

Read through the whole argument on pages 119–20 again to remind yourself of its conclusion and supporting reasons. If necessary, also look again at the analysis of its structure on page 123. Once you have it clear in your mind you can move on to the next range of questions: Is it a good argument? Does it work? Does the reasoning succeed in supporting the conclusion?

It is now that the work you did on analysing and mapping the argument really starts to pay off. It has split the argument up into a number of manageable bits that you can consider one by one. It has also put the different parts of the passage in their place, so that you know exactly what their function is. So, for example, we can pass over the first paragraph because it is mostly introductory, and move straight to where the argument really begins, in paragraph 2.

Paragraph 2 draws the intermediate conclusion that the law doesn't go far enough and should apply to ex-criminal celebrities (as well as ex-drug dealers, bank robbers etc.).

Activity

What reasons are given in paragraph 2 for this conclusion? Are they convincing?

The reasons given are that these celebrities often make big money *and* that they would not do so if they had not been criminals in the past. Provided you accept that both statements are true, then they do give support to the suggestion that the law needs extending, which paves the way for the main conclusion (in paragraph 5) that such income should be confiscated. For if it is a fact that some people do profit from having been law-breakers – and for no other reason than being law-breakers – then the principle referred to in the introduction is (arguably) being broken.

The big question is whether the reasons *are* both acceptable, especially the second. The first claim is fairly obviously acceptable because it is a known fact that ex-convicts who become presenters etc. make big money. It could easily be checked and figures produced to support it if anyone doubted its truth. But what grounds has the author got for the second reason, that these celebrities 'would never have had such careers if it weren't for their crooked past'? Certainly none that are stated. It is an *unsupported claim*, which the author is expecting the reader to take on trust.

Assumption

If you cast your mind back to Unit 9 you will recall that many, if not all arguments, rest on *assumptions* as well as on stated *reasons*. By drawing the conclusion that she does in paragraph 2, the author is making certain assumptions, for example the assumption that celebrities do not have talents that could have made them famous or successful even if they had not been criminals. Unless you assume this you cannot accept the conclusion. But since the reader has no more reason to accept than to reject the assumption, it is a potential weakness in the argument.

Flaw

It could even be said that the need to make this assumption is a flaw, or reasoning error, in the argument, particularly if you consider it to be an unwarranted assumption (an unwarranted claim, or assumption, is one that lacks support). Recall, from Unit 11, that a common flaw in reasoning is the assumption that because two things are both true, one is therefore the cause of the other. Does the author make that mistake here? Is she saying that because a celebrity was once a criminal, that must be the cause of their rise to fame, and consequent wealth?

If you think that is what she is saying, then it would be right to identify this as a flaw in the argument. If an argument depends on an unwarranted assumption, then it is fair to say it is flawed, or that it is unsound, or that there is a 'hole in the argument'.

If you are unsure about some of the terms being used here, remind yourself by looking again at Units 9, 10 and 11.

Blocking the hole

But the author is no fool, and is obviously aware of the potential weakness in paragraph 2. That is why, in the next paragraph, she 'anticipates' a counter-argument that challenges her assumption(s). The purpose behind this is not to admit to a weakness in her argument, but to repair it. In other words, she is trying to block the hole that the counter-argument opens up.

The challenge is that celebrity wealth does not come *directly* from crime, but from 'redirected talent'. The author's response is firstly that the producers and others who make this challenge take a cut of the profits and therefore 'would say something like that'; and secondly that gangsters have no talent: their criminal reputations are enough. And she concludes that the income from becoming a celebrity is therefore still profit from crime, whether it is direct or not.

Activity

How successful do you think the author's reply is? Does it 'block the hole' or sweep away the objections, or not – and why?

It does not sweep away the objections; and it doesn't give any good reason to warrant the author's assumptions. We'll take the second part of the response first. This is simply that the ex-convicts in question do *not* have talent. It might seem like an answer to the challenge, but if you look carefully at it you find there is no further reasoning here. It is just repeating the earlier assumption in a slightly different way. We are still given no evidence of criminals lacking talent.

The first part of the reply is no better. In fact it is no more than an insinuation. The author wants us to believe that the producers and others are all motivated by profit, and would therefore say whatever was needed to protect their 'cut'. It doesn't answer the actual claim that ex-convicts may have talents as well as notoriety. There is also a fresh assumption here, namely that the only people who claim that ex-convicts have talents are producers, or others who have a vested interest. In reality there may be many people, with *no* vested interest, who would also agree with the counter-argument.

Attacking the person

This line of argument is a very common kind of flaw, which needs to be remembered and guarded against. It has its own Latin name – *ad hominem* – meaning literally an argument directed 'at the person', rather than at the argument. What makes it a flaw is that the argument could be perfectly sound and effective, even if the person who is supposedly making it is unreliable or wicked or deceitful or stupid; or anything else that the opponent wants to say to attack their reputation.

If the people who have succeeded in becoming celebrities *do* also have talent, then the counter-argument is a strong one, whether or not some of the people who say so have selfish reasons for wanting it to be true. You cannot make the argument go away just by discrediting those who may use it. Yet it is surprising how often this strategy is used.

What you can legitimately say is that if the only support for some point of view comes from an obviously unreliable source and from no other, then we ought to treat it with some suspicion. But that is a very different matter from saying, as the author does in this case, that because certain people 'would say that, wouldn't they!', it must be unacceptable.

> ### Activity
>
> Another counter-argument and response follow in the fourth paragraph. Critically evaluate the reasoning in this paragraph, identifying any assumptions and/or flaws that it contains.

You probably picked up straight away that there was another *ad hominem* argument here. The claim that a concern for the rights of ex-convicts is 'typical of … woolly-minded liberals' is obviously directed at the person rather than their argument. However, the author does go on to say *why* such concerns are misplaced, and here the argument is much stronger. Thus if you ignore the *ad hominem* part of the paragraph you are still left with two or three reasons that do respond to the objection, and (if true) also support the author's own argument. These are the claims that:

- victims also have rights, one of which is the right not to see those who hurt them enjoying wealth and celebrity;
- victims don't get the same chances (of celebrity) as ex-convicts.

These are powerful persuasive points. You can easily imagine how insulting it would be for someone who had been attacked or robbed later to watch the person who had done this hosting a television show, or seeing his best-selling autobiography serialised in the newspapers or made into a successful film. The victim might be forgiven for thinking, 'Some of that fame has been got at *my* expense. The criminal gets the money and I get nothing. What is more, I am not a celebrity because no one is really interested in my injuries or losses, only in his wickedness.'

But, persuasive as it may be, is this reasoning *sound*? Are there any assumptions hidden behind the strong language? Arguably, yes. For a start you would have to assume that there really is a 'right' of the kind the author claims for the victim. People have rights not to be harmed by others, but those rights are dealt with by the courts when they hand out their sentences. Once such sentences have been served, is there really a *continuing* right for the victim never to see the criminal doing well? Arguably, no – as we shall see when we look at further argument in the next unit.

What the author is asking us to accept in this paragraph is that allowing criminals to exercise their rights to a fresh start is *unfair* to their former victims. But this requires another major assumption. It is the assumption that if victims and criminals both have rights, the victim's rights should come first. Without this assumption there is no ground for the conclusion; for if, as the counter-argument claims, an ex-convict has the same rights as anyone else, then it is hard to see how the author can claim that the victim should have some *special* right over the criminal. This is a potential weakness in the argument, and it is one we will return to in Unit 22.

Conclusion

So we come to the last paragraph, which consists of the conclusion and a further short argument. It has two strands. One is that people freely choose to become criminals; and that if they make that choice they should be barred from future ('respectable') wealth. The other is that if people thinking of becoming criminals know they will be effectively outlawed in this way they may have second thoughts about turning to crime at all.

Activity

As you did with the earlier steps in the argument, critically evaluate the reasoning in the last paragraph.

This is possibly the strongest part of the argument. It places the responsibility for becoming a criminal firmly on the individual, and suggests, reasonably enough, that if that individual then faces having his wealth restricted, he has no one to blame but himself. Opponents of the argument cannot say that the criminal has not been warned. The argument is strengthened further by the claim that this may also deter people from crime, which is probably the best argument there is for punishment of any sort.

But here, too, there are certain questionable assumptions. One is that young people tempted by crime would even *think* about becoming legally rich and famous, far into the future. And if they did, would they care that they would be prevented from doing so? Probably not. Another is the assumption that people do all freely choose their lives; that none is ever drawn into bad ways by their upbringing, or the influence of others, or through knowing no better. Without the assumption that there is truly free choice, it would be harsh to say no one should ever be given a second chance.

Power of persuasion: the use of language

If you read this piece of text casually, and uncritically, it is easy to be impressed by the argument. Your first reaction might be: yes, many criminals *do* profit from the fact that they have done wrong and become well known because of it. And this does not seem right or fair. But, as we have seen, the argument is not necessarily as sound or as conclusive as it may at first seem: there are a number of hidden assumptions and even flaws in the reasoning, when you come to consider it critically.

Part of the persuasiveness of this argument comes from the language the author uses to press her case. Look at two of the phrases used in paragraph 2: 'glitzy new careers' and 'crooked past'. Both help to build up a picture of something both cheap and nasty. In the next paragraph we are told that a 'notorious gangster needs no talent', reinforcing the negative impression that is being created of the convict-turned-celebrity.

Of course, this might be the right impression, or at least one you wholeheartedly agree with. Many of the celebrities that the author has in mind may well be thoroughly unpleasant, untalented people. But that should not blind you to the fact that well-chosen language can heavily influence the way you respond to an argument; that there is always a danger that the *reasoning* can take second place to emotions or sympathies. And if that happens you are not responding critically.

We also saw, in paragraph 4, how potential opponents of the argument are dismissed as 'woolly-minded'. According to the author they are 'endlessly ready to defend the rights of thugs and murderers without a thought for their victims'. And we are presented with the image of these same thugs and murderers 'strutting about enjoying … a mega-dollar income'. The language leaves us in no doubt which side the author is on. But more than that, the author wants to manoeuvre us into a kind of trap, where the choice seems to be between defending the bad guys or supporting their innocent victims.

A critical approach reveals that this argument is strongly biased when it comes to describing the different groups of people involved. There is no concession that there may be some ex-convicts who have genuinely turned their backs on crime, who have real talent as actors or writers, and who do what they can to put right the harm they have caused. Does the author include such people in the same category as those whom she describes as 'strutting about' in their 'glitzy new careers'? The fact is we don't know, because she has conveniently – and no doubt deliberately – left them out of the picture.

Decision time

So, do we rate this as a good argument, or a poor one – overall? That final verdict is left to you. You will probably agree that it is quite a persuasive argument, but that it has weaknesses as well as strengths; and that it makes some claims and assumptions that are, at the very least, questionable. Whether or not these are enough to make you reject the argument, you must decide. You will have the chance to do so in the end-of-unit assignment.

Be careful, however, that in making this decision you are not just saying whether you agree or disagree with the author's opinion or her conclusions. You could quite reasonably think that the conclusion is right but that the argument is poor. Alternatively, you might think it is a strong and compelling argument, but, for reasons of your own, disagree with its conclusion.

The argument from harm

We turn now to the argument you analysed in the previous end-of-unit assignment, *Say no to cheats*. It contains a very common line of argument that occupies the first two paragraphs. It takes the following form: 'Such-and-such is harmful, or could be harmful. Therefore it should be prohibited.'

> ## Activity
>
> Re-read paragraphs 1 and 2 of the passage on page 124, and remind yourself of the reasons given there to support the main conclusion. In arguing for the main conclusion, what underlying *assumption* is also made? Do you think it is a warranted assumption?

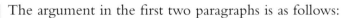

The argument in the first two paragraphs is as follows:

- Medical evidence and past experience suggest that performance-enhancing drugs (PED) are harmful.

- Young athletes are reckless.

- To stand by while they harm themselves would be irresponsible.

(therefore)

IC: The governing bodies have a 'duty of care' for athletes.

Therefore

MC: They are right to prohibit PED.

This seems a reasonable argument. If you accept the truth of the premises – and there is no reason not to – then a strict ban on PED would seem like a sensible policy to follow. But 'sensible' does not necessarily mean 'right', and that brings us to the big assumption that the argument makes: that athletes don't have the right to make these choices for themselves; or that the authorities *do* have the right to make the choices for them, just on the grounds of the dangers PED may pose to their health.

The argument from harm (or risk or danger) to the need for prohibition is often underpinned by this kind of assumption, that those in charge have the right to tell grown men and women what they may or may not do to their own bodies. Is it a warranted assumption? In general, no. Of course, authorities do on occasions impose rules for our own good or safety. Many countries prohibit the riding of motor-cycles without a crash-helmet, or driving of cars without a safety-belt. But there are many other dangerous activities which we are not prevented from doing – mountaineering, sky-diving, etc. – on the grounds that although they are dangerous, we nevertheless have the right to do them if we want. Usually a prohibition needs other arguments beside the argument from *self-harm*, for example that the harm extends to others as well. For example, the strongest argument for banning smoking in public places is that non-smokers as well as smokers are affected. If the argument were only that smoking harms the smoker, it would not have anything like the force that it does have.

So the argument contained in the first two paragraphs alone looks a bit wobbly after all, not from what it states but what it assumes. However, the author was probably well aware of this because her argument does not end there. It goes on to say (paragraph 3): 'But there is another reason … (for not tolerating PED)'.

The argument from fairness

The second main strand of the reasoning is the argument that it is unfair, in fact cheating, to take PED, and that they should be prohibited for that reason as well as the health-risks. Paragraph 3 concludes that if drugs can be driven out of sport we will (once again) be able to identify the 'real champions'.

There is another assumption lurking here: that there are not some other ways, besides PED, of gaining unfair advantages. To meet that possible objection, the author sets out, and responds to, a counter-argument that there are indeed some practices that are perfectly legitimate but are cheating of a sort. The author's response is that PED are in a different class, precisely because they are prohibited.

Activity

Give your evaluation of the author's response to the counter-argument. Is it sound reasoning, or can you see any flaws in it?

 There are in fact three serious flaws that need to be looked at very carefully. These are known as the 'straw man', the 'slippery slope' and 'begging the question'. Two of them relate to the last sentence of paragraph 5:

> 'Anyway, if you start saying that drug-taking is fine because it is no different from energy-giving food you would end up having to allow athletes to run races with jet engines strapped to their backs.'

A straw man

A 'straw man' argument is one in which the opposing argument has deliberately been made weak, to the point where no one would be likely to make or support it. It gets its strange name from the custom of making human figures out of straw for target practice, for example to shoot arrows at.

This is what the author does here. Whether or not you knew the name 'straw man', you should have noticed that in the counter-argument there is no suggestion that drug-taking is 'fine', or that it is no different from eating food. The counter-argument is much more subtle than that: it merely points out that there is a difficulty in distinguishing between permitted ways of getting an advantage and prohibited ones. That does not mean that anyone raising the objection thinks PED should be permitted, only that the problem is not as simple as it seems.

Thus the author is arguing against an opponent who doesn't really exist. It *looks* as though she has scored a point, but it doesn't count because it is such a cheap point. You will often find this flaw in arguments that you read. It can be persuasive if you fail to spot it. And, if it's done deliberately, it is *cheating*!

A slippery slope

Even if there were no 'straw man' fault in the argument, there is another flaw in the same sentence. It has a curious name, too: it's often called a 'slippery slope'. This comes from the idea that once you are on a slippery slope you can't stop yourself going all the way to the bottom. In this case, if you say that some PED are very like some food supplements, then, according to the author, there is nothing to stop you saying that anything athletes do to gain an advantage is all right.

This is obviously nonsense. The difference between special diets or training techniques and the use of certain drugs is really quite narrow. Even the experts have some difficulty drawing a line between, say, a 'food supplement' and an actual drug. This is why the counter-argument has to be taken seriously even if you are in favour of prohibiting PED. The idea that athletes could use jet-propulsion is in a completely different league, and it is perfectly possible to argue for one without having to go to the other extreme.

Begging the question

The third flaw relates to the second sentence in the paragraph: the claim that PED are different from other ways of improving performance *because they are banned*, and that that is what makes it cheating to use them. But the main conclusion is that drug-taking *should* be banned. You cannot validly say that something should be banned just because it is banned already. This is what is known as 'begging the question'. You can see why it is called begging the question with the argument simplified as follows:

It is right to ban PED (conclusion).

Why?

Because using PED is cheating.

Why is it cheating?

Because PED are banned.

Another way to describe this flaw is to point out that it is circular reasoning, or a circular argument. The author is arguing *for* the ban on PED *from* the ban on PED. Many of the flaws you find in arguments are due to circular reasoning or question-begging. Sometimes the circularity is obvious, as it is in this argument. In others it is much more carefully disguised, and you have to be vigilant to spot it.

The argument as a whole

We have found a number of weaknesses, flaws and questionable assumptions in the argument for prohibiting performance-enhancing drugs. That does not mean that we have to reject the argument as a whole, and it certainly doesn't mean we have to reject its conclusion. Most people find the practice of taking PED totally unacceptable and are in full agreement with its prohibition. Most people also consider it to be cheating and believe that it harms the health of athletes.

But the converse is also true. Just because we agree with the author's main conclusion of an argument does not mean we have to approve of the reasoning. As critical thinkers we need to be able to evaluate an argument objectively whether we agree with it or not. In fact, agreeing with the author can often make the job of evaluation more difficult because we are likely to be making the same assumptions and wanting the same outcome.

Summary

A critical evaluation means deciding whether the claims and assumptions made in an argument are warranted.

It means identifying any flaws in the reasoning.

It means assessing the strength of the support that the reasons, if true, give to the conclusion.

It means recognising the persuasive influence of the language used in the argument.

End-of-unit assignments

1 Choose one of the two arguments studied in the unit. Summarise the critical comments that were made, and respond to them with your own observations. Finally, give an overall evaluation of the argument, saying how successfully or unsuccessfully it supports its conclusion(s).

2 Consider the following short argument. Is it sound? If not, identify the flaw or flaws.

> The dinosaurs obviously became extinct because of some catastrophic event such as a large meteorite or dramatic change in the climate. This would mean that they did not disappear gradually over several centuries or millennia, as was once assumed, but that they were wiped out almost overnight. That being so, the cause of their extinction must have been a sudden event rather than a gradual process. A gradual process could not have had such dramatic consequences.

Answers and comments are on page 263.

22 Further argument

Evaluating an argument means deciding whether or not the claims made in it are acceptable, and whether or not they support the conclusion. Further argument goes a bit further: it is your opportunity to put some of your own ideas on the table, either supporting or challenging the author's conclusions.

It has to be said straight away that further argument is not any old argument: it must relate directly to the text you are working on. It is not a chance just to set off on some favourite argument of your own that happens to be on a related topic. You would get no credit in an exam if you read the article 'Time to get tough' – which featured in the last two units – and then wrote about prison reform, or the abolition/ reintroduction of the death penalty. There may be issues that connect these topics to the argument about profiting from crime, but they are not central issues. Your further argument must be for or against the conclusion, or it is just digression.

Evaluation often leads very naturally into further argument, and it is sometimes difficult to say where one ends and the other begins. For example, here is part of a student's response to the third paragraph of *Time to get tough*:

> The author says that notorious gangsters don't need any talent to attract an audience, and that their reputations are enough. This may be true, but it doesn't mean that notorious gangsters don't ever have some talent. They may be very talented. People often think of a gangster being a stupid person, who just uses violence to get their way, but there are gangsters who have got where they are by their intelligence. It takes brains and imagination to plan a big crime and get away with it. It takes brains to be a television presenter. So you can't say that because someone has been a criminal they haven't got the ability to be a celebrity. I read a book by a reformed drug addict who had stolen to buy drugs, and it was brilliant, as good as any other writer could do. It wouldn't have been published and sold in the bookshops if he was stupid and couldn't write. Therefore this statement by the author is misleading.

Activity

Would you describe this extract from the student's essay as evaluation or as further argument, or both? If both, say which bits are which.

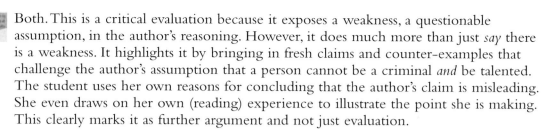

Both. This is a critical evaluation because it exposes a weakness, a questionable assumption, in the author's reasoning. However, it does much more than just *say* there is a weakness. It highlights it by bringing in fresh claims and counter-examples that challenge the author's assumption that a person cannot be a criminal *and* be talented. The student uses her own reasons for concluding that the author's claim is misleading. She even draws on her own (reading) experience to illustrate the point she is making. This clearly marks it as further argument and not just evaluation.

Of course it is not a *decisive* further argument. It doesn't completely undermine the author's case: it merely kicks away one of the supporting planks. To this extent we can say it damages the argument rather than destroys it: it seriously weakens it, but not fatally.

Counter-example

Counter-examples – i.e. examples that challenge a claim – are very powerful weapons for attacking arguments. As we saw in the above extract, just one example of an ex-criminal who arguably does have talent challenges one of the author's main premises.

Interestingly, the part of the argument that the student is attacking is already a response to an anticipated counter-argument, and is therefore a 'counter-counter-argument'. That makes the student's response a 'counter-counter-counter-argument'! This might sound confusing, but there is a simple way to remember which side a piece of reasoning is on: an odd number of 'counters' signifies a challenge to the original argument. An even number means an answer to a challenge, i.e. support.

Activity

Look again at paragraph 4 of *Time to get tough* (if you don't already know it by heart!) and find a claim that could be challenged with a counter-example. If you know of a real-life counter-example, raise it. If not, suggest a possible one. And develop the counter-example into a short further argument.

An obvious target is the last sentence of the paragraph: the claim that victims don't get the chance to become celebrities. It is highly vulnerable to counter-examples and, whether you were able to think of an actual one or not, it is clearly not far-fetched to suggest that a victim of, say, a high-profile kidnapping or hostage-taking could become famous as a result, and gain financially from telling their story.

Such an example could be developed as follows:

> A number of victims of crime have themselves become celebrities and made big profits from publishing their stories or appearing on the media. Is this fair? There are many other people who have suffered from accidents or misfortune who have never been heard of. If you are going to ban some groups of people from celebrity income, simply because other people have not had the same opportunities (like the author does), then you would have to ban everyone from making income from their pasts – criminals and victims alike. Otherwise how would you decide who deserved their celebrity status and who did not?

New lines of argument

But further argument does not have to begin from a particular point of evaluation. Provided you do not wander off the central issues, you can launch your own argument from the passage as a whole. You may, for example, feel that the author has missed out an important consideration that has an impact on her conclusions. Raising it would be a legitimate form of further argument.

For example, there is no discussion in the article about the motives criminals have for becoming celebrities. Nor is there any mention of the consequences. The author seems to assume that the motives are always selfish, on the part of either the criminal or the producers etc. who take a cut; and that nothing, apart from satisfying greed, comes of it. Here are three pieces of further argument, adapted from student responses, which take a completely different line:

[1] Criminals are selfish people. They take what is not theirs and what others have worked hard to get. They disobey laws. They evade taxes. No one is going to tell me that when and if they decide to go straight and become big show-biz personalities, they suddenly change into decent, law-abiding citizens. All they are in it for is themselves, and they will do whatever is necessary to get as much as they can. Leopards don't change their spots. Cheats and thieves don't become honest, they just find other ways to cheat.

[2] Some criminals grow up while they are in prison and come out looking for legal jobs, and some go into acting or writing to make a living. The parts they play in films and the books they write will usually be about criminals or about prison, and they have the experience to make this realistic and true to life. This has a very useful purpose because it lets other people know what it is like to be a criminal or a prisoner. It is not glamorous or romantic like it is in fiction, it's ugly and dangerous.

[3] Young people admire celebrities and want to be like them. If you let big-time gangsters and murderers become celebrities you give young people a very bad example to follow. Criminals become role models. Also you give them the idea they can be rich and famous by being wicked and violent.

Activity

What point is being made in each of these lines of further argument? Do they support the argument in the article, or do they challenge it?

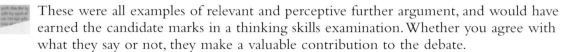

These were all examples of relevant and perceptive further argument, and would have earned the candidate marks in a thinking skills examination. Whether you agree with what they say or not, they make a valuable contribution to the debate.

The first supports the author's conclusion far more than it challenges it, though it takes a quite different line of approach. It would make a good response to any suggestion that criminals can turn over a new leaf or put crime behind them. It implies that criminal celebrities will go on being dishonest if it suits them. As you might expect, this student went on to conclude that, given their records, they do not deserve to keep the money they make.

The second extract introduces the idea that there can be good consequences from criminals becoming actors and writers. This is not an angle that is covered by the author, but it is a relevant point to consider. Experiences of life in the criminal world and in prison do add to public awareness. If this is a good thing – and the student evidently assumes it is – then allowing criminals to become writers and actors etc. does have a useful purpose. It would follow that there is some justification for rewarding them, which of course challenges rather than supports the argument.

The third piece also considers the consequences of allowing criminals to become role models. It obviously supports the argument.

Rights – and wrongs

Probably the most important part of the argument in *Time to get tough* is the issue of people's *rights*. As observed when we were evaluating the argument, the author clearly assumes – and wants us to assume – that ex-convicts don't have the same rights as other people, especially their victims, because they have chosen a life of crime. Opposed to this is the view that once the criminal has served their prison sentence, then their debt to society has been paid in full, and they come out with all their human rights restored. As we know, the author tries to rubbish this view as 'woolly-minded' thinking. But that doesn't stop you from developing it more sympathetically in your further argument. For example:

> It is the job of courts to punish criminals who are caught. Unless their crime is bad enough for a life sentence, they only lose their human rights while the sentence lasts. When they are released they become ordinary citizens again, and should have the same rights as all other citizens, especially if they have learned from their mistakes and are trying to 'go straight'. This is not woolly-minded at all. What is woolly-minded is using our feelings of sympathy for the victims as an argument for punishing ex-convicts for the rest of their lives. That's unjust. As for the victim's right, yes, they do have the right to see the person who has harmed them punished. But the court decides how much, not the victim, or the media.

Balancing 'for' and 'against'

Of course you may not disagree with the author's reasoning in the way the last critic does. Instead you may agree with the author that the law as it stands gives too little consideration to the victim's feelings. You might argue that whereas a convict gets a limited sentence to serve, the victim may carry the injuries or scars for a lifetime. Where that is the case, doesn't it add insult to injury if the criminal later makes a lot of money by telling or selling the story?

But there is another possible response that we have to consider before we finish this unit. Sometimes, not infrequently, we hear arguments for both sides of some difficult issue and we are impressed by both of them – or alternatively by *neither* of them. For example, you may feel, after evaluating and thinking carefully about this argument, that those who champion the victim and those who champion the ex-criminal both have a point, and that whichever way you decide you will benefit one at the expense of the other. In other words, if you stand by the rights of one group, you affect the rights of another group.

That very often happens in real life, and it makes it difficult, or even impossible, for those who have to make decisions to do the 'right thing' by everyone. There is not always a clear choice.

Concluding that there is a balance between equally strong arguments – or equally weak ones – is a perfectly acceptable position to take. It should not be used as a cowardly way of avoiding an uncomfortable decision; but if your critical reasoning leads you to that conclusion, then you have no choice but to declare a 'draw'. The next and final example demonstrates how further argument can lead to a balanced or neutral position:

It is obviously not much of a punishment for a vicious criminal to come out of prison and make a million dollars out of a film about the crime, none of which is given to the victims who suffered from what he did to them. But equally it is not very just if someone has completed their sentence and is then punished again by having doors closed on certain careers. It might even drive them back into crime, instead of going straight, which would create other victims. It all depends on whose side you look at it from.

I think talking about 'rights' is the wrong way to approach this problem. We should think about what is best for society rather than about individual people: criminals or victims. Perhaps if we were all less interested in wealth and celebrity, the problem wouldn't arise in the first place, meaning that we are all a bit to blame.

Summary

Further argument can arise out of evaluation, or it can be a new line of reasoning altogether.

Further arguments can be raised in support of the author's conclusion(s), or in opposition to them.

Sometimes further argument leads to a balanced or neutral conclusion.

End-of-unit assignment

Remind yourself of the argument in *Say no to cheats*, on page 124.

Following some of the examples presented in the unit, produce and develop two lines of further argument. They can be used to support the author's conclusion, or to argue against it. Or they can be balanced to support a neutral position.

23 The appliance of science

Critical thinking has much in common with science. Scientists draw conclusions from observations and experimental data; they make and test predictions and hypotheses; they evaluate evidence. A great many of the thinking skills you have thought about in the units of this book are forms of *scientific* thinking, even though they may be applied to non-scientific topics such as history, politics, sport or entertainment.

In this unit we look at an article that does have a scientific content, and that also takes a scientific approach to its subject-matter.

Read the following article once through. Do this quite quickly without trying to absorb every detail, and answer the first, general question that follows. After that there will be further questions that will require closer reading of the article.

Warning signs

The BSE ('mad cow disease') epidemic in the UK first surfaced in 1987. It was thought that the occurrence of the disease was due to the practice of feeding ground-up animal remains to cattle in the form of 'meat and bone meal' and, in particular, the brains of sheep. Sheep had, for over 100 years, exhibited a similar disease known as 'scrapie'. The practice of feeding cows with meat and bone meal was ended in July 1988 and the subsequent decline in the disease, especially among cattle born after the feed ban, indicated that this feed might well have been the source (see table on page 140).

The disease was not eradicated overnight; this was thought to be partly because some cows passed it to their calves and partly because some farmers continued to use feed they already had in stock.

There was always a fear that the disease might be passed to humans from cattle, and an improvement in slaughterhouse practices was ordered to prevent suspect tissue from cattle (especially parts of the central nervous system) entering the human food chain. In any case, humans had been eating all parts of sheep for many hundreds of years without any obvious major problems. However, the worst fears were realised in 1995 when the first cases of a human disease (called vCJD) were reported with similar symptoms and a similar infective agent[1] (a modified protein known as a 'prion') to BSE. vCJD is fatal to humans in 100% of cases.

At the time, it was feared that human deaths may rise into the thousands or hundreds of thousands, but this was not realised and human deaths appeared to peak in the year 2000 (see table).

Year	Reported BSE cases (total)	BSE cases in animals born after meat and bone meal ban (by year of birth)	vCJD deaths in humans
1987	442	–	–
1988	2 469	11 978	–
1989	7 137	12 726	–
1990	14 181	5 730	–
1991	25 032	4 736	–
1992	36 682	3 459	–
1993	34 370	2 913	–
1994	23 945	2 065	–
1995	14 302	1 010	–
1996	8 016	55	10
1997	4 312	35	10
1998	3 180	17	18
1999	2 274	4	15
2000	1 355	n/a	28
2001	1 113	n/a	20
2002	877	n/a	17
2003	458	n/a	18

'n/a' means 'not applicable'

This did not resolve all fears, as the incubation period[2] of vCJD is thought to be very long, possibly 20 years in some cases. There was no reliable test to indicate whether a human was incubating the disease so, in 2003, research was carried out to examine retained human tissue samples (e.g. tonsils and appendices) for the agent that carries the disease. In 12,674 samples investigated, 3 were found to contain the disease-carrying agent. There are still a lot of unknowns: it is not certain whether the research finding may include false positives[3] or may have missed some possible cases. The research is continuing on a much larger sample. However, extrapolated[4] to the population as a whole this indicates that as many as 3,800 people may, unknowingly, be incubating vCJD.

Glossary:

[1] **infective agent:** anything that carries an infection from one animal or person to another

[2] **incubation period:** the time it takes for an animal or person who has become infected to show any symptoms or develop the illness

[3] **false positives:** positive results that are found in error

[4] **extrapolate:** to estimate from what you do know to what you don't know: for example, from a small sample to a much larger one.

What makes this a 'scientific' text? Identify two or three features of the passage that mark it as a scientific piece, not just a 'general-interest' article about farming and public health.

There are many features of the passage that mark it as a piece of scientific writing. One obvious one is the subject-matter, which is combination of medicine, food science and agriculture. But subject alone is not enough. As the question implies, this topic could be dealt with in a much more general way. What makes this article scientific is the way it approaches the subject, and in particular its reliance on factual evidence.

A large proportion of the evidence is contained in the table. This is intended to show the trends or patterns in the number of cases of both the animal and the human form of the disease. The text, too, is primarily factual. Conclusions are drawn, but only those that can be seen to follow from the facts. One of the most recognisable features of *good* scientific writing is the care that is taken to evaluate and analyse evidence and not to jump to conclusions. Such care is very evident in this passage, especially in the last paragraph.

One of the functions of scientific investigation is to provide, or at least to consider, explanations. Note how this author offers two possible explanations for the observation that the disease 'was not eradicated overnight' (i.e. as soon as the ban was imposed). Note, too, that these explanations are not presented as facts but as opinions. They are *plausible* explanations, in that they would account for the trends shown in the table; but that does not mean that they are necessarily the right explanations, and the author is careful to make that clear by using the phrase 'this was thought to be'. A less scientific commentator might have seized on this and made a headline of it: 'FARMERS IGNORE FEED BAN' or 'BSE IS GENETIC'. Plenty of such headlines did appear at the height of the epidemic, and many had little or no scientific basis. They were written to sell papers, not to carefully sift the evidence. By contrast this author makes no such wild claims. There is nothing sensational in the way the material is presented.

Some of the terms used are technical or semi-technical, and the style is quite formal, which are further clues that this is a scientific piece. If you are not familiar with the subject, a glossary, as provided above, can help. Other words and expressions you can work out from the surrounding context.

A closer look

The questions that follow ask you to take a closer and more focused look at the text, and to respond critically. The questions are similar to those set in thinking skills and critical thinking exams.

The incidence of BSE in cattle has fallen consistently since 1992. Give two reasons why deaths from vCJD in humans might not follow the same pattern.

The clue to this answer is given in the final paragraph: the belief that the incubation period for vCJD may be as long as 20 years. Therefore, although the deaths from vCJD may have started to fall from their peak in 2000, there is no guarantee that this trend will continue. Many people may have been infected but not yet have developed any symptoms. In that case the third column would contain only the figures for people who developed the symptoms unusually quickly, not all those who have been infected.

The other reason why the downward trend in vCJD deaths may not continue is that the research findings may be faulty. As the author points out, there are 'still a lot of unknowns'. There may be some false positives in the available data; and some cases may simply have been missed. As already mentioned, this kind of careful evaluation of evidence is central to good scientific work, just as it is to good critical thinking.

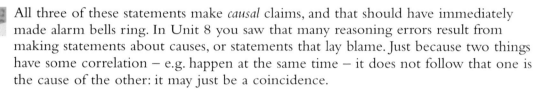

Activity

Comment briefly on whether the three following conclusions can reliably be drawn from the information given in the passage and the table:

A The BSE epidemic was caused by the feeding of material containing sheep's brains to cattle.

B vCJD in humans is caused by eating meat from cattle with BSE.

C BSE may be inherited, i.e. passed from the parent to its calf.

All three of these statements make *causal* claims, and that should have immediately made alarm bells ring. In Unit 8 you saw that many reasoning errors result from making statements about causes, or statements that lay blame. Just because two things have some correlation – e.g. happen at the same time – it does not follow that one is the cause of the other: it may just be a coincidence.

Conclusion A has considerable support, but it cannot be drawn with 100% confidence. Yes, there is a correlation between the practice of feeding animal remains to cattle and the outbreak of BSE. What is more, there is a further correlation between the ending of the practice and the fall in cases. So, the feeding practice could explain the outbreak, especially given that 'scrapie' in sheep and BSE are similar. You could even say that the practice of feeding cows in this way is a very plausible or likely explanation. But from the correlations alone it cannot be inferred that it is the right or only explanation, which is what you would have to prove to identify it as the cause.

The temptation to jump to this conclusion A is increased by the natural feeling of disgust that many people felt, and still feel, about the practice. Cattle eat grass, not meat, and the practice was widely condemned as unnatural, profit-driven and (with the benefit of hindsight) dangerous. Farmers and meat producers were criticised for doing it; and it was an easy step from there to blaming them for BSE. Elsewhere there may be published evidence that the farmers etc. were to blame. But no such evidence is provided in this article, and its author is right to say no more than: 'this feed *might well* have been the source'.

As you would expect, conclusion B is similarly unsupported, and there are scientists who do not accept it. The point that has to be borne in mind is that although vCJD first appeared just after the BSE epidemic, and had the same infective agents (prions), there may have been some, as yet unknown, cause of both BSE *and* vCJD. That would explain the shared agent just as well as a causal connection between the two diseases. Correlations can be very strong evidence of a causal connection, but on their own they are rarely proof positive.

Conclusion C picks up on the author's suggestions as to why the feed ban did not get rid of the disease at once. Note that C is just one of two possible explanations, the other being that some farmers may have used up stocks of feed after the ban. But C is worded cautiously enough to make it acceptable as a conclusion. The trouble with C is not that it is too strong, but that it doesn't say much at all. Yes, of course BSE may be passed from parent to calf, but equally it may not. It remains no more than one possible answer, and that is why it is safe to infer C.

Another way to look at C is as a hypothesis. We can say that *if* BSE could be passed from mother to offspring then it *would* explain why the disease was not eradicated overnight, as the figures indicate. That makes it worth investigating as a possibility by looking for further evidence to support it.

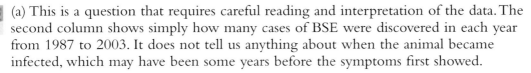

Activity

(a) Why do the figures in the third column of the table (BSE cases in animals born after the feed ban) not show a similar pattern to that in the first column? What, briefly, is the significance of the figures in this column?

(b) What would explain the lack of data in the last four rows of column 3?

(a) This is a question that requires careful reading and interpretation of the data. The second column shows simply how many cases of BSE were discovered in each year from 1987 to 2003. It does not tell us anything about when the animal became infected, which may have been some years before the symptoms first showed.

Column 3 on the other hand does not tell us when the animals in question developed the disease: only when they were *born*. For instance, of all the animals that were born in 1989, 12,726 at some later time developed BSE. Because the disease does not show up straight away, the numbers of cases would have continued to rise after the feed ban because of the animals that had been infected before it. This would affect the figures in column 3, because none of the animals were born before 1987 when the ban was imposed.

The significance of column 3 is that it concerns only animals that should never have eaten any of the suspected feed containing animals. Compared with the overall figures, the number of post-1987 calves that contracted BSE began to fall almost at once, and more rapidly than the overall number of victims.

If the number of cases in animals born from 1988 onwards had immediately dropped to zero (or to negligible numbers), that would have been virtually conclusive evidence that the feed was the source. The fact that it didn't requires some explanation (as we have already seen). The steep decline in column 3 numbers is still quite powerful support for the hypothesis.

(b) The last four rows of the column read n/a – not applicable. This could be because the numbers had by then fallen to so low a level that they were no longer significant: below about 4 they would be below the margin for error, and therefore mean little or nothing statistically. Alternatively it could be because it is still too early to tell whether animals born in the last three or four years are going to get BSE. Column 2 establishes that many animals born before 1987 were still developing the symptoms 10 to 15 years later.

Activity

What is the author's prediction in the final paragraph, and why is he so wary about drawing it as a conclusion? Is it an acceptable conclusion?

His prediction comes at the end of the paragraph: 'as many as 3,800 people may, unknowingly, be incubating vCJD'. He draws this conclusion despite noting that the figure of 3 in 12,674 is not really very reliable and that a bigger sample is needed, especially given that there may have been mistakes in gathering the data. Just 1 missed case would alter the prediction from under 4,000 to over 5,000! And 1 mistaken case would reduce it to 2,500.

Nevertheless, it is an acceptable conclusion because the author acknowledges that it is an extrapolation from a small sample to a whole population, and that it can only be regarded as a rough guide. It can neither be taken as a worst-case scenario nor as grounds for optimism. It does, however, warn us that the vCJD scare may not be over despite the falling numbers of cases given in the table.

This is good, responsible science by an author who does not want to make headlines but does want to work towards the truth as accurately as it can be told.

Summary

Scientific texts are characterised by presentation and evaluation of evidence.

Scientists try to avoid making unwarranted assumptions or jumping to conclusions.

Scientists draw hypotheses and test them against the evidence available.

Scientific method and critical thinking overlap in many respects.

End-of-unit assignment

Find a short article in a non-specialist science magazine (e.g. *New Scientist, National Geographic*), or in the science section of a newspaper, or on the Internet.

Analyse it carefully to identify the findings it comes to or hypotheses it supports.

List some of the characteristics it has which identify it as a scientific text.

If you can work with another student, or in a group, exchange and discuss the articles you have found. Try to think of points to discuss like the questions you were set on the BSE article.

24 Conditions

A 'condition' is a familiar idea. It is the same as a requirement, something that is met or satisfied – or not as the case may be. For instance, it might be a condition of entry into a certain college or university that you score 70 in an entrance exam. If you get 70 the condition is met; if you get 69, it's not.

This might sound quite plain and straightforward. But really what has just been said is thoroughly ambiguous. For there are three ways of interpreting a condition like this one, and how you do interpret it can make a lot of difference to the consequences.

Necessary and sufficient conditions

Conditions fall into two categories according to whether they are necessary or sufficient.

Scoring 70, for example, could be a *necessary* condition, in which case you will not get into the college if you score 69 or less. But if it is only a necessary condition, then a score of 70 may not, on its own, be enough to secure you a place. The exam may be followed by an interview to choose the best students from all those who scored 70 or more. This practice is very common, especially in colleges where there is a lot of competition for a limited number of places. Under such a condition, therefore, a score of 70 would be *necessary*, but not *sufficient* – which could be quite a shock if you scored 80 and still got turned down!

Alternatively, scoring 70 may be a *sufficient* condition. If you score 70, you are in – end of story. There are no other hurdles to clear. But when you say something is a sufficient condition that doesn't mean it is also a necessary one. For example, there may be a second chance for anyone who scored, say, 60 or more to be interviewed, and to gain a place that way. So that, as well as those who automatically qualify by exam, there are others who may qualify by interview. This, too, is a common practice, in circumstances where there are more places than there are students likely to get the qualifying score.

There is, of course, a third way of applying the condition, and that is to make it necessary *and* sufficient at the same time. This would mean that you get in if you score 70 or more and don't get in if you score 69 or less. This is not such a common practice in a context like entry requirements, for the very good reason that it would allow the admissions tutors no flexibility. If they make the conditions both necessary *and* sufficient they could end up with fewer students than they want, or with more than they can give places to.

To summarise all this:
- Sufficient condition: all the students who score 70 or more get in.
- Necessary condition: only the students who score 70 or more get in.
- Necessary and sufficient condition: all and only students who score 70 get in.

Tree diagrams

Another way to present this kind of data is in a tree diagram, sometimes called a 'decision tree'. From the diagram you can read off the information that a score of 70 is a sufficient condition for an offer, because a Yes response leads straight to an offer. But it is not a necessary condition, because a No response can also lead to an offer. This is a fairly simple scenario, with only two paths leading to a positive outcome. In more complex situations, with several branching paths, a diagram can be a very useful aid for 'reading off' the conditions.

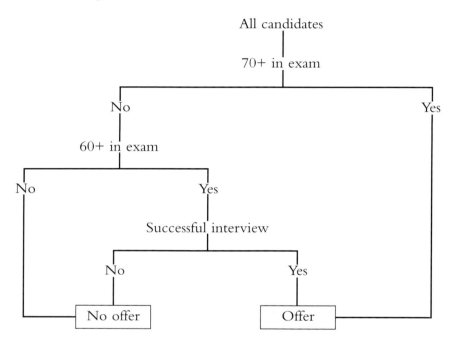

Activity

Explain, using the diagram, what a score of 60 or more in the exam means in terms of necessary and sufficient conditions.

 A score of at least 60 is a necessary condition, because the No branch leads straight to a refusal. But it is not a sufficient condition because there is still another condition to be met after a Yes, i.e. another branching of the tree.

Conditional statements

Conditional statements, that is statements that stipulate conditions, typically contain the word 'if', or 'if' followed shortly by 'then'. For example:

A If you score 70 or more then you will be offered a place.

In this sentence getting more than 70 is a *sufficient* condition. It could also be a necessary condition, but the sentence doesn't tell us whether it is or not. To express necessary conditions you may need to employ other words such as 'not', 'only' or 'unless'.

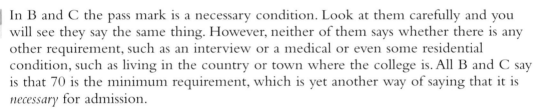

Activity

Here are six more conditional statements. For each one say whether scoring 70 or more is a necessary or a sufficient condition, or both:

B You will be offered a place only if you score 70 or more.

C If you don't get 70 or more you won't be offered a place.

D You will be offered a place if and only if you score 70 or more.

E If you get 70, you are in.

F Unless you score 70, you have no chance of a place.

G If you score 70 you're in, but if you don't you can always re-sit the exam.

In B and C the pass mark is a necessary condition. Look at them carefully and you will see they say the same thing. However, neither of them says whether there is any other requirement, such as an interview or a medical or even some residential condition, such as living in the country or town where the college is. All B and C say is that 70 is the minimum requirement, which is yet another way of saying that it is *necessary* for admission.

D sets a necessary and sufficient condition. It is an abbreviation (or 'contraction') of two statements: 'You will get in if you score 70' and 'You won't if you don't.' In logic such statements are called biconditionals, 'bi–' meaning 'two'.

In E the condition is sufficient: it doesn't say whether it is necessary as well. Compare it with A, and note that E is just another way of expressing A.

F obviously states a necessary condition but, unlike B and C, it emphasises that scoring 70 is not also a sufficient condition. G appears to do the opposite: it states a score of 70 in the exam is a sufficient condition but adds that you can re-sit if you get less. However, you may still have to get 70 or more at some time, so it is unclear whether the mark is necessary or just sufficient.

The structure of conditionals

A conditional is a complex statement that is true or false *as a whole*, regardless of whether the parts of it are true or not. Take the following statement, which we will assume to be true on the grounds that we have read it in a particular college prospectus.

H If Mia scores 60, (then) she will be invited to an interview.

A statement is 'complex' when it contains two or more shorter sentences within it. In grammar these are called clauses. In H, for instance, there are two clauses: 'Mia scores 60' and 'She (Mia) will be invited to an interview.' They are joined logically and grammatically by the connective 'if … then' to form the whole complex, conditional statement, H.

Logicians show this structure of complex statements by substituting letters (*p*, *q*, *r*, etc.) for the actual clauses. H, for instance, has the form:

> If *p* then *q*.

B and C (from earlier in the unit) have the form:

> If not-*p*, then not-*q* (where 'not-*p*' means the candidate *doesn't* get the pass mark and 'not-*q*' means the candidate *doesn't* get a place).

Don't worry if you find symbols and formulas off-putting. Some people – mathematicians for example – find some elementary logic helpful, because it is a bit like algebra; others don't. If you are one who does, you can use formulas (like '*p*', 'not-*p*', 'if *p* then *q*', etc.) to help clarify your ideas, but if not you can just as well do it in words. There is no need to know any formal logic to think critically, any more than there is a need to know about formal grammar to speak a language fluently. As with any skill, you have to select the tools that work for you.

Hypotheticals

You will often find conditional statements being referred to as 'hypotheticals'. 'Hypothetical', in this context, means 'conditionally true'. Politicians are often asked hypothetical questions, particularly by journalists, to try to get them to commit themselves to some future course of action. For example:

> 'Minister, what will you do *if* these allegations of bribery turn out to be true? Will you resign?'

To which the politician will typically reply:

> 'I am not going to answer that question, because it is purely hypothetical. The allegations aren't true.'

If she is persistent enough, the journalist may get the minister to concede:

> 'I would resign if I had taken the bribe. (But I haven't.)'

This is not a statement that the minister will resign, only that he *would* under certain conditions. It is thus a hypothetical statement.

Statement H is also hypothetical. What makes it true, if it is true, is that it was a condition stated in the college prospectus. But that doesn't mean that either of the two clauses needs to be true by itself. H is true even if Mia *doesn't* get 60 and *doesn't* get a place.

The only combination that could make H false would be if Mia did get 60 and still wasn't invited to interview. That is because the claim H is making is that scoring 60 is a *sufficient* condition.

Conditions and reasoning errors

We have looked in some detail at conditions and conditional (hypothetical) statements because some of the most serious weaknesses and flaws in arguments come from confusing them.

Activity

Look at the following passage and ask yourself what is wrong with it. There are several ways you could describe the fault, but try to do it in terms of necessary and sufficient conditions.

> [1] Under French law you must have a first-aid kit in your car – bandages, scissors, plasters, etc. If the police stop you and you can't produce these you can be prosecuted for not being equipped to deal with an emergency. As it happens I've got a good first-aid kit that more than meets the legal requirements, because I think it makes sense to carry one and to know how to use it. I approve of the French law. So at least if I'm stopped by a patrol car I won't be liable to any nasty fines.

As an everyday piece of conversation, all that is wrong here is a rather sloppy use of the word 'any'. Someone overhearing it would simply assume that the speaker was talking about fines specifically for not carrying a first-aid kit. However, you were asked to consider it critically, as an argument, in which case you would have to say it was invalid. This is because the requirement to carry a first-aid kit is necessary – but far from sufficient – to avoid 'any nasty fines'. For example, drivers in France and in many other countries also have to carry a fire extinguisher. Carrying a fire extinguisher is therefore another necessary condition for avoiding fines, along with many other legal requirements. To set conditions which were sufficient, as well as necessary, you would have to list every French traffic law!

Too strong

Another, more general, way to identify the fault here is to point out that the conclusion is too *strong*. A 'strong' claim, in this context, is one which says a lot, or says something in a very definite or sweeping way.

Words like 'any', 'all', 'only', 'always', 'never', etc., are naturally strong words, and if you use them in the conclusion of an argument you will need equally strong reasons to support them. Or you will need to weaken or soften the conclusion in some way to balance it with the conditions. For instance, if the speaker in [1] had concluded that by carrying a first-aid kit he was reducing the risk of getting fined, the flaw in the argument would vanish. Recall the analogy of the see-saw in Unit 11.

Evaluate and compare the following two arguments. Are there flaws in either or both of them, and if so what are they?

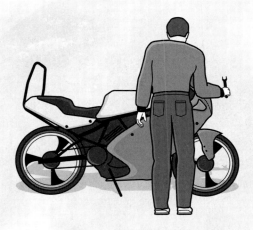

[2] There appears to be an air-lock in the fuel line. That would definitely account for the engine failing to start. Therefore if we bleed the system to get rid of the air-lock, the problem will be solved and the bike will run perfectly.

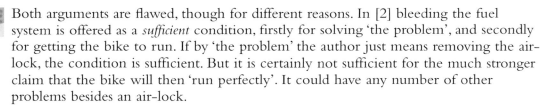

[3] If there is a blockage in the fuel line, there would be no fuel reaching the engine, and that would explain why the bike is not starting. So if you want to get it running today, you'll have to bleed the system.

You don't need to know anything about motor-cycle engines. Your job is just to check for faults in the reasoning.

Both arguments are flawed, though for different reasons. In [2] bleeding the fuel system is offered as a *sufficient* condition, firstly for solving 'the problem', and secondly for getting the bike to run. If by 'the problem' the author just means removing the air-lock, the condition is sufficient. But it is certainly not sufficient for the much stronger claim that the bike will then 'run perfectly'. It could have any number of other problems besides an air-lock.

One way to repair [2] (even if it doesn't fix the motor-bike) would be to qualify the conclusion in some way, for example by adding the phrase: 'unless there is another fault as well' to the end of the sentence.

In [3] the claim is that bleeding the system is a *necessary* condition for getting the bike to run. The grounds for this conclusion are that a blockage would be sufficient to explain why the bike won't start. There is also an implicit assumption that bleeding would unblock the system. But whether it would unblock the system or not, it does not follow that you *have* to do this. If the problem is in fact something else altogether, such as an electrical fault, then obviously it is not necessary to mess around with the fuel system to get the bike going.

Errors like these are very common in reasoning where conditionals play a big part. In both [2] and [3] the conclusion is itself a conditional (or hypothetical) statement. In [3] the main premise is as well.

Summary

Conditions can be divided into two kinds: necessary and sufficient.

Conditional, or hypothetical, statements typically have the form: 'If p then q'.

Confusing necessary with sufficient conditions often results in reasoning errors.

End-of-unit assignments

1 A tutor made the following prediction to a group of students: 'If you have not read the course-book, you won't pass the exam.'

   (a) Explain this prediction in terms of necessary and sufficient conditions.

   (b) Which of the following has to be true if the tutor's prediction was correct – and why do the others *not* have to be true?

   A   All those who read the book passed the exam.

   B   All those who had not read the book failed the exam.

   C   The same number of students read the book as passed the exam.

   D   Only those who passed the exam had read the book.

   E   None of those who failed the exam had read the book.

OCR, AEA Paper 1, June 2002

2 A city council gives generous grants to sports clubs and community centres that can show they provide facilities for local people, by which they mean inner-city residents. The council awards this grant in full to any leisure club located within the city limits that has a membership of 200 or more. If, as is usually the case, all the available money is not taken up by organisations in this category, some further grants are available for a limited number of organisations in outlying districts, provided they have at least 300 members and access to regular public transport to and from the city. The grants are for improvements to leisure facilities, which otherwise the council would have to provide itself.

   (a) Draw a decision-tree diagram which represents the information in the above text.

   (b) Use your diagram, and/or the text, to say whether each of the following statements is correct or incorrect – and why:

   A   For a club with exactly 250 members, being inside the city limits is both a necessary and sufficient condition for the award of a grant.

   B   For a club with 300 members, having access to public transport to and from the city is a sufficient condition for the award of a grant.

   C   For the award of a grant, access to good public transport is a necessary condition for a club with 299 members or less.

   D   For a club with 300 members, being within the city limits is not necessary but it is sufficient for getting a council grant.

Answers and comments are on page 264.

25 Principles

One particular type of claim on which arguments are often based is a principle. A principle is a *general* claim that, if true, is true under all circumstances. A principle is not something that can be applied selectively.

Activity

Read the following dialogue, preferably aloud with a partner, taking a part each. Then complete the activity that follows.

Carla Can I borrow your new CD?

Dieter What do you want it for?

Carla To make a copy. I'll give it straight back.

Dieter But it's illegal.

Carla So what? No one is going to find out.

Dieter They might. And if they do it's not just you that gets in trouble, it's me as well.

Carla Dieter, am I hearing this? Do you think the police are going to burst into your room in the middle of the night because they suspect you of lending me a CD? Get real.

Dieter I am getting real. I work for a shop that sells CDs, or had you forgotten? If I get caught making pirate copies, I'll lose my job.

Carla But I've told you; you won't get caught. No one will know.

Dieter *I'll* know.

Carla You mean you'll inform on yourself!

Dieter Don't be silly, Carla. I mean, I'll know I've done something wrong. I'll be guilty of cheating.

Carla Cheating! Cheating who?

Dieter The record company, the song-writers, the band, the retailers ...

Carla Oh, poor them! Do you know how much profit they all make out of people like you and me? If they didn't charge so much, we wouldn't need to copy CDs. They're greedy. And if piracy is denting their profits, good for piracy! Anyway, it's not like I'm walking into a shop and taking something off the shelf.

Dieter It's still theft. You're helping yourself to something without paying for it. And you are cheating the owners of the copyright out of what is theirs. If it's all right for you to take from them, you can't complain if someone takes something of yours. Remember how you felt when your mobile phone was stolen. Are you now saying that was all right?

Carla That was different. You know it was. It cost a lot of money to replace. If I copy your CD, some fat-cat bosses are going to lose a fraction of a cent that they won't even miss.

Dieter Well, then, where do you draw the line? One cent? Twenty? A Euro? If it's okay to take a small amount, it's okay to take a little bit more. Then a little bit more, and a little bit more still ... In the end you'll be saying it's okay to walk into a shop and fill your pockets with anything that takes your fancy – as long as no one finds out.

Carla That's shoplifting. And if you really think it's the same as copying one little CD you've got some very mixed-up ideas.

Dieter *I've* got mixed-up ideas. You're the one ...

Carla Oh, I'm not listening to any more of your pompous rubbish. Keep your CD. I'll borrow one from someone else.

Compare Carla's argument with Dieter's. How would you describe their different standpoints, and the kind of reasons they offer to support their positions? Do you think there is a *winner* in this argument, and if so who?

The main difference is that Dieter's is an argument from principle. At least, it *becomes* an argument from principle as a result of Carla's persistence. At first Dieter simply resists lending the CD on the grounds that it is illegal to make 'pirate' copies and you can get into trouble for it. When Carla points out that there is no risk of being found out, Dieter changes his direction and argues that it is *wrong* to do it – on principle. He claims that pirating CDs is cheating, and really just the same as any other kind of theft: it makes no difference what the amounts are or who the loser is. Stealing is stealing, whether you take a fraction of a cent from the profits of a huge corporation, or take goods from a shop, or steal someone's mobile phone when she is not looking.

Carla's argument invokes no such principle. She clearly believes that there is a significant difference between copying a CD and committing a serious theft. She even implies that because of the very small loss involved, and the very large incomes of those who incur the loss, that there is some justice served by pirating CDs. It is not that she thinks stealing is all right: she thinks copying a CD is not the same as stealing.

Who you pick as the winner depends on whether you agree with Dieter that this issue is wholly a matter of principle. If it is, then Carla's argument cannot stand up to it. Clearly, the pirating of a CD is a form of theft, and Carla is wrong to do it, however negligible the sums are. That is what distinguishes a principle from other kinds of claim. You can't wriggle out of a principle by saying that it applies under one set of circumstances and not under others, especially if the 'other' circumstances are ones that happen to suit you. So, if you agree with Dieter that this is a question of principle, you would really have to say that he wins the argument. If, however, you think that the principle doesn't stretch to 'harmless' actions like copying a CD, then possibly you would say that Carla's argument shows more sense of proportion, and that Dieter's is too extreme and inflexible.

The point to remember, however, is that arguments from principle *are* inflexible. If something really is a principle, then there are no exceptions. You could not have it as a principle that stealing is 'all right sometimes', and that people have to decide when it is and when it isn't all right. You might agree with Carla that it is not the biggest crime in the world to cheat the music industry out of a few cents, but you couldn't defend it on principle. In fact, if you accept that cheating is wrong, and that what you have done is cheating, then you also have to accept that you are in the wrong – even if you think it is a very minor offence.

So how might Carla defend her position? One of her lines of argument is to claim that the companies who make and sell CDs charge an unjustly high price, which to some extent justifies cheating them. This is, in fact, quite a common argument that people bring against big and powerful organisations. It implies that overcharging is itself a form of theft; or, if not theft, then at least an abuse of position. As Carla says:

'Do you know how much profit they all make out of people like you and me? If they didn't charge so much, we wouldn't need to copy CDs. They're greedy. And if piracy is denting their profits, good for piracy!'

'Two wrongs don't make a right'

The trouble with this argument is that it infringes another principle that many people rightly stand by: the principle that two wrongs don't make a right. Basically this means that if someone takes advantage of you, it doesn't make it right for you to behave in the same way. Of course, we all know of occasions when it seems quite appropriate to say that so-and-so 'asked for it', or 'deserved it', or 'had it coming to him'. Suppose a politician has come to power by spreading malicious lies about his opponents, only to meet his downfall because someone has finally done the same thing to him. You might say with good reason that he 'deserved' the shame and humiliation it caused him. But that would not make it *right* to publicly tell lies about him.

Spreading a malicious lie is *wrong*, whichever way you look at it. It is harmful; it is untruthful; and (since it is malicious) it is obviously done with *intent* to do harm. No matter how 'deserved' it may be, it remains a *bad* thing to do. In fact, by saying that it is 'deserved', you have already made the judgement that the original act was bad. So you can't have it both ways: it can't be a bad thing when one person does it and a good thing when another person does it – whatever the reason. That is what it means to say: 'Two wrongs don't make a right.'

If you accept the principle that two wrongs don't make a right, you can't really accept Carla's defence that the big music companies have 'asked for it' by charging inflated prices. You can sympathise with people who feel that they are being overcharged. But you can't rationally argue that *therefore* cheating is good behaviour.

Differences of *degree* and differences of *kind*

But there is another line of reasoning that Carla uses that we also need to consider. Straight after her attack on the music industry she says: 'Anyway, it's not like I'm walking into a shop and taking something off the shelf.' To which Dieter replies: 'It's still theft. You're helping yourself to something without paying for it. And you are cheating the owners of the copyright out of what is theirs.'

Activity

Carefully consider or discuss the question: 'Is it still theft?' Is there a difference between, for example, shoplifting or stealing someone's phone, and infringing the copyright law in the way Carla intends to? And if so, what is the difference?

 The difference, according to Dieter, is one of *degree*. According to Carla it is a difference in *kind*. If these expressions are not familiar to you, their meaning should soon become clear.

A difference in degree is just a difference that can be measured or counted: for example, degrees of temperature, or degrees of strength, or of intelligence, or of wealth. The list could go on and on. If we ask two people what their earnings are, and find that one receives just a little more than the other, we would call the difference one of degree, not one of kind. If we ask the same two people what they do for a living, and one says she is a doctor, the other says a farmer, that is a difference in kind. There aren't degrees of being a farmer: you either are one or you aren't.

Here is another example. The capital of Canada is situated on the Ottawa river, which not only divides the city in two, but also forms the border between the English-speaking province of Ontario and the French-speaking province of Quebec. Judged on the basis of where you live, you are either an Ontarian or a Quebecois. You are not more of an Ontarian if you live three miles from the river than you are if you live one mile from the river. In other words, the difference is of kind, not degree. The river draws a line between the two residential areas, and you live in either one or the other.

If we apply this distinction to Dieter's argument we see that he thinks the difference between copying a CD and stealing goods from a shop is just a matter of degree. In effect he says there is no difference, other than the amount that is taken. Petty cheating is the same as stealing – in principle. And on principle it is dishonest to do either.

Carla, by contrast, sees a difference in kind. She fails to come up with any sort of definition that shows how they are different, but she clearly assumes that they are. Comparing the copying of a CD with the theft of her mobile phone, she says: 'That was different. You know it was. It cost a lot of money to replace.' And comparing it with shoplifting: 'if you really think it's the same as copying one little CD you've got some very mixed-up ideas'.

Drawing the line

Dieter's response is a rhetorical question: 'Where do you draw the line? One cent? Twenty? A Euro? If it's okay to take a small amount, it's okay to take a little bit more. Then a little bit more, and a little bit more still. … In the end you'll be saying it's okay to walk into a shop and fill your pockets with anything that takes your fancy – as long as no one finds out.'

In other words, Dieter sees no difference in principle between the two ends of the scale, because there is no point at which you can draw a line and say, 'This is where petty cheating ends and where real, grown-up stealing begins.'

Who is right? In the strict sense Dieter seems to have a better case. If all that Carla can say is that her mobile phone cost much more than the small amounts she is going to take from the music corporations, and that they can afford it much more than she can, then it looks like a difference of degree and not of kind. And therefore the principle applies. But it is not always as simple as that.

Take the example of degrees of wealth that we looked at a moment ago. Although there is only a difference of degree between one person's income and another, no one would say that there is therefore no difference between wealth and poverty. Just because we cannot say exactly where one ends and the other begins, it doesn't mean that 'wealthy' and 'poor' are not differences in kind. Similarly, if an employee takes a paper-clip home from work, surely she is a different kind of offender from someone who systematically swindles the company out of millions. Even if our principled friend Dieter would say that they are both taking something that isn't theirs, and are therefore both thieves, no rational person would say that they were in the same league.

And so Carla has a point. Sometimes differences in degree are large enough to become differences in kind. The truth is we can distinguish between minor offences and serious crimes, just as we can distinguish between the wealthy and the poor. Dieter is right to say that they do differ in degree, but wrong to argue that we can't tell the difference.

The slippery slope

Dieter's argument in fact contains quite a well-known flaw: a version of what is called 'slippery slope' reasoning, which we met up with first in Unit 21. The underlying assumption in a slippery slope argument is that if you accept one conclusion you have to accept another conclusion that is only a little bit different, and so on. But if you do that you eventually have to accept some completely outrageous conclusion. For example, if you tell me that putting one grain of sugar in my tea won't make it taste *noticeably* sweeter than it did with no sugar at all, I would have to agree with you. I would also have to agree that putting two grains of sugar in the tea wouldn't make it taste sweeter than one grain did, and so on. I would even agree that there will not be a single point at which the tea tastes noticeably sweeter than the moment before. The 'logical' conclusion would seem to be that the tea will never taste noticeably sweeter, *however* much sugar I put in. This is obviously untrue, which means that a string of evidently true premises have led to a false conclusion! That shows that the argument is unsound.

Dieter does something similar by saying that if you accept the premise that a very small-scale offence is fairly harmless, then we have to accept that a slightly more serious one is also fairly harmless, and so on until we end up being stuck with the conclusion that any offence, however serious, is harmless. Stealing a paper-clip is not significantly different from a massive fraud!

Principles vs. pragmatics

A more general way of criticising Dieter's reasoning would be to say that he pushes principle too far. He may have right on his side, strictly speaking, but his use of the principle is too heavy-handed. There are further arguments he could have used which might have been more appropriate, and would have left him looking less 'pompous', as Carla calls him when she runs out of more reasoned arguments.

For example, he could have developed the argument that copyright infringement is against the law for good reasons, even if it is not taken as seriously, by most people, as directly stealing goods. If copyright isn't respected, the best singers and song-writers may not find it worthwhile producing records, causing the general quality of musical output to fall. Alternatively, the recording companies may respond by charging even more for their products to cover the costs of fighting lawsuits or researching ways to beat the pirates. Then, the argument would go, everyone suffers because of the ones who cheat; or, conversely, if people respect the law, everyone gains in the long run. This is similar to the argument against fare-dodgers on public transport. It is the law-abiding passengers who pay in the end, not the transport companies whom the fare-dodgers think they are cheating.

Reasons like these are called *pragmatic*, meaning practical or sensible. Arguments using reasons like these contrast with arguments from principle. The two examples we have examined could be summarised:

> Laws protecting copyright should be respected because it is in everyone's best interest to do so (pragmatic argument).

> Laws protecting copyright should not be broken because it is a form of stealing and stealing is always wrong (argument from principle).

Summary

Principles, especially those that are generally accepted by society, provide strong arguments. However, if principles are stretched too far, the effect can be to weaken the argument.

End-of-unit assignment

Find or construct an argument that has a principle for its main premise. Consider some of the counter-arguments that could be raised against it.

26 An argument under the microscope

In this unit we examine a piece of argumentative text in close detail. It is an argument that raises its ugly head every four years, and which has done so for over a century. This article, by Janet Sender, appeared in May 2004.

Whose are the Olympics?

It's that time again when everyone starts running and jumping with excitement over the Olympic Games. I don't mean running and jumping on the athletics track, either. This is not sports fever, it's politics. Nor is the excitement about the next Olympics, but the one after the one after next. Yes, it's that time when the International Olympic Committee (IOC) decides which city will stage the world's biggest sporting extravaganza eight years from now.

So why all the fuss? One simple answer – money. National pride may have something to do with it, too; but money is the real driving force. But the truth is that neither money nor national pride should play any part in the debate. The Olympic Games rightfully belong in one country, Greece, for the very good reason that Greece is where the Olympic Games were invented and where the name comes from. This is not a political or an economic issue. There is only one sensible and justifiable place to have the Games, and that is Athens, the capital of Greece – this time, next time and always.

Of course some of the competing nations will ask why all the benefits of holding the Olympics, especially the huge revenue that they allegedly generate, should always go to one country. Alternatively, it is often pointed out that hosting the Olympics is a risky business, requiring massive investment to make it a success. A country the size of Greece cannot be expected to bear those costs every four years. Sharing the burdens, as well as the benefits of the Games, is the fair and proper way to do it, with the richer countries being the safest choice.

But these self-seeking and contradictory arguments are precisely what you would expect to hear from big business. Of course those with most to gain from the building programmes needed to provide the facilities and infrastructures will say that the present system is the most workable. It is a view that gets much of its support from North America and Western Europe, which have had more than their fair share of playing host to the Games. The economic case for retaining the existing arrangement is therefore flawed from the start.

The Olympic Games, properly understood, are an international movement dedicated to friendship and peace world-wide. The Games are no nation's property. The countries that take part should pay for the Games according to their wealth, with the poorest nations contributing least and benefiting most. That approach alone would reflect the true Olympic ideal. But it is only possible if the Games have a permanent site.

Last but not least, there is a practical but compelling reason for returning the Olympic Games to their ancient roots, and that is the ever-present threat of terrorism. Everyone who is old enough remembers the tragic events that marred the 20th (Munich) Olympiad in 1972. Today the Games are an obvious target for an atrocity that would put 1972 in the shade, especially if the games are seen, rightly or wrongly, as a symbol of US world dominance. By holding the Games in the historical location, rather than a different national capital every four years, the issue becomes depoliticised, and the danger of a terrorist attack is greatly reduced.

Activity

What is the overall conclusion of the above argument?

The conclusion comes at the end of the second paragraph. It is the whole of the sentence: 'There is only one sensible and justifiable place to have the Games, and that is Athens, the capital of Greece – this time, next time and always.'

If you choose (or you are asked) to paraphrase your answer, rather than lifting it word-for-word from the text, remember that you must still give the conclusion *in full*. This is not a simple, one-part claim: there are several elements to it. It is not enough to say that the Games should be in Athens. The actual conclusion is that there is only one 'sensible' *and* 'justifiable' location for the Games, *and* that Athens should become the permanent site.

The need to capture the whole of the conclusion becomes clear when you move on to evaluating the supporting argument. If the reasons supported only the claim that it was *justifiable*, without saying why it was also *sensible*, the argument would be unsound, because it would be incomplete. Similarly, if the argument didn't establish that one *permanent* site was more justifiable and sensible than a different site each time, again the reasoning would be inadequate.

'Athens should be the site of the next Olympic Games' would not be a sufficiently accurate and inclusive answer. 'The Greek capital should be the permanent home of the Olympic Games. No other solution can be justified or makes sense' would be fine.

Activity

(a) What is the function of the first paragraph?

(b) How would you describe the style, or tone, of the first paragraph; and how is it achieved? Give one or two examples of the author's use of language.

(c) What effect does the style or tone of the first paragraph have on the reader? How might it influence the reader?

(a) The first paragraph is introductory. It sets up the context for the argument as a whole without giving either the conclusion or any supporting reasons.

(b) You could describe the author's style of writing in the first paragraph in a number of ways: humorous, sarcastic, scornful, dismissive, pejorative etc. It is achieved by means of phrases like: 'running and jumping ... (not) on the athletics track', which makes the excitement she is talking about seem childish; and the word 'extravaganza', which suggests that the current Games are over-glamorised.

(c) The author is probably trying to make the reader feel that the 'fuss' over the hosting of the Games is all a bit unnecessary, and a bit ridiculous. If it works, this can have the effect of 'softening the reader up' for the reasoned argument that is to come. In other words it is a persuasive device, rather than straightforward reasoning.

When you are evaluating argument it is important to look out for features of persuasive writing and distinguish between them and the reasoning itself. By the reasoning itself we mean the underlying claims, which could be expressed in any number of different ways. By the writing style we mean the claims as they are expressed in a particular piece of text, complete with any emotional appeals, sarcastic touches, colourful phrases. etc. In paragraph 1 there are plenty; so it is more than just an introduction.

Activity

The author offers various reasons for choosing a permanent site in Greece. Identify (a) a pragmatic reason and (b) a reason justifiable on the grounds of principle.

(a) One pragmatic reason the author offers is that a permanent site will, arguably, reduce the threat of terrorism by depoliticising the Games. This would obviously be of practical benefit to athletes and spectators, and even to the organisers whose profits would be affected if the threat of terrorist attacks deterred people from attending the Games. The inclusion of the word 'practical' in the text marks this as a pragmatic reason.

(b) By contrast there is no obvious practical benefit behind the argument that Greece is where the Games were invented and where the name comes from. We are told that the Games are 'rightfully' the property of Greece for these historical reasons, and for that reason alone they should be held there. The general principle underlying this strand of reasoning is that the inventor or originator of something has a moral and/or legal ownership of it. This applies not just to this particular context, but to authors, artists, explorers and others – in fact any person or group who can claim to have discovered or created something.

Activity

In paragraph 2 the author makes the explicit assumption that money and national pride should have nothing to do with the debate. What *implicit* (i.e. unstated) assumption does she also make – and is it warranted?

There is clearly an assumption that historical reasons should play a part in the debate. Without this assumption the conclusion just doesn't follow. Another way to say this is that there is a missing premise. If the author wanted to spell this premise out it would have to be something like: 'The issue is a historical one.' Merely saying that it is not political or economic does not establish that it *is* historical.

Activity

What is the function of paragraph 3?

It is a counter-argument. You may remember back in Unit 20 that the strategy of *anticipating* a counter-argument – i.e. setting it up and then knocking it down – is a common argument strategy. That is clearly what the author is doing here.

Activity

Is the charge of being 'contradictory' (paragraph 4) a fair assessment of the counter-argument?

You can see what the author means. The way she has set up the counter-argument, it looks as if those who support it want it both ways: they want to say no one country should get the profits, and that no one country should have to bear the costs. But you could equally say that the counter-argument is simply looking at two possible outcomes, and claiming that either way it would be unfair. Thus the charge of contradiction does not really stick.

Activity

Paragraph 4 is a response to the counter-argument (i.e. a counter-counter-argument). What is your evaluation of it?

It is a very weak response. In fact it is an example of a classic fallacy, known as an *ad hominem* argument, which was introduced in Unit 21. *Ad hominem* means attacking the person(s) who holds the belief or makes the claim, rather than attacking the argument itself. It may be perfectly true that the economic argument for the present system does suit big business, and that it finds favour in North America in particular. But that does not make the argument bad; and it certainly doesn't make it flawed, as the author concludes. The flaw is much more evident in the author's argument than in the counter-argument she unsuccessfully tries to demolish.

Activity

In paragraph 5, the author writes: 'The Games are no nation's property.' Is this claim contradicted anywhere else in the passage? If so, does the contradiction weaken the argument to any extent?

This is a tricky question because it appears to have a very straightforward answer. In paragraph 2 the author says, quite plainly, that the Olympic Games 'rightfully belong in one country, Greece'. This looks like a blatant contradiction of the later statement that they are the property of no one nation. And if it is a clear contradiction, it also appears to be a serious flaw in the reasoning. For surely, if the Games *do* belong to no single nation, then the present system of rotating the host country would seem the right one, and giving it permanently to Greece, as the author proposes, would seem to fly in the face of one of her premises.

But is it as blatant a contradiction as it seems? Not necessarily. You could defend the argument by clarifying what exactly is meant by the words 'belong' and 'property'. 'Property' suggests ownership or possession. If the Games were the out-and-out *property* of one country, that country would presumably have the right to do as it pleased with them for its own benefit – choose the time and place, make the rules, keep all the profits. But the author is not saying anything as extreme as that. Just belonging somewhere is not the same as being a possession, especially when followed by the word 'in' rather than 'to'.

This may seem a small detail, but accurate analysis often depends on small detail: a word here, a phrase there. It might be perfectly reasonable to say that the Olympic Games belong *in* Greece, but that they are not the property *of* Greece. In other words the Olympics remain the property of all the nations that compete in them, but historically their rightful location is Greece. It could even be pointed out that 'Greece' means a region of the world where the ancient Olympics took place, not the modern country called Greece; and that is all that it means to say the Games belong there. Under that interpretation there is no contradiction.

Of course, an opponent of the argument could just as reasonably reply that this is a quibble: 'belonging in', 'belonging to', 'property of' all mean the same when it comes to deciding whether the Games should be in one country or shared around. The author cannot have it both ways. If the Games don't belong to Greece, they don't belong in Greece either, and that is all there is to it.

The principle of charity

Which of these is the right interpretation is ultimately for you to decide. However, there is a guideline that a good critical thinker should follow in cases like this one, where one interpretation is seriously damaging for an argument and another is much less so. It is sometimes called the principle of charity, because it allows the author the best interpretation. What it amounts to is giving the benefit of the doubt. One way to apply the principle of charity here would be to ask the question: Would the author have made these two statements if she thought they contradicted each other? The answer is, almost certainly, no. Why would she? She doesn't need to say that the Olympic Games belong to Greece in the sense of being Greece's property. It is quite sufficient for her argument to say that the Olympic Games belong in their traditional location. And she has no need to deny that they also belong to the whole world, and should be governed by the International Olympic Committee as they are now. You would only insist on the worst interpretation if you wanted to find fault with the argument, which is a form of pre-judging. The whole point of the principle of charity is not to be kind, but to be fair. You assume the best interpretation; then if you still want to make negative criticisms, or present counter-arguments, they will be much stronger for it.

Another way to put all this would be to say that accusing the author of a contradiction in this context would be a rather 'cheap' objection. It would be like picking someone up for a slip of the tongue, or for saying something that they never really meant. In this respect it has some resemblance to the 'straw man' argument that you saw in Unit 21.

Activity

Bearing in mind exactly what the conclusion of the argument is, does the argument adequately support it?

No. The conclusion is a very strongly worded claim that the *only* sensible and justifiable place for the Games is Athens – now and *always*. Words like 'only' and 'always' require equally strong premises to underpin them. The weakness of the author's arguments is that she has not eliminated all the possible alternatives, or looked at all the possible counter-arguments. She could reasonably conclude that there is some justification for a permanent site in Athens, and that it makes good sense. For that she has provided some support. She has not come near to establishing that this is the only acceptable conclusion.

You could say that this imbalance between reasons and conclusion amounts to flawed reasoning. Alternatively, you could describe it as a serious weakness. Either way, the right evaluation of the argument is that it falls short of its purpose.

Activity

'The ancient Olympic Games were for competitors from all over Greece. The modern Olympics are for competitors from all over the world.' If true, what impact does this observation have on the argument?

It is fairly damaging. The historical argument is an important part of the author's case. She is using the fact that the Games were originally in Greece to support the conclusion that they should always be in Greece. If someone objects that the original Games were located in the region from which all the athletes came, and that this is no longer the case, that would be grounds for arguing that circumstances have significantly changed.

Again, however, the objection is not a fatal one. There are still defences that could be made: for example, the age of air-travel has made the world a much smaller place. It probably takes less time to fly from Sydney to Athens than it took to travel from Sparta to Athens in ancient times. Therefore the place where the athletes come from is not really relevant to the case for a single permanent site.

Critical questions

Questions like the ones you have been answering provide a useful way of focusing on the key features of an argument, which is why such questions are included in thinking skills exam papers. The questions were quite tough, and required some serious critical thinking on your part. But they are also a bit of a luxury because they guide you in your analysis and evaluation. When you are confronted with real arguments – on television, in print, or just conversation – you have to know what questions to ask, as well as how to answer them.

Many of the questions above are worth remembering because they, or questions very like them, will be relevant to most arguments, not just to this one. You will almost always need to ask: What is the main conclusion? Are there any missing premises (assumptions)? Are there contradictions? Are the reasons strong enough to support the conclusion? What use does the author make of persuasive language, emotion, or popular appeal? And so on.

End-of-unit assignment

Find an argument in a recent newspaper, or on the Internet, and make a copy of it. Using some or all of the questions you were asked in the unit, produce a list of your own questions based on the text you have chosen.

You can then either answer the questions yourself; or, if you are working in a group with other students, exchange texts and questions and discuss the answers together.

27 Synthesis

In the previous unit you studied a single document and answered some specific questions on it. These tested your skills in analysis and evaluation.

In this unit we introduce a further skill that you need to develop for more advanced levels of critical thinking. It is the skill of bringing together information, evidence and opinion from a range of different sources to support an argument or conclusion. This skill is called synthesis. In higher-level thinking skills examinations it is assessed by means of an extended piece of writing that you have to plan and construct yourself.

Synthesis requires first selecting and organising material that is relevant to a particular task. In the exercise that follows the task is to extend the debate on the Olympic Games that arises from Janet Sender's article on pages 158–9 (Document 1). The questions she was addressing were fairly narrow ones: 'Whose are the Olympics?' and 'Where should the Olympics take place?' Her conclusion was that they should be held permanently in Athens, and her reasoning was largely historical and political. Among its weaknesses was the fact that she gave little in the way of factual information, examples or evidence to back her claims.

The three new documents that follow are largely informative. Not every part of them is directly relevant to the debate, and there is more information in them than you would need for an argument on the specific question of where the Games should be held. Nor do the additional documents enter directly into the debate, although they contribute to it.

Read the new documents now; and if necessary re-read Janet Sender's argument. Do this quickly, to get an overview of the material rather than trying to take in every detail. Look out for parts of the texts that are most relevant to the debate. Then go on to the activity that follows.

Document 2

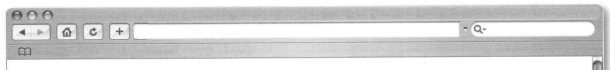

The History of the Olympic Games – Ancient and Modern

Introduction

The modern Olympic Games are always hosted by a city – not by a country.

The first Olympic Games of the Modern Era were hosted by Athens (Greece).

The Olympic Games were hosted by Sydney (Australia) in 2000 and by Athens in 2004.

Host Cities and the Calendar known as the OLYMPIAD

The ancient Olympic Games were always in the same place – OLYMPIA – a sacred city in western Greece known as **ELIS**. The Games were a religious event, a **FESTIVAL** that honored the Greek God **ZEUS**. The ancient Games were hosted by the **ELIANS** who were the guardians of the sanctuary to Zeus. They tried – and succeeded for a few hundred years – to be *neutral*, that is, un-allied to other Greek city-states, similar to modern day Switzerland. But in the fifth century BCE (or BC) they allied themselves with Sparta and warred against their neighbors. The Elians lost control of the sanctuary to the Spartans, then to other Greek city-states, then finally to the conquering Romans. In 80 BCE the Roman general Sulla moved the Olympic Games to Rome and only a single race for boys was held at Olympia, the *stade race*. But then Sulla died and the next Games returned to Olympia in 76 BCE.

The ancient Olympic Games and the modern Olympic Games are **QUADRENNIAL**, meaning they are held every four years. This four year period of time is known as an **OLYMPIAD**. To the ancient Greeks it (an OLYMPIAD) was their calendar, a way of designating time. However, this calendar was not used by every Greek city-state and there is great difficulty in studying ancient history because of the calendar and attempts to 'date' things. There was no accurate dating system in the ancient era and every civilization used a different calendar system. There were calendar s for the Babylonians, Hebrews, Greeks, Romans and many others. The one thing they all had in common was that they were conquered by the Romans. Julius Caesar created the *Julian calendar* in 46 BCE. Our modern calendar is based upon revisions to the Julian calendar, made and instituted by the Catholic Church in 1582 by Pope Gregory XIII, known as the *Gregorian Calendar*. This becomes an issue when trying to date the ancient Greek Olympiads from 776 BCE, which was year 'one' of the 1st Olympiad. To make it very simple – your birthdate this year would not have been the same date in ancient Greece.

Just as in ancient Greece, the modern Olympic Games are held every four years at the beginning of the *Olympiad*. The *1st modern Olympiad* began in 1896 when Pierre de Coubertin revived the Olympic Games and they were held in Athens. Therefore, these Games are referred to as 'The Games of the First Modern Olympiad.' More specifically, the Games were held in 'year one' of the 'first modern Olympiad.'

During the early years of the Modern Olympic Movement there was a disagreement over who should host the Olympic Games. The Greek Government wanted the Games in Athens permanently while Pierre de Coubertin, the French 'founder' of the Modern Olympic Games, wanted the Games to rotate around the world to major sporting cities. So the Olympic Games of the second Olympiad were held in Paris, France and the Games of the third Olympiad were in St Louis, Missouri, USA. The Greeks went ahead and scheduled their own Olympic Games in 1906, a tenth anniversary celebration of the 1896 Games. At that time these Games were considered 'official,' in spite of the calendar – not being a **QUADRENNIAL** event. From an historical perspective – the 1906 Olympic Games must always be included in Olympic record keeping. They happened – they cannot be ignored. However, they are not called the Games of the fourth Olympiad – because the Games of the Fourth Olympiad were held in 1908 in London, England. Is this confusing you? Don't worry – it was confusing to everyone back then too. The Greek government did not hold any future Olympic celebrations in the twentieth century because it was to expensive. The modern Games have continued to be hosted in cities around the world. The Greeks tried to get the 1996 Games because it was the centennial (100th birthday) of the Modern Olympic Games, but the Games were hosted in Atlanta (USA). However in 2004 they did return to Athens.

The ancient Greeks celebrated their Olympic Games without interruption for over 1,000 years, from 776 BCE to 261 CE (AD). Quite remarkable! After the year 261 it is unknown what happened to the Games because records are lost. Actually – they abruptly end, probably because there was an invasion by the *Heruli*, a barbarian tribe from the coast of what is now southern Russia. Invading in a fleet of 500 ships they devastated Byzantium and Greece before the Romans forced them to retreat. The Elians erected defensive walls with towers around the Olympic sanctuary, but we have no evidence that any celebrations were held.

There must have been something happening at Olympia. It must have remained a religious site to the Greek god **Zeus**. We know this because in 391 CE the Roman emperor **Theodosius** I, who accepted the new religion known as Christianity, outlawed all pagan religious festivals throughout the Roman Empire. It is believed that the last Games held at Olympia were in 393 CE. By 395 CE it is known that the great statue of **Zeus**, one of the Seven Wonders of the Ancient World, had been removed to a Roman palace in Constantinople, the capital of the Eastern Empire, where is was destroyed in a fire in 462 CE. But evidence has been found that there were even later Olympic Games until 425 CE. In 426 CE *Theodosius* II, grandson of *Theodosius* I, issued an edict to destroy all pagan temples. The temple of Zeus at Olympia was burned to the ground. Rome itself had already been sacked by Allaric and the Visigoths in 410 CE. The 'Dark Ages' had begun. Keep in mind that all these dates have been calculated by historians who have tried to use mathematics to 'date' events.

Almost 1500 years had passed when Pierre de Coubertin, of France, organized a revival of the ancient Olympic Games and the first celebration was held in Athens, Greece in 1896. In the first 50 years of the Modern Games they have been cancelled three times. In 1916 the Games were cancelled due to World War I and in both 1940 and 1944 the Games were cancelled due to World War II. In 1980 the United States led a boycott of the Moscow Olympics and in 1984 the Soviets retaliated and led a boycott of the Los Angeles Olympics. Wars, politics, corruption – these are forces that affect the modern Games as much as they affected the ancient Games. It affects the Host of the Games and it affects the calendar. Although an Olympiad cannot be cancelled because it is a period of time, the Games of an Olympiad can be cancelled. Below is a list of the host cities of the Ancient and Modern Olympic Games with Arabic numbers being used instead of Roman numerals (21st Olympiad instead of XXI Olympiad).

Host cities of the modern Olympic Games

1896	1st Olympiad	**Athens**, Greece
1900	2nd Olympiad	**Paris**, France
1904	3rd Olympiad	**St Louis**, Missouri, USA
1906	3rd Olympiad, year 3	**Athens**, Greece (sometimes called the 'interim Games')
1908	4th Olympiad	**London**, England
1912	5th Olympiad	**Stockholm**, Sweden
1916	6th Olympiad	cancelled because of World War I (scheduled for Berlin, Germany)
1920	7th Olympiad	**Antwerp**, Belgium
1924	8th Olympiad	**Paris**, France
1928	9th Olympiad	**Amsterdam**, The Netherlands
1932	10th Olympiad	**Los Angeles**, California, USA
1936	11th Olympiad	**Berlin**, Germany
1940	12th Olympiad	cancelled because of World War II (scheduled for Tokyo, Japan; then re-scheduled for Helsinki, Finland and cancelled a second time)
1944	13th Olympiad	cancelled because of World War II (London considered, but war continued)
1948	14th Olympiad	**London**, England
1952	15th Olympiad	**Helsinki**, Finland
1956	16th Olympiad	**Melbourne**, Australia and **Stockholm**, Sweden (horses were not permitted to be imported into Australia so the equestrian events were in Stockholm)
1960	17th Olympiad	**Rome**, Italy
1964	18th Olympiad	**Tokyo**, Japan
1968	19th Olympiad	**Mexico City**, Mexico
1972	20th Olympiad	**Munich**, Germany
1976	21st Olympiad	**Montreal**, Canada
1980	22nd Olympiad	**Moscow**, Soviet Union (USSR)
1984	23rd Olympiad	**Los Angeles**, California, USA
1988	24th Olympiad	**Seoul**, South Korea
1992	25th Olympiad	**Barcelona**, Spain
1996	26th Olympiad	**Atlanta**, Georgia, USA
2000	27th Olympiad	**Sydney**, Australia
2004	28th Olympiad	**Athens**, Greece
2008	29th Olympiad	**Beijing**, China
2012	30th Olympiad	–

Document 3

Q Hello, I found your site very informative. I was wondering if you could tell me how a city is chosen to host the Olympics? Thanx so much. Sarah, New York.

A Cities (not countries) are chosen by the International Olympic Committee (IOC) to host the Olympic Games. There is a formal procedure that must be followed by all the cities desiring to host the Games. This process is called the 'bid'. Cities bid to host the Games. Usually a city will form a committee or a commission to prepare the bid. The bid is like a book that gives details such as sports facilities, hotels and restaurants available, transportation network, and many other aspects of holding such a large function as the Olympic Games. The bid must answer questions like 'where would the ten thousand athletes stay'. 'What sports facilities exist now, and what would have to be built?' 'What public transportation exists and could it handle huge crowds for all the sports?' 'Who would finance the cost of the Games?' Hundreds of other questions need to be answered. The 'bid book' is then submitted to the International Olympic Committee for review. It used to be that the entire IOC would then visit all the cities that submitted bids. Six years prior to the Olympic Games that are being bid for, the IOC schedules a meeting and votes for a host city.

However a problem has come up in this bid procedure – corruption. Recently it has been revealed that some members of the IOC were actually bribed in order to get their votes for bidding cities. Salt Lake City, the host of the Winter Olympic Games in 2002 apparently earned some votes through bribery. The IOC has always had a very good reputation for honesty and character, but this reputation has been tarnished through the bribery scandal. The IOC investigated its members and kicked some of them out. Others were warned. Then they changed their procedure. In the future only a small group of the IOC (there are over 100 members) will visit each city and report back to the rest of the membership.

Q Are the winter Olympics the same as the main Olympics?

A They are in a different time and place. Obviously they have to be somewhere with snow. And there were no ancient winter Olympics either, because the Greeks hadn't invented skiing! Otherwise, yes, the same rules and procedures apply for choosing a venue for the winter games.

Q What do the Olympic rings mean and where did they come from? (From several students, different schools).

A The Olympic rings were designed by Pierre de Coubertin around 1913. Contrary to popular belief, the Olympic rings never existed in ancient Greece. This myth was created by an error published in a popular book about the ancient Olympic Games in the 1960s. The authors did not know what they were looking at and concluded (wrongly) that the Olympic Rings were 3000 years old. In Greece, inside the ancient stadium at Delphi, there was a stone engraved (actually not engraved, but in 'relief') with the five Olympic rings. This stone was actually  created by German stonemasons in 1936 for Leni Riefenstahl's film OLYMPIA. Many authors have perpetuated this myth by including this information in their ancient Olympic chapters. But it's wrong! Just goes to show that not all historians know what they are talking about.

The Olympic rings designed by Pierre de Coubertin actually represented the first 5 Olympic Games (1896, 1900, 1904, 1908, 1912) when they were first used in 1913. Later they came to represent five continents. The three rings on the top row are blue, black and red with the two rings in the lower row yellow and green. When all are connected, the order of colors is: blue, yellow, black, green and red.

Document 4: The Olympic Charter – Rule 11

> The Olympic Games are the exclusive property of the IOC (International Olympic Committee) which owns all rights relating thereto, in particular, and without limitation, the rights relating to their organisation, exploitation, broadcasting and reproduction by any means whatsoever, whether now existing or developed in the future ...
>
> All profits derived from the celebration of the Olympic Games shall be applied to the development of the Olympic Movement and of sport.

The task

Before you can begin to select and organise relevant material from sources like these, you need to be very clear what you are doing it for – the task or assignment that has led you to the documents in the first place. The task on this occasion is as follows:

> You have been asked to speak in a debate on the future of the Olympic Games to an audience of athletes, business people, sports fans and others who are concerned that the Games are falling into disrepute and straying from their original ideals. The previous speaker in the debate was Janet Sender: your job is either to support or to oppose her proposal.

Activity

Go through all the items again, including Ms Sender's article, and note down, or highlight, any points that you feel to be relevant to the argument you will be constructing. There is no need to sort or organise it at this stage: just compile a rough list of points that you could make, and others that you may need to respond to.

Selection

There are some parts of the texts that are of obvious significance, and some that are just as obviously irrelevant. For instance, if you are going to take up the author's argument that the interests of western Europe and the USA have been served much better than those of other nations, especially in the Third World, the table of host cities would clearly be useful evidence. Even if you decide to oppose the previous speaker, you would need to anticipate the accusation that the west has had the lion's share of the Olympic cake. Hence the data in the table are *relevant* whether or not they will strengthen your conclusion or challenge it.

The list of points you select will usually be a mixture of fact and opinion, and it is important not to confuse them. Facts, generally speaking, are neutral, unlike opinions or judgements. A footprint in the snow is just that, an outline of a foot, unless or until some significance is attached to it. If it turns out to have the same pattern as the boots owned by a defendant in a murder trial, the footprint becomes a piece of evidence. Similarly the fact that the Olympic Games were held in Atlanta in 1996 is a neutral fact unless, for instance, it is coupled with the fact that they had been held in Los Angeles only twelve years earlier, and that both these cities are in the United States.

Something else to remember is that the same piece of evidence can be a 'two-edged sword'. It may, depending on how it is presented and interpreted, give support to either side in an argument. Take the information about the earliest records of the Games, in the second paragraph of Document 2:

> The ancient Olympic Games were always in the same place – OLYMPIA – a sacred city in western Greece known as **ELIS**. The Games were a religious event, a **FESTIVAL** that honored the Greek God **ZEUS**. The ancient Games were hosted by the **ELIANS** who were the guardians of the sanctuary to Zeus ...

This could be presented straightforwardly as support for the claim that the Olympics belong in Greece on historical and geographical grounds. This is very much Janet Sender's take on the facts. But the few lines of information could just as well be used to argue that the ancient Games were nothing like the modern ones, and the only connection between them is that they share the same name. Therefore the event we call the Olympics now is no more a Greek invention than it is French or American or Chinese.

At this stage in the exercise you should try, as far as possible, to keep an open mind, even if you do sympathise with one side more than the other. Critical thinking should never be reduced to a game in which the sole purpose is to 'win' an argument. The primary object of learning to think critically is to make good judgements, not to score points. The right approach is to look at the facts and ask yourself: 'What conclusion does this information most strongly support?' Not: 'How can this information be manipulated to back up my already-formed opinion?'

The points you select from the documents may be similar to the bullet points below – though the exact way in which you make notes is up to you and your tutor to develop. And if you are writing them in an exam, they can be even more abbreviated, as only you need to understand them. All the same, don't rush the reading and note-making stage of the exercise: the time you spend reading, thinking and planning will save you time when you come to writing your finished essay.

Document 1 – Argument
- conclusion: should be permanent venue in Greece.
- reasons: historical right / present system driven by money / would depoliticise games / lessen terrorist threat.
- evaluation: contradictory in parts.

Document 2 – Historical
- early OGs held at Olympia – religious festival – hosted by Elians (neutral but later allied and hostile). Moved to Rome in 80 BC, then back.
- took place every four years and were like a calendar.
- lasted 1000 yrs! Then 1500 years passed before games restored.
- records, especially dates unreliable / different calendars.
- modern games – Coubertin – Frenchman. Disagreement and confusion at first.
- Games affected by wars, politics and corruption.

Data table
Shows most games held in Europe or America.

Document 3 - Internet discussion site

- complex bidding system
- IOC then decide
- open to corruption e.g. Salt Lake City winter games
- Olympic rings mean the five continents / designed in modern times

Document 4 - official statement

- games belong entirely to IOC and so do all profits

You may have left out some of these points and you may have included others. But it is hoped that your list will have been similar. Clearly, many of the notes above are relevant and could be used by one or other side in the debate.

Notice how this exercise has condensed several passages, some quite long ones, into a handful of bullet points. You may need to go back to the document later to find specific details, but mostly you can now work from the notes in planning and writing your 'speech'.

Inference

In a much earlier unit you studied the skill of drawing inferences (conclusions) from information in various forms. Once you have selected the relevant points from the documents, the next task is to decide what can be inferred from them, both individually and collectively. You must also decide what *cannot* be inferred, so that you do not jump to conclusions.

Take the table of host cities in Document 2. As raw data it just tells you each of the venues of the Summer Olympics in modern times. But the data support a number of quite striking facts. For instance, the modern Games have never been held in Africa. They have been awarded to Asia only twice, South America just once, and so on. You can count up yourself how many times the Games have been in Europe.

Facts like these are simply a matter of data extraction, which you will encounter in more detail and complexity in the problem-solving section of this book (Units 29–44). If someone had wished to make the point about the unequal distribution of the host cities, they could have presented the data in other ways, e.g. percentages or pie charts. But here there are no points being made overtly. The inferences are left to the reader to draw, and that is what you must do.

Drawing direct, factual conclusions from the data is one thing. Making further inferences and value judgements on the basis of the data is another, and you must do it with care. It would be a safe enough observation to say that the international spirit of the Olympic Games has not been reflected in the choice of host cities. It would not be a safe conclusion to say that there has been favouritism and corruption in the IOC. You would need evidence of a different kind altogether to go that far. The most you could infer in that direction is that the obvious imbalance towards certain regions of the world raises questions about favouritism, and that this is not good for the reputation of the Olympic movement, whether it is founded or not.

Synthesis

We now come to the final and most demanding part of the exercise: *drawing together* the various pieces of information, inference and opinion to make a cogent argument for one side or the other. This is the part we call 'synthesis'.

> **Activity**
>
> Review the points you have listed showing what you consider the most relevant items in the documents. (You may want to add or delete some after comparing your list with the suggested one above, but if you are happy with yours, then use it.)
>
> Look in particular for links between them, or natural ways to group them. There are a number of different ways to do this: highlighting, numbering, drawing connecting lines, etc.

Not wanting to do the work for you, here is just one example of the kind of links that can be made. It follows up on the inferences we drew earlier from the data in Document 2.

Data table

Shows most games held in Europe or America.

Document 3 – Internet discussion site
- complex bidding system — *adds to suspicion*
- IOC then decide
- open to corruption e.g. Salt Lake City winter games
- Olympic rings mean the five continents / designed in modern times

so what does symbol mean?

Three points are drawn together as being relevant to the question of favouritism or worse in the selection process. The 'student' has highlighted them and made a brief note as to the possible connection between them: (1) the data add to any suspicion there may be about corruption; and (2) even if there is no corruption there is something wrong with a movement that embraces five continents but usually excludes three of them from the honour of holding the games. Developing these themes would provide a substantial paragraph or section in the student's eventual essay.

Decision time: 'resolving the dilemma'

All worthwhile arguments have two sides to them. An argument with only one side – or an argument to which there is no reply – may exist but it is hardly worth making. An argument for something that is already a known fact would fall into this category. It is uninteresting.

Interesting arguments, on the other hand, present us with dilemmas. A dilemma is a difficult choice. It is difficult either because there are good reasons for either side of the argument; or because, whichever choice you make, there are some unwanted consequences. Therefore you will often hear people talk about the horns of a dilemma: if you avoid one horn, there is another waiting for you!

The choices for the Olympic Movement – and for you now you are involved in the debate – are whether it would be better to keep to the present system of rotating the Games at different venues, with all the problems and criticisms that gives rise to; or to opt for one permanent site and risk angering some member countries who want their turn to host the event. The dilemma is that whichever the IOC decides, it will not please everyone. The dilemma is compounded by the fact that there is no third way. This *is* a case where the options *are* restricted to two (see unit 19). You have to hold the Games somewhere, or not hold them at all.

When faced with a dilemma, you just have to make a decision, or duck it and get caught on both horns. Reaching such a decision, and satisfying yourself or others that it is the right decision, is what is meant by 'resolving the dilemma'.

Shortly you will have to make a decision about which side you support, based on what you know from reading the texts. You will have to justify your decision by giving reasons why it is the better of the two choices.

Summary

Using all the skills: synthesis, of the kind just described, not only involves drawing together information, it also means drawing together your *skills*, the skills you have been acquiring and practising throughout this course.

In the assignment you are about to complete, you will find yourself calling on them all: analysing, evaluating, inferring, justifying, explaining, and further argument.

End-of-unit assignment

Write a speech that will be given to an audience of athletes, business people, sports fans and others who are concerned that the Olympic Games are falling into disrepute and straying from their original ideals.

The previous speaker in the debate was Janet Sender: your job is either to support or to oppose her proposal.

Base your argument on the four documents provided. It is important that you make reference to them. This is not a test of your own wider knowledge of the subject.

28 Critical marking

This final unit in the critical thinking section is a bit different from the others. This time you will not be producing work for your tutor to mark: you'll be having a go at the tutor's or examiner's job instead.

The subject will be a familiar one because you recently completed an assignment on it at the end of the last unit. There are three student essays below. They vary in quality and in approach, and what you have to do is rate them on a scale from A to E.

You can only do this if you have some criteria to base your assessment on, so here are what are called *descriptors* for three of the grades, A, C and E. They are the kind of descriptors that examiners typically use when marking thinking skills papers. The object of the exercise – apart from the fun of being an examiner for a day – is to help you understand what is expected of you when you take your exam.

An A-grade candidate has:
- selected all (or nearly all) the relevant information from the documents;
- drawn sound and justifiable inferences from available evidence;
- distinguished accurately between fact and opinion;
- evaluated available evidence and argument critically and perceptively;
- brought together (synthesised) ideas in a clear and well-organised way;
- reached a sound conclusion backed by well-developed reasoning.

A C-grade candidate has:
- selected a reasonable amount of relevant information;
- drawn inferences from the documents, most of which are sound or justifiable;
- observed that some of the information is fact and some is opinion;
- offered some evaluation of evidence and argument;
- brought together (synthesised) some of the ideas and information;
- drawn an acceptable conclusion with some supporting reasoning.

An E-grade candidate has:
- made some reference to the documents;
- drawn some acceptable inferences from the information;
- evaluated or discussed some of the material in the documents;
- reached a conclusion, or offered an opinion, on the subject of the debate.

For essays that meet 3 or more but not all of the A-grade criteria, award B.
For essays that meet 3 or more but not all of the C-grade criteria, award D.
For essays that do not meet 3 or more of the E-grade criteria, award F.

Mark the three essays according to the above descriptors. As well as giving a grade, comment on why you think the essay deserved the grade you gave it. You can also make comments on specific parts of the essays.

No account should be taken of the quality of the writing. So long as the student's meaning is understandable, that is all that counts: this is a test of reasoning, not of writing skill.

After you have marked the essays you can find out what grades an examiner gave them – and why – by turning to pages 265–6.

Essay 1: Maria

I agree with Janet that the Olympic Games should remain in Athens where they originally started. This would be a good thing because it would mean that organisation of the Games would not be so full of corruption – it would not be possible for members of the International Olympic Committee to be bribed, as happened in respect of the Winter Olympics held in Salt Lake City in 2002 (Doc. 3) as there would be no selection procedure for them to influence. Of course the Winter Olympics are a recent offshoot event as they are for Winter sports and there was no skating or skiing at the ancient meetings at Olympia, but the point is the same.

Janet Sender says that the Olympics rightfully belong to Greece because that's where they began, but she also says that they are no nation's property, which looks like two contradictory opinions. Rule 11 of the Olympic Charter (Doc. 4) on the other hand says that the Games are the exclusive property of the Committee. I think that it's not so much that they belong to Greece as that it's better if they are held in one place always – and Athens is the obvious place for it to be.

There would be less risk of danger to the participants and the spectators because less political interest would be attached to the Games without the long competition and bidding process (Doc. 3). I agree that one result of this would be that the feeling of United States' dominance, which might make the event a target for a terrorist attack, would lessen. If there was no big battle to host the Games during the preceding Olympiad – this is the proper name for the four-year period between the events (Doc. 2) – then there would be no dimension of international political rivalry at all and the relations between the competing countries would be friendlier.

The whole meeting has also become very commercialised, with sponsorship, advertising, and ranges of logo-covered sportswear. As well as that, there is enormous financial benefit to the host location in terms of increased trade and tourism. Rule 11 says that all profits derived from 'celebration' of the Games have to be used to develop sport and the Olympic movement, but a lot of money is made from the Games by individuals and by cities rather than by the Olympic movement, and this does not seem part of the spirit of the original Greek sporting meeting.

Of course it would not be fair to expect Athens to pay all the costs involved in hosting the Olympics, and it would be right for all the participants to make a fair and appropriate contribution. The history of the Games given in Document 2 shows that they began as a religious event to honour Zeus. That aspect has now been lost completely but it would be more in the spirit of world-wide peace and friendship that cities and countries did not try to outdo each other during the bidding process, and stuck to the competition that goes on inside the stadium.

Essay 2: Gudrun

The Olympic Games began in Olympia in Greece in 776 BC as a religious event to honour the god Zeus. They continued to be held until 261 AD, although they sometimes moved from one Greek city to another. There was then a long gap until they were started again by a Frenchman called Pierre de Coubertin in 1896 and held in Athens again, although there is a lot different now in the way they are arranged.

They are always held by cities rather than countries, and those cities that want to host them have to put in a bid several years before. The bid has to contain information about how the city will manage to house all the athletes and provide the sports facilities and everything else necessary. This means that there is a lot of rivalry and secrecy while the Olympic committee is choosing the city that will win. If the Olympics were held in one place, as they usually were to start with, then there would be no rivalry beforehand.

The Olympic Games were held in Munich in 1972 and there was a terrorist attack. In 2002 the Winter section of the Olympic Games was held in Salt Lake City and it was found that there had been corruption with members of the Olympic committee accepting bribes to allow the event to go there. If the Olympic Games were held just in one place there would not be no risk of attack because the countries competing in them would not have been hostile to each other during the bidding process, and also they could only be in one place so there would be no point in trying to bribe the committee.

The rules are saying that all the money that is made during the Games belongs to the committee, but of course it would be unfair if Athens had to pay every time to put up all the athletes and maintain all the sporting facilities to the highest standards, so it would be fair for all the competitors to pay a fee to the city. That could be calculated by how many athletes would be attending and entering the events. It would also have to be counted in that Athens would make a lot of money from people who wanted to attend the Games, and from tourism. But many tourists go to Athens anyway.

The Olympic Games have a long history in Greece and were supposed to be neutral. It is for that reason that I consider that Janet Sender's opinion is the right one. She makes a good point and there are no weaknesses in her argument.

Essay 3: James

Janet Sender has offered these arguments in favour of the Olympic Games taking Athens, Greece, as its permanent home:

1 The Games were born in Greece, and owe their name to the fact.
2 Financial contribution to the Games should be split worldwide amongst the competing nations relative to their means, as this is in accordance with the Olympic ethic of friendship and peace worldwide. For such a system of finance to work the Games require a permanent home.
3 'De-politicising' the issue of where the Games are held by locating them permanently in Greece – their historical home – greatly reduces the threat of terror attacks.

Miss Sender has stated that the Games are no nation's property. If this is the case then how can she justify her proposal to take away the right of the rest of the world to be hosts?

Reference to Document 2 will show those that do not already know that the Games of the ancient era began in Olympia, Greece. When they first began Greece as a country was not the host; instead the city state of Olympia was. Were Miss Sender to be completely true to the history of the Games she should be trying to convince us that the ancient site of Olympia should be restored to its former Games-hosting glory – after all it did host them for something approaching a millennium. The fact that Athens is in Greece bears no relevance in the argument that the Games should return to their ancient home, as for accuracy's sake Athens might as well be on the other side of the world.

Perhaps if Miss Sender were to argue that the Olympic Games should return to the site of their rebirth, a little over a century ago, then maybe she would have a case for Athens hosting the Games on a permanent basis. Remember, though, that the right to host the Games would not only be taken away from the world outside Greece, but also from everywhere within Greece bar Athens – a strange view to take if she is of the opinion that the Games are no-one's property.

Document 3 provides further confirmation that it is particular cities that are selected to host the Games, and not countries. Essentially, the IOC votes on the basis of how good a host it believes each city could be, regardless of the country in which it is located.

Document 4 reveals another important flaw in Sender's speech: she specifically tells us that the Olympics are 'no nation's property'. The Games are however the property of the IOC, as stated in Rule 11 of the Olympic Charter. Whilst the Games might well not belong to any particular country, it certainly is not the property of the people either. It is controlled and run by a governing body with exclusive rights to all things Olympic. Miss Sender might do well to address this issue if she is going to argue against any sort of exclusive ownership of the Olympic Games. So what of Sender's two other presented reasons that the Games should be permanently in Athens? That a permanent home is required for it to be possible to split the cost of the Games amongst the competing nations is a poor argument. Firstly, the current system of rotating the Games around the world already does the very thing which Sender is hoping to achieve – split the cost; only by locating the Games permanently in Greece would the problem of one nation/city bearing all the burdens arise. In fact, the poorer nations are getting a much better deal under the current system. I can certainly imagine there being murmurs of discontent from countries both rich and poor were a system introduced whereby all nations are expected to play their part in funding the Games every quadrennial. Secondly, Sender offers no qualification of her claim that to split the cost fairly the Games must have a permanent home. I can only presume that Sender thinks it would be impossible to accurately divide up the bills if the bills themselves were varying every four years in accordance with the development costs and economy in the country of the host city. However, presumption is not a satisfactory basis for accepting an argument, particularly when, as in this case, that which is being presumed is unconvincing.

Finally, Sender appeals to the big buzzword of the moment: 'terrorism'. Apparently, locating the Games permanently in Greece would de-politicise the whole affair, thus reducing the risk of terrorist attacks against certain host countries. But keeping the Games in one place does not change what they symbolise. The same athletes will compete and the same fans will watch – if a terror group has issue with the Games then the venue is inconsequential, if the terror group has issue with the country then what is to stop them blowing up any crowded football stadium on a typical match day?

In summary, of the three arguments Sender provides, I am dismissing two of them on the grounds that they are completely unqualified. The first point Sender makes is the most convincing, that the Games should return to their historical home. However, this does not strike me as reason in itself for keeping the Games in Athens, rather it seems like an answer to the question of where the Games should be held were they to take up permanent residence elsewhere. In the absence of any compelling reason to ask this question I must disagree with Janet Sender and give my full support to the current system.

PART 2 Problem solving

29 What do we mean by a 'problem'?

Consider the action of striking a match. The processes you need to go through are quite complicated. You must find the box, open the tray, take out a match, hold it by the plain end, close the box, and rub the match against the correct side of the box. In fact one could break this down even more: I didn't, for example, tell you to hold the box in one hand and the match in the other.

Although this is complicated, it is an everyday task that you do without thinking. However, if you encounter something new, which may be no more complicated, the processes required to achieve the task may need considerable thought and planning. This thought and planning are what constitutes problem solving.

Imagine, for example, trying to fit a number of rectangular packages into a large box. There are two ways of starting. You can measure the large box and the small packages and calculate the best way of fitting them in. You may make some initial assumptions about the best orientation for the packages, which may turn out later to be wrong. Alternatively, you may do it by trial and error. If you have some left over at the end that are the wrong shape to fit into the spaces left, you may have to start again with a

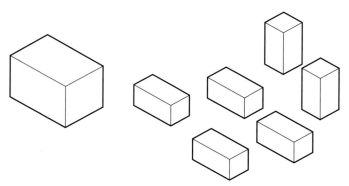

different arrangement. Either way, you will have to be systematic and need some sort of strategy. Developing strategies for tasks is at the heart of problem solving.

With some problems, the method of finding an answer might be quite clear. With others there may be no systematic method and you might have to use trial and error from the start.

The word 'problem' is used in different ways. It can mean something that is causing us a difficulty. The word 'problematical' implies a situation where we cannot see an easy solution to something. However, not all problems are like this. In some cases we may enjoy problems and solve them for fun, for example when reading a puzzle book or doing a crossword.

The words 'problem solving' are also used in a mathematical sense, where the solution sought is the proof of a proposition. Although a lot of the problems we are looking at here use numbers and require numerical solutions, the mathematics is very simple – only that which is normally learned in primary education. A lot of problems do not use numbers at all.

There are three clearly defined processes that we may use when solving problems:

- identifying which data are relevant when faced with a mass of data, most of which is irrelevant;
- combining pieces of information that may not appear to be related to give new information;
- relating one set of information to another in a different form – this involves using experience: relating new problems to ones we have previously solved.

These processes are the fundamental building blocks of problem solving and can be expanded into areas of skill that may be brought together to solve more complex problems.

The activity below gives an example of a simple problem – you can give either a simple answer or a more complicated one, depending on the degree of detail you consider necessary.

Activity

Roger has a meeting in a town 50 miles away at 3 p.m. tomorrow. He is planning to travel from the town where he lives to the town where the meeting is by train, walking to and from the station at both ends.

List the pieces of information he needs to decide what time he must leave home. Then work out how you would proceed to plan his journey from these pieces of information.

The chances are that you missed some vital things. You may have thought that all he needed was a railway timetable. Unless you approached the problem systematically, you may not have thought of everything.

Let us start by thinking of everything he does from leaving his house to arriving at the meeting.

1 He leaves his house.
2 He walks to the station.
3 He buys a train ticket.
4 He goes to the platform.
5 He boards the train when it arrives.
6 He sits on the train until it reaches the destination.
7 He leaves the train.
8 He walks to where his meeting is being held.

You can construct the pieces of information he needs from this list. They are:

1 The time taken to walk from his house to the station.
2 The time needed to buy a ticket (remember to allow for queues!).
3 The time to walk to the platform.
4 The train timetable.
5 The time taken to walk from the station to where the meeting is held.

Did you find them all? Perhaps you thought of some that I missed. For example, I didn't think of allowing for the train being late. You could estimate this by experience and allow some extra time.

Now, to find out when he should leave home we need to work *backwards*. If his meeting is at 3 p.m., you can work out when he must leave the destination station to walk to the meeting. You can then look at the timetable to see what is the latest train he can catch (allowing extra for the train to be late if necessary). You can then see from the timetable when this train leaves his home town. Continuing, you can determine when he should have bought his ticket, and when he should leave home.

Of course, you could do the whole thing by guesswork, but you might get it all wrong and, more to the point, you cannot be confident that you got it right.

In the sense we are using the word in this book, a 'problem' means a situation where we need to find a solution from a set of initial conditions. In the following units we will look at different sorts of problem, different kinds of information, and how we can put them together to find solutions to the problems. These units will lead you through the types of problem-solving exercises you should encounter in thinking skills examinations and give some indications about how you might approach such problems. However, learning to solve problems is a generally useful life skill and also, we hope, fun!

Summary

In this chapter we have looked at what a problem is and how the word can be used in different ways.

We have seen how information is used to contribute to the solution of a problem.

We have looked at how various methods of using information can lead to more or less effective solutions.

1 List the operations involved in making a cup of tea. In what order should you do them? First list the main things, then try to break each down into smaller parts.

2 Consider something you might want to buy (for example a car, hi-fi system or a computer). Make a list of the pieces of information you would need in order to make a decision on which one to buy.

3 Here is a problem for which you should find some information or make up some so you can produce a solution:

Find a mileage chart that gives the distances between various towns (these can be found in most road atlases). Pick a base town and four other towns. Consider making a journey that starts at the base town, takes in the other four and ends at the base town. In what order should you visit the towns to minimise the journey?

4 Here is a series of questions based on a very simple situation, but which require clear thinking to solve. Some are easier than others.

A drawer contains 8 blue socks and 8 black socks. It is dark and you cannot tell the difference between the two colours.

(a) What is the smallest number you will have to take out to ensure that you have a matching pair?

(b) What is the largest number you can take out and still not have a matching pair?

(c) What is the smallest number you can take out to be sure that you have one of each colour? (This seems a silly question but some people like to wear odd socks.)

(d) What is the largest number you can take out and still have all of one colour?

(e) What is the smallest number you can take out to be sure you have a blue pair?

Answers and comments are on page 266.

LEARNING RESOURCE CENTRE
FILTON COLLEGE
FILTON AVENUE
BRISTOL
BS34 7AT

0117 9092228

30 How do we solve problems?

We have seen that a problem consists of a set of information and a question to answer. In order to solve the problem we must use the information in a certain way. The way in which we use it may be quite straightforward – it may for example be simply a matter of searching a table for a piece of data that matches given conditions. In other cases, instead of searching for a piece of data, we may have to search for a method of solution. The important thing in either case will be to have a strategy that will lead to the solution.

Many publications give (in various forms) the procedure:

Data ⇒ Process ⇒ Solution

This is all well and good, and indeed represents a way problems can be solved. It says nothing about what the words and, in particular, the arrows mean. It is in this detail that the key processes are found.

There are several ways problems may be approached. A term that is used a lot is heuristic (see for example *How to Solve It* by G. Polya – a book on mathematical problem solving (Penguin 1990)). This word comes from the Greek 'to find' and refers to what we might call 'trial and error' methods. Alternative methods depend on being systematic – this may involve either using previous experience or searching for solutions in an organised manner.

Imagine you are going out and can't find your house keys. Finding them is a problem in the sense meant by this section of the book. The heuristic method is to run around all the likely places to see if they are there. After the likely places, you start looking at the less likely places, and so on until they turn up or you have to resort to more systematic methods. There are two systematic ways of searching. The first (using experience) involves thinking carefully about when you last came into the house and what you did – this is often the most reliable and can be the quickest method. The other (which in mathematical terms is often known as the 'brute force' method) involves searching every room of the house thoroughly until they are found. This is often the most reliable method but can take a very long time.

When people are solving problems, they may use all of these methods in the order given above. This is quite logical, as the heuristic method can lead to a very rapid solution whilst the systematic search is slowest. One of the prime skills you need in tackling problem-solving questions in examinations is to make a good judgement of which method is the most appropriate one to use in any set of circumstances.

In any problem you will be presented with some initial pieces of information – these may be in the form of words, a table of numbers, a graph or a picture. You will also know what you need to produce as a solution (the answer to a question). The first thing to do is to identify which pieces of information are most likely to be useful in proceeding to the solution and to try to identify how these pieces of information may be used.

Here is a very simple example that illustrates methods of finding solutions. The information given is in the form of a train timetable:

Oldsville (depart)	5.45	7.15	8.45	10.15	11.45	13.15
Middleham (depart)	6.50	8.20	9.50	11.20	12.50	14.20
Newton (arrive)	8.30	10.00	11.30	13.00	14.30	16.00

Suppose you have an appointment in Newton at 11.30 a.m. It will take 15 minutes to walk from the train station to your appointment. Which is the latest train you can catch from Oldsville?

The first important thing to do is to read and understand the question. Make sure you know where you are leaving from and where you are going to: this immediately shows that the information about Middleham is irrelevant. You also know the time by which you must arrive at the appointment.

The method of calculation should be clear in this simple case: work backwards from the appointment time. If your appointment is at 11.30 a.m., you must arrive at Newton station at 11.15 a.m. at the latest. Therefore you must catch the 7.15 train from Oldsville. If you did not read the question properly, or jumped to an answer without thinking, you might have thought that the 8.45 from Oldsville would do as it arrives in Newton at 11.30.

Although this example is simple, it illustrates many of the methods used in solving problems:

- Identify clearly and unambiguously the solution that is required – reading the question carefully and understanding it are very important.
- Look at the data provided – identify which pieces are relevant and which are irrelevant.
- Do you need to make one or more intermediate calculations before you can reach the answer? This defines a strategy for solving the problem.
- You may need to search the data given for a piece of information that solves (or helps to solve) the problem.
- Past experience of similar problems helps. If you had never seen a railway timetable before, you would have had to spend more time understanding it.
- The problem is solved using a systematic, stepwise procedure (in this case working backwards in time from the appointment).

The activity below involves a slightly different type of problem.

Activity

Geeta runs a small shop. This week she has a special offer on toothpaste. One tube sells at the normal price of $1.20, but if you buy two, the second one is half price. Geeta makes the same amount of profit whether she sells one tube or two.

How much does Geeta pay her wholesaler for each tube of toothpaste?

This is a problem where the method of solution is not immediately obvious. There is a very easy method of solving it (this is where experience of previous similar problems may be useful). However, there are several different methods that could be used.

Firstly, we could guess. If she paid 80¢ per tube, her profit on one is 40¢, but she sells two for $1.80 (second half price) so her profit on two is $1.80−$1.60 or 20¢. This is wrong.

We could then refine our guess by searching. Was 80¢ too high or too low? Try 90¢: this gives profits of 30¢ on one and 0¢ on two, so we went the wrong way. Try 70¢: this gives profits of 50¢ on one and 40¢ on two – we are getting closer so we might find the right answer in the end.

So far, this has taken quite a long time, and little brain-power or 'analysis' of the problem has been used. Let us take a different approach – by thinking more carefully.

We know she makes a certain profit on one tube. If she sells a second one, she makes the same overall profit. This means she makes no profit at all on the second tube, so the wholesale price must be equal to the selling price of the second tube, or 60¢.

That only took a few seconds. It is the sort of solution that you are more likely to come up with if you have seen a lot of similar problems before and you think carefully about the information given.

Finally, to be sure that you got the problem right, check the answer. The profit on one tube was $1.20−60¢ = 60¢, the profit on two tubes was $1.80−$1.20 = 60¢. That's correct!

You should have learnt a little about finding a method of solution from this example. The guesswork method can only work by luck. This may be called the 'pirate's gold' approach – we know the treasure is on the island somewhere so we dig a hole. If it's not there, we dig another one somewhere else. Sometimes this method may seem to work, but it is usually because a little previous experience has been used, even unknowingly. The searching method – this can involve systematic searching or inspired trial and error – is valuable in some cases. Sometimes it is the only method that will work.

In the case above – and in many others – the method of finding a clear strategy was the most efficient. Strategies are not always found by rigorous methods; the discovery of an appropriate strategy usually depends on past experience of similar problems. This will be dealt with in later chapters.

Summary

In this chapter we looked at some methods of solving problems.

We saw how different methods may be used in different circumstances.

We recognised the value of experience in identifying problem types and appropriate methods of solution.

We saw how important it was to read and understand the information and the question.

We looked at the relative merits of guesswork, searching and strategic methods of solution.

1 The petrol usage of a number of cars has been measured. Each car started with a full tank, then made a journey (all journeys were over similar roads). After the journey the tank was filled to the top, the amount of petrol needed to fill it being recorded. The results are shown below. Put the cars in order of their petrol efficiency (km/litre), from lowest to highest.

Car	Length of journey (km)	Petrol used (litres)
Montevideo	120	10
Stella	150	16
Riviera	200	25
Roamer	185	21
Carousel	230	16

2 The votes have recently been cast at the local elections. Voting is carried out using a single transferable vote system. This means that each voter ranks the candidates in order of preference. Votes are counted initially on the basis of all voters' number one ranking. The candidate with the lowest votes is excluded and the votes of those people who placed him or her number one are reallocated using their second preferences.

The results of the first count are shown below. How many candidates still have a chance of winning?

Patel	323
Brown	211
Walshe	157
Ndelo	83
Macpherson	54
Gonzalez	21

3 Rajesh is cooking a meal for some friends. This will involve roasting a chicken – this takes 2 hours cooking time plus 15 minutes resting on removal from the oven. The oven takes 15 minutes to warm up. He will also cook some rice (30 minutes soaking plus 15 minutes cooking), broccoli (5 minutes to prepare and 5 minutes to cook), and a sauce (10 minutes to prepare and 15 minutes to cook).

What should be the timing of events if they are to eat at 7 p.m.?

4 Joseph is making a bookcase. This requires two vertical side pieces of wood 1.2 m high and three shelves 1.6 m long – all 20 cm wide. He will cut these from a sheet of wood 2.4 m x 1.2 m.

Draw a diagram showing how the pieces may be cut to leave the biggest possible uncut rectangle. Are there other ways to cut it?

Answers and comments are on pages 266–7.

31 Selecting and using information

In one very simple form, problem solving involves understanding and making use of information. In the examples considered in this unit, the problem to solve is to select the correct pieces of information and to use them in an appropriate manner.

Information can come in a great variety of forms and, if you want to be good at using it, it is necessary to practise extracting data from a variety of sources.

Here are some possible forms of information:

- Tables: for example, summaries of surveys, specification sheets or transport timetables.
- Graphs: these are used in science and in business to provide information in such a way that it can be absorbed quickly and easily.
- Words: numerical, spatial, logical and many other types of information can be summarised or described in words.
- Pictorial: pictures, for example in the form of engineers' or architects' drawings, can be used not only to show what something looks like, but also to give information about relative sizes and positions.
- Diagrammatic: diagrams come in a wide range of forms: flow charts, maps, schedules and many other things can summarise numerical and spatial information.

Here is a series of activities based on various different forms of information. Try to work them out by yourself before looking at the answers and comments. These activities also introduce some problem-solving methods that are discussed further in later chapters.

Activity

Tabular information

The table shows the results of a survey into portable music player ownership. People in three age ranges were asked what type of portable music player they had.

Age	Type of music player			Total
	CD	MP3	Minidisc	
10–15	45	57	21	123
16–20	119	83	34	245
21–25	54	50	28	132
Total	218	190	92	500

Although the row and column totals are correct, one of the individual figures in the table has been typed incorrectly. Which one is it?

This table has a lot of figures, and finding the incorrect one might seem quite daunting. However, we must look at what we are trying to do and what information we have.

In this case we know that only one individual entry is incorrect and that the totals are correct. All we have to do is check each total in turn. Looking at the column totals, we find that the first two (218 and 190) agree with the entries by adding the three numbers above them. However, the third one does not agree with the entries above it, which add up to 83.

We are not quite there yet – the wrong number could be any of the ones in the 'Minidisc' column. Repeating the procedure for the row totals, we find that the second row (16–20) adds up to 236. The error must be where the wrong totals cross over. The incorrect figure is the '34' in the 16–20 Minidisc entry. It should be 43 – we know it should be 9 higher because both the row and column totals were 9 too low.

Activity

Graphical information

The graph shows the rainfall for a particular island during 2003. The lower end of the bar shows the lowest rainfall for any day during the month and the top end of the bar shows the highest rainfall for any day during the month.

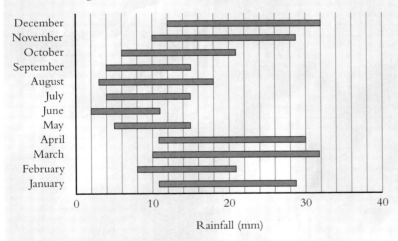

What was the difference between the lowest day's rainfall and the highest day's rainfall during the year?

There are two skills involved here. Firstly one must understand the verbal description of what the graph means. Then, based on the question, one must interpret the graph in the required way.

The solution is quite simple and involves taking the lowest point on any of the bars from the highest point on any of the bars. These values are 2 mm and 32 mm, so the total range is 30 mm.

Verbal information

In an inter-school hockey knockout competition, there are initially 32 teams. Teams are drawn by lots to play each other and the winner goes through to the next round. This is repeated until there are only two teams left, who play each other in the final, and the winner gets a cup. Matches have two halves of 20 minutes each. If the teams are level at the end of normal play, two extra 10-minute periods are played. If it is still a draw, teams take penalty shots at goal to decide the winner.

Chorlton Rangers were eventually knocked out in the semi-final. In one of the earlier rounds they had to play the two extra periods before they won.

For how long in total had Chorlton Rangers played when they were knocked out?

There is a considerable mass of information here, all presented as words. It must be read carefully. The method of solution is not difficult, the skill lies in choosing the correct pieces of information and using them appropriately. First we need to know how many matches Chorlton Rangers played. The first round had 32 teams, subsequent rounds had 16, 8 and 4 when they were knocked out – so they played 4 matches.

Next we need to know how long each match lasts. This is 2 × 20 minutes = 40 minutes. We must also note that Chorlton Rangers played the two extra periods in one match – a total of 20 minutes. So their total playing time was 4 × 40 minutes + 20 minutes or 180 minutes: 3 hours in total.

Pictorial information

The picture shows a tiled wall. Tiles with different printing on them are used to make up the overall pattern.

How many different patterns of tile are needed to make up the pattern?

Solving this requires a systematic evaluation of the picture. We not only need to identify the apparently different tiles, but also to look at how tiles can be used in different orientations. The procedure is to eliminate tiles one by one, noting each time whether a new tile is needed or one we have already seen can be used in one orientation or other.

In fact, only three tiles are needed:

If you did not get the right answer, can you now convince yourself that three tiles as shown is correct?

Activity

Diagrammatic information

The map is a simple representation of the roads joining four towns.

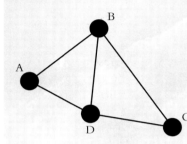

If I live in town B and wish to visit friends in towns A, C and D and then return home without retracing my steps, how many different ways can I do it?

To solve this you need to look at the different orders systematically, always checking with the map to see that any given order is possible. This example introduces the concept of a search, which will be further considered in Unit 34.

From B you can start by going to A, D or C. From A you can then go to D then C and return home. From C you can go to D then A and return home. However, if you start by going to D, inspection of the map will show that you cannot visit both A and C without retracing your steps, so this is not allowed. There are only 2 possible routes.

Summary

In this unit we have seen how data can be presented in several different forms.

We have also seen the importance of reading the question carefully to ensure that the correct pieces of data are extracted from the information given and used correctly.

1 Using the data in the first example above (tabular information), draw a graph (of an appropriate type) showing the proportion of types of portable music player owned by 16–20-year-olds.

2 The pie charts illustrate the change that the introduction of the CD in 1985 had on the recorded-music market. Total annual sales of all types of recording in 1984 were 170 million and in 1994 they were 234 million.

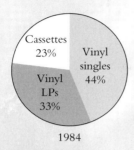
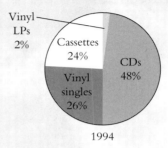

1984   1994

What, approximately, happened to the actual annual sales of vinyl singles between 1984 and 1994?

A   They fell by 14 million.

B   They fell by 5 million.

C   They were unchanged.

D   They rose by 17 million.

E   They rose by 64 million.

3 The table below shows the starting and finishing positions of the rider Claude Chance during the Molivian 2003 Superbike season. He has a bit of a reputation for getting a good grid position by riding fast in practice, but then starting poorly in the race. 'Grid' shows the position in which he started the race.

Race	Grid	First lap	Finish
Alency	2	3	1
Bresville	1	1	1
Argest	3	2	2
Euroland	2	5	3
Saint Croix	2	3	1
Montours	2	1	retired
Stelland	1	1	2
Castelle	1	2	retired
Fertoux	1	4	1
Belle Plage	3	5	3
Grunlande	2	4	retired
Hondoring	3	3	1

In how many races did he lose his position at the start and regain at least one place by the end of the race?

4 A carpenter is fitting some bookcases to an alcove, using as much of the space as possible from floor to ceiling, a height of 2.5 m. The books to be fitted into the shelves are 210 mm high and a gap of at least 30 mm is necessary above each book so they can be removed. The shelves are 20 mm thick. The alcove is 1.2 m wide. The bottom shelf should not be less than 300 mm from the ground as the house owner cannot bend down easily.

How many shelves can be fitted into the alcove?

Answers and comments are on page 267.

32 Processing data

In the previous unit we looked at solving problems by selecting the correct items of data from various sources and using them in the correct way to produce a solution. This unit considers problems where the data are clearly given (i.e. there is no ambiguity about which pieces of data to use). The problems covered here involve using the data in the correct way to find the solution to the problem. The example below illustrates this.

Chris and Sophie are brother and sister and go to the same school. Chris walks to school using a footpath, a distance of 900 m, and he walks at 1.5 m/s. Sophie cycles to school along the roads, a distance of 1.5 km, and she cycles at 5 m/s. They both plan on arriving at school by 8.55 a.m. Who leaves home first and by how much?

A Sophie, by 5 minutes
B Chris, by 5 minutes
C At the same time
D Sophie, by 10 minutes
E Chris, by 10 minutes

This is a multiple-choice question, a type you will see frequently in thinking skills examinations. Some of the examples in this section of the book have multiple-choice answers as in the examinations. However, many have 'open' answers, where you are asked, for example, to give a numerical solution. This is, in many ways, a better way to learn how to do the questions – those with multiple-choice answers will come more easily if you can do the question without needing to know possible answers. If you can come to the solution without looking at the options and then check that your solution is one of the options, this is safer and often quicker than checking the options against the data given. In the case of the example above, it is much better to work out the answer first.

Chris walks 900 m at 1.5 m/s, this takes him $900/1.5 = 600$ seconds or 10 minutes. Sophie cycles 1.5 km (1500 m) at 5 m/s, which takes her $1500/5 = 300$ seconds or 5 minutes. As Chris takes 5 minutes more, he must leave home 5 minutes earlier, so B is correct. (If you are unsure about relating speed, distance and time see the box below.)

The skill in this question is to use the correct pieces of information appropriately and at the right time in the calculation. There are five relevant pieces of data (the two distances, the two speeds and the fact that they arrive at the same time). It is quite clear that the method of solution is to calculate both the journey times, so in this case there is no method to find. Problems where the method is not clear will be discussed in the next unit.

Speeds, distances and times

A lot of problem-solving questions involve calculating one of the variables speed, distance and time from the other two. If you are uncertain how to do this, the formulae below give the method:

speed = distance/time

distance = speed × time

time = distance/speed

If you are worried about remembering these, there is an easy way. Speed is measured in units such as km/h or m/s. This is a distance divided by a time, which is equivalent to the first formula – the others can be worked out from it.

Always check that you use consistent units in calculations. If the speed is in metres per second and the time is given in minutes, you must first convert the time to seconds (or the speed to metres per minute) before applying the formulae.

Also, consider whether your final answer is a reasonable number. If, in the example given above, you had divided Sophie's distance in km by the speed in m/s you would have an answer of 1.5/5 = 0.3. 0.3 seconds or minutes would clearly be ridiculous for 1.5 km and hours did not appear in the calculation – so it is obvious that something is wrong.

Care must be taken when calculating average speeds. Say for example that a river ferry travels between two towns 12 km apart, travelling at 4 km/h upstream and 6 km/h downstream. It might seem that the average speed will be 5 km/h, but this is wrong. In order to calculate the average speed, you must divide the total distance by the total time. In this case, the ferry takes 3 hours upstream and 2 hours downstream – a total of five hours. The average speed is, therefore, 24/5 or 4.8 km/h.

Activity

Pablo has a garden pond, which he tops up at the beginning of each week from a 200 litre water butt which is, in turn, filled by rain water from part of his roof. At the beginning of the summer the water butt is full. The average weekly summer rainfall where he lives is 5 mm. The part of his roof from which he collects rain has an area of 6 m². He uses 60 litres per week on average to top up the pond.

For how many weeks can he expect to have enough water in the butt to top up the pond fully?

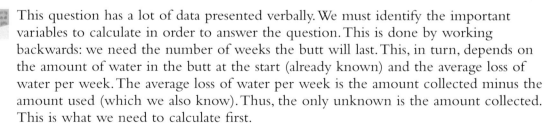

This question has a lot of data presented verbally. We must identify the important variables to calculate in order to answer the question. This is done by working backwards: we need the number of weeks the butt will last. This, in turn, depends on the amount of water in the butt at the start (already known) and the average loss of water per week. The average loss of water per week is the amount collected minus the amount used (which we also know). Thus, the only unknown is the amount collected. This is what we need to calculate first.

The weekly rainfall is 5 mm, which is collected on an area of 6 m². In consistent units (using metres) the volume collected is 6 m² × 0.005 m of rain or 0.030 cubic metres. A cubic metre is 1000 litres, so the volume collected is 30 litres.

As he uses 60 litres per week and collects 30 litres, he loses a net 30 litres each week. Thus his 200-litre butt will last for 5 weeks – at the beginning of the sixth he would only have 50 litres, which would not be enough to top up his pond.

This question illustrates one method of approaching problem-solving questions. We know what answer is required, so which pieces of information do we need to come up with to get that answer? This indicates which calculations need to be made on the given data. This may be represented as shown:

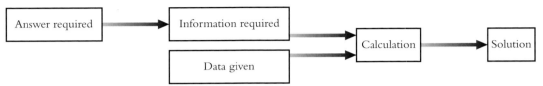

Another type of problem for which the method does not have to be found involves identifying whether there are enough data to solve the problem and, if not, which data are missing. This is a useful building block in problem solving. Identifying which data are needed to solve a problem can save effort in finding unnecessary data or in making unnecessary calculations. Such questions are approached in a manner similar to that shown above. Here is an example:

I recorded a film starting partway through a videotape. The tape counter has four digits and it said 1230 before I started recording. The film finished when the counter said 3265. My brother then took out the tape without rewinding it and put in one of his own, which was partway through. Without resetting the counter he watched a programme he had previously recorded, which he said was 1240 units long. When he finished the counter said 5070. He then rewound his tape to the beginning.

If I put my tape back in without changing the counter, to what setting must I rewind it in order to find the start of my film?

The above problem cannot be solved with the information given. What additional piece of information is needed to solve it?

This question actually has some information that is not needed. I know the length of my film (3265 − 1230 = 2035 counter units), so I know that the tape must be rewound by this much. In order to know where to start, I need to know the counter reading when my brother took his tape out. This is the extra piece of information required.

Which pieces of information in the passage above are not needed? You may like to answer this for yourself.

In this case we were not asked to solve the problem, merely to identify what pieces of information were needed to solve it. In real-life problem solving, the data are not generally given – they have to be found. Having the skill to know which pieces of data are needed can save considerable time and effort. Solving this type of problem does not need particular mathematical skills – just some clear and logical thinking.

Summary

We have seen that, for some problems, the method of solution is not straightforward but needs to be found. In these problems it is the ability to search for and discover an appropriate method that is the primary skill.

We have learned that it can be useful to look for intermediate solutions that can lead to the answer, and have also seen that approaching problems from both ends can be useful.

We also learnt about a different type of problem, in which all the information is not given, and how we might identify which pieces of information are necessary or sufficient to solve a problem.

End-of-unit assignments

1 A department store is having a sale. The advertising hoarding for the sale is shown below:

All goods 40% off marked prices!
If you buy $100 worth of goods or more (at marked prices) you get 60% off all you buy.

Clearly, if you buy just under $100 worth of goods, you would be better off to buy some more in order to qualify for the 60% discount.

For what total purchase values (at marked prices) would it be worth your buying more to qualify for the larger discount and either reducing your total bill, or getting extra goods for free?

2 Sylvia Okwumbe is trying to break her national record of 14 minutes 35 seconds for running 5000 m ($12\frac{1}{2}$ laps of the track). Her average time per lap for the first 5 laps is 1 minute 13 seconds. What average lap time does she need for the remaining $7\frac{1}{2}$ laps?

3 A pancake stall sells sweet or savoury pancakes. The savoury pancakes can have three toppings (eggs, ham, tomato), which may be used in any combination. The sweet ones come with orange, lemon or strawberry jam with either ice-cream or fresh cream. How many combinations does the stall sell?

4 I currently use a conventional light bulb in my living room that is on for an average of 600 hours per year. A conventional bulb costs 60¢ to buy and 2¢ per hour for electricity to run it when it is switched on. It lasts for 2 years on average. I am considering changing to an energy-saving bulb, which will cost $6 to buy but will only cost 0.2¢ per hour to run. It should last for 8 years.

What effect would the change have on my annual electricity bill when averaged over a long period?

Answers and comments are on page 268.

33 Finding methods of solution

The previous unit dealt with problems for which the method of solution was relatively straightforward. In this unit we are looking at problems where the primary skill in solving them is to develop a method of solution. The way of proceeding to an answer in some problems may not be clear either:

a because it is necessary to find an intermediate solution first, or
b because we need to work simultaneously forward from the data (to identify what can be calculated) and backwards from the required answer (to identify what needs to be calculated).

Having a strategy for approaching such problems is important. In particular, it can be very useful if you have seen a problem of a similar sort before, which you know how to approach – this is where experience in tackling problem-solving questions can be invaluable.

One strategy that can help to solve problems when you are not clear how to proceed is to analyse the problem:

* marshal the information you are given
* write down or underline those pieces of information which you feel are important
* simplify – reject unimportant information
* look at the question and decide what pieces of information could lead to the answer
* make a sketch, list or table.

Sometimes, intermediate answers are necessary in order to proceed to the complete solution. This may be regarded as similar to the identifying of intermediate conclusions in Unit 5. The solution of a problem can be like an argument that first leads to one conclusion, then this (possibly using further information) proceeds to the final conclusion.

This may be illustrated in the diagram below. Here, the calculation steps are represented by some of the arrows.

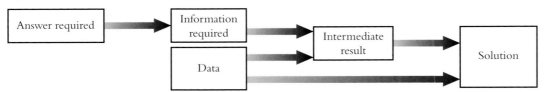

A problem that may be solved using an intermediate result is given in the example below. This is similar to the question in the previous section in that it involves distances, speeds and times but, because of the nature of the question, the method of proceeding is less obvious.

Susan and her brother Jim live 400 km apart. They are going to have a week's holiday by exchanging houses. On the day they are starting their holiday, Susan leaves home at 8 a.m. and Jim at 10 a.m. They both drive at 120 km/h on a motorway that travels directly between their homes.

At what time do they pass each other on the road?

From the data given, it is easy to find out when they both arrive at their destinations, but finding when they cross is not so straightforward. The problem can be made much simpler by using an intermediate step. First calculate where Susan is when Jim leaves. She has been travelling for 2 hours, so she has covered 240 km – that is, she is 160 km from Jim's house. The problem is now quite easy. At 10 a.m. they are 160 km apart and rushing towards each other at a joint speed of 240 km/h. Therefore, they will meet 40 minutes later (160 km/240 km per hour is $\frac{2}{3}$ hour or 40 minutes). The crossing time is 10.40 a.m.

If we had been asked to find the place where they cross, the crossing time could have been used as a second intermediate value. Jim travels 120 km in an hour. 40 minutes represents $\frac{2}{3}$ of this or 80 km, so they cross 80 km from Jim's house.

In this case the numbers were very easy but the same method of solution could have been used whatever the distances, times and speeds.

Activity

Reeta's mobile phone company charges her a monthly sum plus a fixed rate per minute for calls (regardless of the time of day). She said that in her first month she used 300 minutes of calls and the bill was $72. Being horrified by this, she reduced her calls to 180 minutes in the second month and her bill was only $48. She is going to try to keep to 100 minutes per month in future. How much can she expect her bill to be?

This is another problem where an intermediate calculation is necessary. In order to calculate her bill, we need to know the monthly charge and the rate per minute. We know the difference between the first two months' bills – this difference is only due to the reduced calls, so 120 minutes less calls saved $24. This means calls cost 20¢ per minute.

The monthly charge, therefore, is $72 − 300 × 20¢ = $72 − $60 = $12.

If she used 100 minutes in a month, her bill would be $12 monthly charge plus 100 × 20¢ ($20), so the total would be $32.

Another way of approaching problems is to lay out the information in a different way. This is especially so when the information is given verbally – the connection between the different pieces may not be immediately obvious. Consider, for example, the problem given below:

In a class of 32 at a school, all students must study at least one foreign language. French is compulsory, but students may also opt to study German or Spanish or both. 6 students take all three languages. 18 take both French and Spanish. 8 students take only French.

How many are studying German and French but not Spanish?

With a bit of clear thinking, this may be solved in a direct fashion by making an intermediate calculation (those studying only French and Spanish). However, the situation can be made a lot easier by using a Venn diagram.

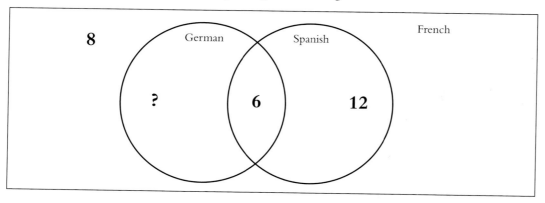

In this diagram, the outer box represents all the pupils (the universal set); in this case they all take French. The left-hand circle represents those taking German (and French) and the right-hand circle represents those taking Spanish (and French).

We know that the number taking only French is 8; this is shown and represented by the area outside both circles. Those taking all three languages are represented by the intersection of the two circles and shown as 6. The number taking French and Spanish is 18; of these 6 take all three, so 12 take only French and Spanish. This is shown by the outer section of the right-hand circle. We can now calculate the number in the area marked by the question mark, as this must be all the students in the class minus the numbers in the other three areas, i.e. $32 - 8 - 6 - 12 = 6$. This is the required answer: the number studying German and French but not Spanish is 6.

Venn and Carroll diagrams

We have seen how a Venn diagram may be used to solve a problem that involves dividing things into categories. Venn diagrams may also appear with more than two categories – these are covered in a later section on more difficult questions.

The same data may also be represented using a Carroll diagram, which is really just a table representing the areas shown in the Venn diagram. Some people may find Carroll diagrams easier to understand. The diagram for the problem above is shown below. All students study French, so this does not appear in the diagram. The figures given in the information for the problem are shown on the diagram: 6 studying Spanish and German, 18 studying Spanish (with or without German) and 8 not studying either German or Spanish. The '?' represents the value we are looking for.

	Studying German	Not studying German	Total
Studying Spanish	6	B	18
Not studying Spanish	?	8	A
Total	C	D	32

It is now easy to see how we can fill in the rest of the table. The value in cell A is 32 − 18 = 14, so the value we need is 14 − 8 = 6 as we found before. Can you calculate the remaining missing values in cells B, C and D and relate these values to areas in the Venn diagram?

Activity

There is one railway on the island of Mornia, which runs from Eastland to Westpoint. There are two intermediate stops at Maintown and Riverford. The trains run continuously from one end to the other at a constant speed, stopping for three minutes at each station. From departing Eastland to arriving at Westpoint takes 42 minutes. From Eastland to Riverford takes 24 minutes. From Maintown to Westpoint takes 36 minutes.

How long does it take from Maintown to Riverford?

 A diagram makes this problem much easier to solve.

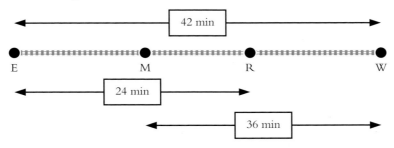

It can now be seen that if we add the time from E to R to the time from M to W, we get the time from E to W plus the time from M to R. The times from E to R and M to W each include one 3-minute stop, whilst the time from E to W includes two 3-minute stops, so when we subtract the EW time from the sum of the ER and MW times, the stops cancel out. Thus the time from M to R is 24 + 36 − 42 = 18 minutes.

We can now look further at an extra useful element in the solution of problem-solving questions − that is, checking that we have the right answer.

If ER takes 24 minutes (including a 3-minute stop) and MR takes 18 minutes (no stop), then EM (no stop) must take 3 minutes (24 − 18 − 3). Similarly, RW must take 36 − 18 − 3 = 15 minutes. We now have the times for all the sections:

EM = 3 minutes
Stop at M = 3 minutes
MR = 18 minutes
Stop at R = 3 minutes
RW = 15 minutes

The total of all these is 3 + 3 + 18 + 3 + 15 = 42 minutes as expected.

Check that the times from E to R and M to W agree with the answer of 18 minutes from M to R as given.

This example once again shows that representing the data in a different way can lead to a simple method of solving a problem that at first appears unclear.

Summary

We have learnt the importance of finding methods of solution for problems for which the way of proceeding to an answer is not necessarily obvious.

We have looked at the value of alternative ways of presenting data and ways of looking for intermediate results that may lead to the final answer.

End-of-unit assignments

1 Anna's neck chain has broken into two parts. She has lost the broken link and is having it repaired by a jeweller who will open one  of the remaining links and use it to rejoin the chain. The chain is made from metal 2 mm thick and each of the broken pieces has a fitting at the end used for closing the chain which each adds 1 cm to the total length.

One of the broken pieces is 33.2 cm long and has 10 more links than the other, which is 25.2 cm long. Excluding the fittings at the ends, how many links will there be in the complete chain?

2 A ferry connects the towns of Upton and Lowside, which are on a river. The river flows at a constant speed of 4 km/h. It takes the ferry 5 hours to go from Lowside to Upton but only 1 hour for the return journey. How far apart are the two towns?

3 Joe and his son Jim are walking along a path. Jim notices that, for every 5 strides he takes, his father only takes 4. Their left feet have just hit the ground at exactly the same time. In how many of Jim's strides will their left feet hit the ground together again?

4 The 23 members of a reception class in a school have done a survey of which cuddly toys they own. Pandas and dogs are the most popular, but 5 children have neither a panda nor a dog. 12 have a panda and 13 have a dog. How many have both a dog and a panda?

Answers and comments are on page 268.

34 Solving problems by searching

Some problems may not always be resolved by using direct methods of calculation. Sometimes, problems do not have a single solution, but many, and we need to find one that represents a maximum or minimum (for example the least cost or shortest time for a journey). In these cases we need to have a systematic method of evaluating the data to come up with all (or at least the most likely) possibilities. Once again, with this type of question, it is important to have a way of checking that the final answer is correct.

Here is an example of a problem that requires a search:

Amir is helping with a charity collection and has gathered envelopes containing coins from a number of donors. He notes that all the envelopes contain exactly three items but some of them contain one, two or three buttons instead of coins. All the coins have denominations of 1¢, 5¢, 10¢, 25¢ or 50¢.

What is the smallest amount of money that is not possible in one of the envelopes?

The easiest way to approach this question is to list the possibilities in a systematic order. We know envelopes can contain 1, 2 or 3 coins. The possibilities with one coin (and two buttons) are: 1¢, 5¢, 10¢, 25¢ or 50¢.

That was the easy part. With two coins (and one button), we need to be a little more careful. First consider that the first coin is 1¢, then look at all the possibilities for the second. We can then continue with the first coin as a 5¢ in the same manner (we do not need to consider repeats). The possibilities are:

1¢ + 1¢, 1¢ + 5¢, 1¢ + 10¢, 1¢ + 25¢, 1¢ + 50¢, then

5¢ + 5¢, 5¢ + 10¢, 5¢ + 25¢, 5¢ + 50¢,

10¢ + 10¢, 10¢ + 25¢, 10¢ + 50¢,

25¢ + 25¢, 25¢ + 50¢, and

50¢ + 50¢.

Listing all the totals we have: 2¢, 6¢, 11¢, 26¢, 51¢, 10¢, 15¢, 30¢, 55¢, 20¢, 35¢, 60¢, 50¢, 75¢ and $1.

Finally, we need to list all the possibilities with three coins. This is slightly more difficult. However, we only need to go on until we have found an impossible amount (you may already have spotted it). The possibilities are:

1¢ + 1¢ + 1¢, 1¢ + 1¢ + 5¢ etc.

1¢ + 5¢ + 5¢ etc.

You should have spotted by now that we have not seen the value 4¢ and that all further sums of three coins (anything including a 5¢ or above) will be more than 4¢. So 4¢ is the answer.

This was actually a trivial example used for the purposes of illustration. There is an alternative way to solve this, which also involves a search. This is to look at 1¢, 2¢, 3¢ etc. and see whether we can make the amount up from one, two or three coins. In this case it would have led to a very fast solution, but if the first impossible value had been, for example, 41¢, this second method would have taken a very long time and we might have been unsure that we checked every possible sum carefully.

Activity

You could try repeating this exercise using coins of denominations 1¢, 2¢, 5¢, 10¢, 20¢ and 50¢ and with 1 to 4 coins in each envelope. This is quite a long search. Consider (and discuss with others) whether there are ways of shortening it.

If you start this search you will find it takes a very long time. It is difficult to be absolutely systematic (especially when considering all options for four coins). It is also difficult to keep track of all values that have been covered at any point in the search. It is necessary to look for short-cuts, and out of boredom you will probably have done so.

The denominations 1¢, 2¢ and 5¢ in combinations of 1 to 3 coins can make all the values from 1¢ to 10¢. This means that, by adding to the 10¢ and 20¢ coins, all amounts from 1¢ to 30¢ can be made. After 30¢ it is necessary to use both the 10¢ and 20¢ or a 20¢ and 2 × 5¢. The former leaves one or two extra coins, which can make 1¢, 2¢, 3¢, 4¢, 5¢, 6¢, 7¢ but not 8¢. The latter leaves only 1 coin, which cannot be an 8¢, so 38¢ is the minimum that cannot be made from 1 to 4 coins. This method involves analysing the problem, which can be a very useful tool in reducing the size of searches.

The type of search shown above involves combining items in a systematic manner. Other searches can involve route maps – looking for the route that takes the shortest time or covers the shortest distance, or tables – for example finding the least expensive way of posting a number of parcels.

With all these searches, the important thing is to be systematic in carrying out the search so that no possibilities are missed and the method leads to the goal. The activity below involves finding the shortest route for a journey.

Activity

The map shows the roads between four towns with distances in km.

I work in Picton and have to deliver groceries to the other three towns in any order, finally returning to Picton. What is the minimum distance I have to drive?

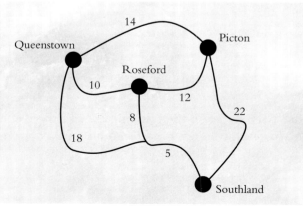

There are only a small number of possible routes. If these are laid out systematically and the sums calculated correctly, the problem can be solved quite quickly.

The possible routes (with no repeated visits to any towns – you should be able to satisfy yourself that it is never worth retracing your steps) are:

PQRSP

PQSRP

PRQSP

PRSQP

PSRQP

PSQRP

This gives six values. In order to see how they are obtained you may note that there are three pairs, each visiting one of the towns first (after leaving Picton). The two routes in each pair take the last two towns in opposite orders.

The distances associated with each route are as follows:

59 km

62 km

67 km

62 km

59 km

67 km

Therefore, the minimum distance is 59 km.

If you were particularly astute, you would have noticed that the routes come in three pairs of the same distance (e.g. PQRSP is the reverse of PSRQP so must be the same). This would have saved you half the calculations.

Summary

We have learned that some problems require a search to produce a solution.

We have seen the importance of being systematic with a search, in order both to ensure that the correct answer is obtained and to be certain that we have the right answer.

We also saw how analysis of the problem can reduce the size of the search and time taken.

1 The notice below shows the prices of admission ($) to the Tooney Tracks theme park.

Adult	12
Child (aged 4–16)	6
Child (aged under 4)	Free
Pensioner	8
Family ticket (for 2 adults and 2 children)	30
Additional child 4–16 or pensioner	5
Additional adult	10
Family ticket (for 1 adult and 2 children)	20
Additional child 4–16 or pensioner	5
Additional adult	10

Maria is taking her 3 children aged 3, 7 and 10 and two friends of the older children (of the same ages) as well as her mother, who is a pensioner.

What is the least it will cost them?

2 I recently received a catalogue from a book club. I want to order 7 books from their list. However, I noticed that their price structure for postage was very strange:

Number of items	Cost of post and packing
1	45¢
2	65¢
3	90¢
4	$1.20
5	$1.50
6 or more	$3.20

I decide, on the basis of this, that I will ask them to pack my order in the number of parcels that will attract the lowest post and packing charge.

How much will I have to pay?

3 Jasmine has been saving all year for her brother's birthday. She has collected all the 5¢ and 20¢ coins she had from her change in her piggy bank. She is now counting the money by putting it into piles, all containing $1 worth of coins. She notices that she has a number of piles of different heights.

If 5¢ and 20¢ coins are the same thickness, how many different heights of $1 pile could she have?

A 5   B 6   C 10   D 11   E 20

Answers and comments are on page 269.

35 Spatial reasoning

Spatial reasoning involves the use of skills that are common in the normal lives of people working in skilled craft areas. Imagine, for example, the skill used by joiners in cutting roof joists for an L-shaped building. It is also necessary for many professionals: the surgeon needs to be able to visualise the inside of the body in three dimensions and, of course, architects use these skills every day of their lives.

Spatial reasoning can involve either two- or three-dimensional tasks, or relating solid objects to flat drawings. Thinking in three dimensions is not something that comes easily to all people, but undoubtedly practice can improve this ability.

In the simplest sense, a problem-solving question involving spatial reasoning can require visualising how an object will look upside down or in reflection. More complicated questions might involve relating a three-dimensional drawing of a building to a view from a particular direction or the visualisation of how movement will affect the view of an object. This unit is shorter in terms of description than most of the others but there are more examples at the end – this is an area where practice is more important than theory.

The example below involves a problem-solving task in two dimensions.

The drawing shows part of the tiling pattern used for a large floor area in a village hall. This is made up of two tiles, one circular (shown in black) and one irregular six-sided tile (shown in white). Approximately what proportion of the two tiles will be needed to cover the whole floor?

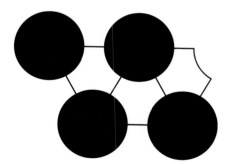

A Three white to one black
B Two white to one black
C Equal quantities of both
D Two black to one white
E Three black to one white

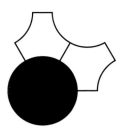

This seems a relatively simple problem, but the answer is not immediately obvious. This is an example of a tessellation problem. There are various ways to go about solving it – one way is to continue drawing the pattern until you have enough tiles that you can estimate how many of each are needed. Another, more rigorous, method is to identify a unit cell that consists of a number of each tile, which may be repeated as a block to cover the whole area. Such a unit cell for this problem is shown in the drawing.

If you now think carefully, you can imagine that this block of three tiles could be repeated over and over again, filling any area without any gaps, to give the pattern shown in the original drawing. So two white tiles are needed for every black tile. B is the correct answer.

The activity below involves three-dimensional reasoning. Because the drawing is not of a familiar object there are no short-cuts – you need to work out what the possibilities are for the unseen side.

Activity

The drawing is a three-dimensional representation of a puzzle piece.

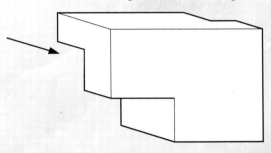

Which diagram is *not* a possible representation of how it looks from the back (i.e. the direction shown by the arrow)? The shaded areas are recesses.

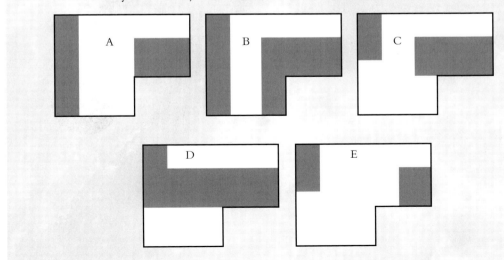

There must be some sort of recess in the top-left corner (top back right as shown on the 3-D drawing). We cannot tell whether it goes right to the bottom as shown in A and B or just some of the way down as shown in C and E.

Similarly, there is a recess that goes through to the right-hand edge (left back on the 3-D drawing). Those shown in A, C and E would all give the same 3-D view from the front. We can now eliminate A, C and E, as both the rear features are shown as being possible. D joins up the two recesses – this would also be possible as the join would not show from the angle originally shown.

We have come to the answer B by elimination – this is a completely valid way of proceeding, but it would be useful to check that this is indeed the correct answer. The recess on the right-hand side of drawing B would be visible at the bottom of the three-dimensional drawing, seen on the right-hand face of the cut-out. So B is not possible.

Once again, this is more difficult than might be expected. We do not actually know what the hidden reverse side looks like – there are an infinite number of possibilities. All we can do is consider what hints are given by the three-dimensional picture. One primary feature of this type of question is that the answer cannot be produced just by considering the information given and the question. This is a backward question. The five options must all be looked at and a decision made on whether each is possible. Backward questions are a regular feature of questions on spatial reasoning and of identifying similarity which is dealt with in the next unit. They do not occur very often in the other types of question. The value of elimination was shown in the method of answering this type of question.

Summary

We have seen the importance of spatial reasoning in many occupations and how problem-solving questions can test this.

The value of practice in solving this type of question has been emphasised.

This unit introduced questions that are backward in that the answer must be found from the options rather than just from the information and the question.

The use of elimination in answering such questions was illustrated.

1 Fred wants to write the letters SFC on his forehead for this afternoon's Sunderland Football Club match. He does it with face paints while looking in a mirror. What should it look like?

2 Draw a simple picture of your house or another building with which you are familiar as seen from above and from the front. How much can you tell about the side and back views from your drawings?

3 Outside the Diorama hotel there is a set of flag poles, as shown in the drawing. The flag poles are all painted different colours (Red, Blue, Yellow, Green, Orange, White).

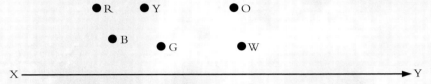

When they are seen from position X, they are seen in the order (from left to right): R Y B O G W.

If somebody walks from X to Y, in how many, and what, different orders will they see the flagpoles (exclude places where one is exactly hidden behind another)?

4 Our local café has an unusual clock on which the minute hand behaves normally but the hour hand goes round backwards. It reads the same time as a conventional clock at 12 noon and 12 midnight. What time is it when the hands are positioned as in the clock face shown?

A 8.50   B 9.15   C 9.45   D 2.15   E 2.45

5 The solid shown, which is a cube with one corner cut off, is made from a shaped and folded piece of cardboard.

Which of the following pieces of cardboard will fold to make the shape (there may be any number correct from 0 to 4)?

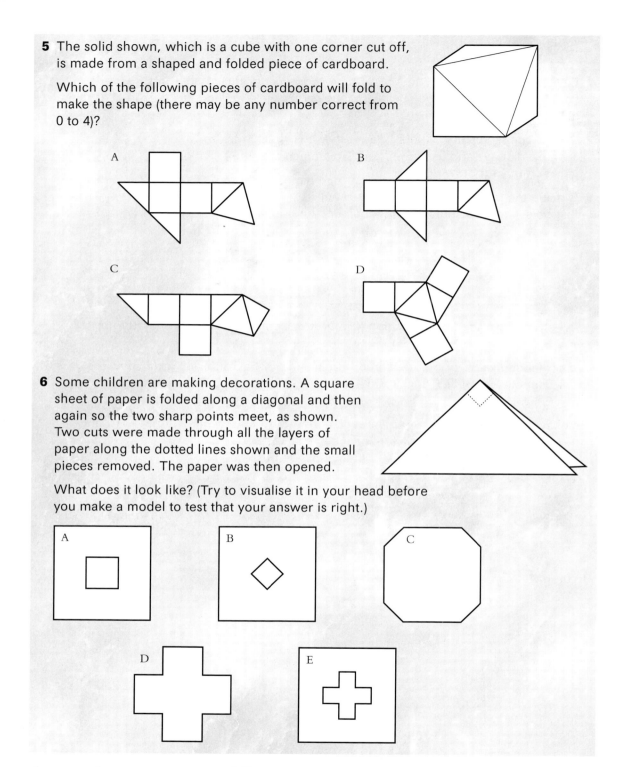

A

B

C

D

6 Some children are making decorations. A square sheet of paper is folded along a diagonal and then again so the two sharp points meet, as shown. Two cuts were made through all the layers of paper along the dotted lines shown and the small pieces removed. The paper was then opened.

What does it look like? (Try to visualise it in your head before you make a model to test that your answer is right.)

A

B

C

D

E

Answers and comments are on page 269.

36 Recognising patterns

In Unit 29 we saw that there are three main skills involved in solving problems. We have already dealt with the first two of these (identifying important information and combining pieces of information). The previous unit on spatial reasoning started to deal with the third main skill: that of using experience to identify relationships between different pieces of information or the same information in different forms. In that unit, we were dealing mainly with visual information. This unit extends that to graphical, verbal and tabular information.

An extension of this skill is to identify possible reasons for variation in data – once again, this springs from past experience as to what causes changes and the types of variation that may be expected. This type of question can be quite similar to those described in Unit 8.

These are best illustrated using examples. The first deals with identifying the similarity between two sets of data.

The table shows the results of a survey into ownership of various household appliances by families who live in a town.

Appliance	Dishwasher	Vacuum cleaner	Washing machine	Microwave oven	Food processor	Toaster
% ownership	68	98	77	54	34	92

Which of the bar charts accurately represents the data shown above?

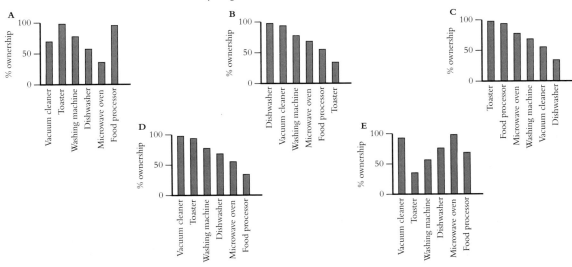

This question is actually quite easy. It is only a matter of being careful and matching appliance to bar length correctly. The main complication (and this is a potential trap for those who don't look at the question and the graphs carefully) is that the order of the appliances in the graphs is different in some cases from the order in the table. Also, the exact heights of the bars cannot be read accurately enough at the scale on which the graphs are drawn, so it is necessary to look at the relative heights of the different bars.

In fact D is the correct graph. The appliances have been put into order by their percentage ownership. A has the appliances ordered as for D but the bars are in the order of the table. The other graphs have similar errors – you might like to identify the error in each case.

The next example looks at identifying reasons for variations in data.

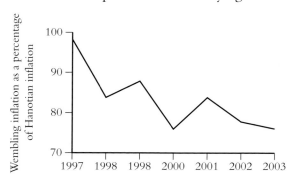

The graph shows the inflation rate in the province of Wembling as a percentage of inflation in the country of Hanotia as a whole over the period from 1997 to 2003.

Which of the following could explain the variations shown in the above graph?

A Hanotian inflation has been high over the period shown.
B Hanotian inflation has risen over the period shown.
C Food prices in Wembling have risen less than in Hanotia as a whole.
D Food prices in Wembling are subject to higher seasonal fluctuations than in Hanotia as a whole.
E The inflation rate in Wembling is falling due to high unemployment.

Let us look at these five answers in turn. It is important to remember that the graph represents the inflation in Wembling as a percentage of the inflation in Hanotia, not the *actual* inflation rate in Wembling.

A The graph represents only the ratio between Wembling and the whole of Hanotia; high inflation in Hanotia cannot explain the shape of a graph of the ratio.
B A rise in Hanotian inflation would only cause the fall in the ratio shown if the inflation in Wembling was less: we know nothing about this.
C If food prices rose less in Wembling than in Hanotia as a whole, this could explain why the ratio fell – even if inflation in Wembling was rising.
D Seasonal fluctuations would only manifest themselves within a year, not between years.
E Even if the inflation rate in Wembling is falling, we know nothing about the inflation rate in the whole of Hanotia, so we cannot conclude that the ratio would fall.

Thus C is the only reasonable answer. The others depend either on reading the graph incorrectly or reading more into the graph than we can safely conclude. This illustrates the importance of reading and understanding the information given (both verbal and in other forms) and of reading the question correctly. Beyond that, the deductions that can be made follow from the application of correct logic.

Solving these two types of problem depends on the skill of recognising an identity between data presented in two forms. As with spatial reasoning, this skill comes with practice and it can be useful to look at data in newspapers to see how they are presented and to consider whether they are always presented in the clearest way.

Activity

The table shows the results of a questionnaire, asking the five colleges in a town the proportion of students taking 1–4 A-level subjects.

	Percentage of students taking number of A-levels shown			
College	1	2	3	4
Abbey Road	13	25	42	20
Barnfield	5	18	55	22
Colegate	24	36	28	12
Danbridge	16	18	61	5
Eden House	10	14	48	28

The local newspaper (forgetting that there might be different total numbers of students in the five colleges) just added the numbers together and divided by 5 to produce a percentage graph for the town as a whole. However, they forgot to add in the data for one college so their percentages did not add up to 100.

Which one did they forget?

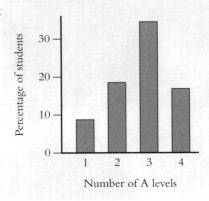

 This question is a little more difficult than some we have seen so far. There are several ways to approach it. We can note that if we knew the actual averages for the four colleges the newspaper *did* include, it might be possible to see if these averages disagreed with an estimated average for the five colleges and the direction of the error would give some indication of which one was forgotten.

Looking at the 'averages', the approximate values (we have to estimate these from the graph) are 9, 19, 35 and 16 respectively for 1, 2, 3 and 4 A-levels. Multiplying these by 5/4 (to correct for the fact that they were divided by 5 instead of being divided by 4), we get (approximately): 11, 24, 44 and 20.

If we were being very systematic, we could now compare these with all sets of four averages, but it would take a long time. Instead, let us note that the 11 looks a little low for the averages of 1 A-level, as does 24 for the averages of 2. 44 for the averages of 3 looks very low and 20 for the averages of 4 looks far too high. From this, we may suspect that Danbridge has been missed as it is higher than the others for 3 A-levels and lower for 4.

We can check this by averaging one of the columns for the other four colleges (preferably use 3 or 4 A-levels as they look to have the biggest discrepancy) and comparing the results – try this for yourself and see whether you can confirm that Danbridge is the college whose results are missing.

Summary

We have learnt how data may be represented in more than one way and the importance of systematic comparisons between two sets of data in ascertaining that they are the same.

We saw that reading graphs and tables carefully is necessary in order not to make errors in identifying similarities.

The use of careful logical deduction was seen to be important in identifying the reasons for variations in data.

End-of-unit assignments

1 Look in the newspapers (business pages are often useful) or on the Internet to find examples of numerical data in various forms (verbal, graphical, tabular). Express the data in a different form. Consider which form makes the data clearest to understand.

2 Four-digit personal identification numbers (PINs) are used to withdraw cash from banks' machines using plastic cards. It can be very difficult to remember your personal number. I have a method of remembering mine. It is the two numbers of my birth date (i.e. the date in the month) reversed, followed by the two digits of my month of birth reversed (using a zero in front if either is a single number so, for example, May would be 05).

Which of the following could not be my PIN?

A 3221   B 5060   C 1141   D 2121   E 1290

3 Four house teams play each other in a school hockey league. The scoring system gives 3 points for a win, 1 point for a draw and 0 for a loss.

They all play each other once, and the league tables before the last round of matches are as follows:

	Played	**Won**	**Drawn**	**Lost**	**Points**
Britons	2	0	2	0	2
Danes	2	1	1	0	4
Normans	2	1	0	1	3
Saxons	2	0	1	1	1

Which of the following is a possible table of the scores after the last two matches are played? (Hint: you first need to decide which games have already been played, so you know what is left.)

	A	**B**	**C**	**D**	**E**
Britons	5	3	5	5	2
Danes	5	4	7	5	5
Normans	3	4	3	4	6
Saxons	2	4	1	1	2

4 The graph shows the charges made by a book club for sending out various numbers of books. All books cost the same amount.

Which of the following pricing structures would give the graph shown?

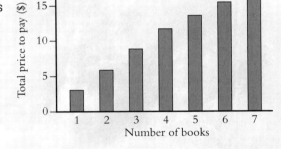

A $2 plus $1 postage and packing per book

B $2 per book plus $3 postage and packing for any number of books

C $2 plus $1 postage and packing per book, postage and packing free on any books over 4

D $2 plus $1 postage and packing per book, postage and packing on all books free if you order over 4

E $2 per book plus $3 postage and packing for 1–4 books, $1 extra postage and packing per book if you order any more than 4

Draw the graphs for the other price structures.

Answers and comments are on pages 269–70.

37 Making choices and decisions

A lot of the problems we encounter in everyday life involve making choices and decisions. To buy or not to buy? Which one to buy? How much to buy? Which train to take? All these are types of choice and decision that contribute to problem-solving processes and involve the use of skills that can be tested by problem-solving questions.

A lot of these questions can involve skills that have been covered in earlier units: extracting information, processing data and finding methods of solution can all be involved. The example below is of a question where a choice has to be made:

My local shops all have different discounts on jars of coffee.

Which of the following represents the best value for money?

A Everlo: $1.29 for a 150 g jar
B Foodland: $2.89 for 200 g, buy one get one free
C Springway: $3.36 for 300 g, buy one get the second half price
D Superval: $1.57 for 150 g, 50¢ voucher off the next 150 g (one voucher per customer)
E Massive: $1.57 for a 150 g jar with 50 g extra coffee free

In this case it is easiest to express all the prices to a 300 g equivalent – you may see that this requires fewer calculations than, for example, converting them all to 100 g.

A is 2 × $1.29 = $2.58 for 300 g
B gives 400 g for $2.89, so 300 g is $\frac{3}{4}$ × $2.89 = $2.17
C gives 600 g for 1.5 × $3.36 = $5.04 or 300 g for $2.52
D First 150 g is $1.57, second is $1.07 so 300 g is $2.64
E $1.57 for 200 g or $2.35 for 300 g

So B is the best value.

This is quite straightforward; no skills that have not already been introduced are involved. It is just necessary to work efficiently and correctly, finding the most effective way of approaching the problem.

The activity below involves making a decision.

After school on 5 days a week, my 3 children usually have an apple each. If they have friends visiting (this may happen to any of them, but only on 3 days a week), their friends also eat an apple. I buy small apples in pre-packs that can contain anywhere from 5 to 8 apples. How many packs should I buy a week to make sure they can all have apples when they want?

This is a maximum and minimum type problem: we have to combine the most apples that could be eaten with the smallest number in a pack.

The most that could be eaten is 6 (the most children I may have) × 3 days per week plus 3 (my children) × 2 days per week or 24 per week.

The minimum in a pack is 5, so I could need as many as 5 packs.

You might also like to work out what is the minimum number of packs I might need.

This illustrates a particular type of decisions question – where the decision is based on the minimum (or sometimes the maximum) to fulfil a criterion.

Summary

We have seen how problems may involve making choices and decisions.

These may involve selecting one item from a number or options or making a decision on an action.

In solving these problems it is important to choose an efficient way of working so the correct answer is obtained and calculations are carried out in the most effective and simplest way in order to reduce the chance of error.

End-of-unit assignments

1 In a game of pontoon dice, you continue throwing a single die until the sum of all your throws exceeds 21 (bust) or you decide to stop. You win plastic counters depending on the score you stop at.

Stopping score	Counters won or lost
1 to 12	0
13 or 14	Win 1
15 or 16	Win 2
17 or 18	Win 3
19	Win 6
20	Win 8
21	Win 10
Over 21	Lose 4

After 4 throws you have 17. Should you throw once more? Consider the chances of getting different scores and how much you will win or lose. What is best on average?

What should you do if you have a score other than 17?

2 Anna's local supermarket has an offer on petrol, depending on the amount you spend in the store. If you spend $20–$30 you get a voucher that gives you 2¢ per litre off petrol; if you spend $30 to $50, you get 3¢ per litre off and if you spend over $50 you get 4¢ per litre off. Anna's car will take 30 litres of petrol.

Consider for what range of total purchase prices in the supermarket it is worth her buying a small amount extra, so that the reduction in the petrol cost will make her total bill smaller.

3 Pupils at a school have to decide what subjects they are going to study next year. English, science and mathematics are all compulsory, but they can choose the remaining four subjects.

The table shows how the choices can be made. They must choose one subject from each column. The fourth subject may come from any column.

1	2	3
geography	French	history
technology	German	religious studies
art		physical education
music		Latin

Which of the following combinations would not be allowable?

A   French, geography, physical education, art

B   French, German, Latin, music

C   technology, German, art, history

D   French, German, geography, music

E   geography, music, French, religious studies

4 The country of Hanotia prints stamps in the following denominations:

1¢, 2¢, 5¢, 9¢, 13¢, 22¢, 36¢, 50¢, $1.00, $5.00

A mail order company sends out equal numbers of three sizes of package, which incur postal charges of 34¢, 67¢ and $1.43. They want to stock as few different denominations of stamp as possible (but not only 1¢ stamps as sticking lots of these on envelopes would be a nuisance!).

Which ones should they stock?

Answers and comments are on pages 270–71.

38 Using models

In the sense used in this unit, the word model means an abstract representation of an object or a process, not for example a small copy of the Eiffel Tower.

Models are usually mathematical or graphical. They help us to understand how things work and give simplified representations that can enable us to do 'what if?' type calculations.

A very complicated example of a model would be the type that governments set up to simulate their economies. These usually consist of large numbers of mathematical equations and are implemented on computers. They can predict (with varying success) things such as what will happen to the inflation rate if interest rates are raised. Such models are gross simplifications because there are too many variables contributing to the condition of a national economy and not all can be included.

Models are also used by scientists, for example in predicting population growth. A model such as this, which may be used to predict fish stocks in commercial fishing areas, can be invaluable as it may be used to control quotas on fish catches to ensure that fishing does not reduce stocks to unsustainable levels.

In both of these cases, the model has been produced as a result of a problem-solving task. Clearly, such large models are beyond the scale of a thinking skills examination, but some of the skills used in modelling can be developed and tested.

Here is an example where you are asked to choose between several different models based on a simple real-life scenario. This is based on Pablo and his water butt, which we first met in Unit 32.

Pablo has a garden pond, which he tops up at the beginning of each week from a 200-litre water butt which is, in turn, filled by rain water from part of his roof. At the beginning of the summer the water butt is full. The average weekly summer rainfall where he lives is 6 mm. The part of his roof from which he collects rain has an area of 8 m². He uses 60 litres per week on average to top up the pond.

Which of these graphs represents the volume in Pablo's water butt from the beginning of the summer?

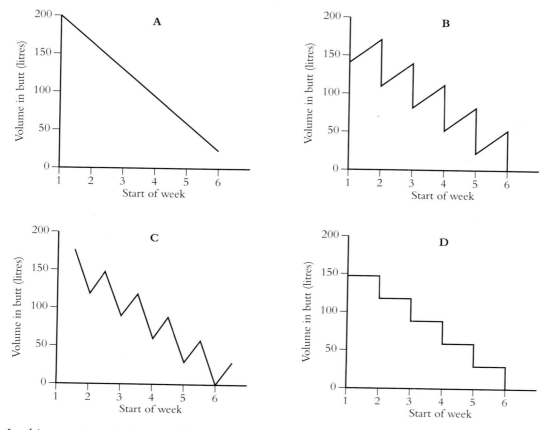

In this case, it is the form of the model that we are trying to recognise. The water level drops suddenly at the beginning of each week when he fills up the pond and rises gradually during the week due to rainfall. Graph B shows this. Graph A only shows the average loss of 30 litres per week – this would only be correct if he trickled water gradually into his pond during the week instead of filling it in one go. What is wrong with graphs C and D?

Graph B is a *model* of the way Pablo's water butt works. It is, of course, an approximation, in that rainfall does not come as regularly as is shown, but it is the best we can do as we do not know exactly how the rainfall will vary. This type of model can be used to predict what would happen in the future and could be modified to allow for any changes, for example if he installed another water butt.

Many people use models in their everyday lives without even realising it. An efficient shopkeeper will, for example, have a set of rules that tells her how much ice-cream to order so she has enough in the summer months and less in the winter.

The activity below requires you to go some way towards developing a mathematical model of the situation in order to solve the question.

Activity

Naraya has a small part-time business making greetings cards. The cost of materials for each card she makes is 45¢. Her fixed overheads (heating, lighting, use of computer etc.) come to $2,000 per year. She can sell her cards to shops for $1.20 to $1.60 (they will double this to get their selling price to the customers) but she knows that for every 10¢ increase in her price, she loses 10% of her customers.

Investigate the relationship between her sales volume and profit. She would like to make a profit of around $3,000 per year. How does she calculate the optimum price at which to sell cards?

At a selling price of $1.20, she makes 75¢ per card. Thus, to cover her overheads and make her desired profit, she needs to make and sell $5,000/0.75 or approximately 6,700 cards per year. If her price were increased to $1.30, she would only have to make $5000/0.85 or approximately 5,882 cards. This is a decrease in required sales of more than 10%, so it is better for her to charge the higher price.

Plot or tabulate the price against profit and consider whether there is a price above which a rise would not be worthwhile. Remember that the sales reduce 10% for every 10¢ rise in price. If there is an optimum, can you find a way of discovering it by any method other than trial and error?

Summary

We have learnt how a mathematical or graphical model may be used to approximate real-life processes.

We have seen how models can be set up so they can be used for prediction.

A graph of any sort is a model from which it is possible to get a visual idea of how variations can occur.

End-of-unit assignments

1 A novelty marketing company is selling an unusual liquid clock. It consists of two tubes as shown. The right-hand tube fills up gradually so that it is full at the end of each complete hour, and then empties and starts again. The left-hand tube does exactly the same in 12 hours. The time shown on the clock is 8.20.

Draw what the clock looks like at 3.45 p.m.

2 Jerome likes to go hill-walking. He is planning a walk up a 1000 m high mountain, a distance from base to top of 15 km. He will retrace his steps on the way down. He knows that on a mountain of this height he will average 2 km/h going up and 5 km/h on the way down, spending 15 minutes at the top. It is a very hot day, and the local tourist information centre is recommending that anyone walking should drink $\frac{1}{2}$ litre of water every hour. There is a spring two-thirds of the way up the mountain at which he can refill his water bottle.

How big a water bottle will he need to take?

3 A telephone company's rates consist of a fixed charge of 60¢ for calls up to 3 minutes then 0.1¢ for each second thereafter.

Which column in the following table represents the average price per minute of calls?

Call time (min)	Average cost of call per minute				
	A	B	C	D	E
1	60	60	60	20	60
2	60	30	30	20	33
3	60	20	20	20	24
4	6	16.5	6.5	16.5	7.5
5	6	14.4	6.4	13.7	7.2
6	6	13.0	6.3	11.4	7.0
7	6	12.0	6.3	9.4	6.8
8	6	11.2	6.2	7.7	6.7
9	6	10.7	6.2	6.0	6.6
10	6	10.2	6.2	6.0	6.6

Answers and comments are on page 271.

39 Combining skills – using imagination

The next five units deal with more advanced problems. In some cases these are just harder examples based on the skills you have already learned. In other cases, slightly more advanced use of mathematics is required. This does not go beyond algebra and probability at relatively simple levels but, if you are not confident with this, you can move straight to Unit 44, which deals with checking whether you have the correct answer. The problems may involve the use of several different skills in one question, require extra stages of intermediate result or require more imagination in developing methods of solution. The examples in this section, some of which are longer and harder than those you are likely to encounter in AS-level thinking skills tests, will help you to improve your skills and make the standard questions seem easier. They will be particularly useful for those candidates taking higher-level tests, including A-level.

This unit deals with problems that seem more intractable at first sight and need more imagination in coming to a solution.

The problem below is an example of one that needs this type of imagination – although data extraction and processing skills are needed to solve this problem, the main difficulty is in finding a method by which to solve it.

Gurning is an activity held in Cumbria where competitors have to contort their faces into the most extreme shapes. Several Cumbrian villages have a gurning competition each year. Each village puts up a champion gurner who demonstrates his or her skills, then the villages vote one by one (they are not allowed to vote for their own gurner). Each village awards 8 votes to their favourite, 4 to the second and 2 to the third and 1 to the fourth. Clearly, tactical voting is important, so the order of voting is changed every year. This year, they vote in order from most northerly to most southerly. The results before the last two villages have voted are shown (in voting order). Who still stands a chance of winning?

Northwaite	6
Kirkby Morton	5
Blackport	6
Hawgig	24
Garthdale	12
Heatherside	9
Wibble Moor	24
White Peak	4
Feldene	13
Buncastle	17

This is mainly a data-extraction type question. Such questions are normally quite straightforward but this one includes a large amount of information to digest and a method of solving it also needs to be found.

There are three important things (the first skill is to identify these):

1 The scoring system, which means that with two villages left to vote, the maximum extra votes that any one village can score is 16.
2 The fact that a village cannot vote for itself, which means that Feldene and Buncastle can only receive a maximum of 8 more votes.
3 Some villages might score no more, so any village that can pass the mark of 24 can still win.

Given these three things, the method becomes much clearer. The appropriate maximum available must be added to each team and the result compared with 24. The allocation of the lesser votes is unimportant, as they could go to villages who have no hope anyway.

Adding 16 to the first 8, we see that 4 of them can exceed 24: Hawgig, Garthdale, Heatherside and Wibble Moor. Adding 8 to the last 2, Feldene cannot reach 24 but Buncastle can reach 25. So 5 teams can still win. Buncastle would be best advised not to vote for Hawgig or Wibble Moor!

You may see that this question required no new skills, and the mathematics was limited to simple addition and counting. The difficulty in this question was in using the information correctly and seeing how best to proceed.

The activity below gives an example in which the main problem is in identifying a method of proceeding. The information in this case is much simpler.

Activity

A survey of UK petrol prices showed the average to be 82.5p per litre. Filling stations in East Anglia made up 5% of the survey and the East Anglian average was 86p per litre.

On average, how much more expensive is petrol in East Anglia than the rest of the country?

This problem is not, in principle, any harder than those we have encountered earlier. It is mathematically slightly more complex and a clear idea of the meaning of an average must be retained.

We can quickly note that 5% is $\frac{1}{20}$ of the total. One easy way to proceed is to assume that there were 20 filling stations in the survey, one of which was in East Anglia.

The sum of the prices at all UK filling stations must have been $20 \times 82.5 = 1650$p. The price in the East Anglian filling station was 86p. Therefore the sum of the prices in the remaining 19 was $1650 - 86 = 1564$. The average in the rest of the country was $1564/19 = 82\frac{6}{19}$ or about 82.3p. So East Anglian prices are, on average, 3.7p more expensive than in the rest of the country.

Since all the numbers are just over 80p, we could make life easier by subtracting 80p from everything, leaving smaller numbers to work with. As long as we remember to add the 80p back on at the end, this will still give the right answer. For example, if we wanted the average of 82 and 86, we could say this was $(82 + 86)/2 = 84$. It would be much easier to note that the average of 2 and 6 is 4, then add this back on to the 80. In the example above the calculations reduce to:

$20 \times 2.5p = 50$

$50 - 6 = 44$

$44/19 = 2\frac{6}{19}$

Once again, experience and a lot of practice is the way to become efficient at solving the harder problems. The more different types of problem you have seen, the more you will be able to build on your skills and combine skills you have previously learnt into techniques for solving new types of problem.

Summary

We have looked at more difficult problem-solving questions that require a combination of skills to solve them.

The value of experience has been emphasised in recognising the skills needed for a question and applying them in an appropriate manner.

We have seen the importance of recognising the important things in a question and simplifying it by concentrating on these.

We have seen how imagination may be required to come up with methods of solution for types of problem that you may not have previously seen.

End-of-unit assignments

1 There are four teams in the netball league on the island of Naldia. In a season, they play each other once. Three points are awarded for a win, one for a draw and none for a loss. At the end of the season, the points were as follows:

Dunrovia: 6

Arbadia: 4

Brindling: 4

Crittle: 2

(a) How many matches were drawn?

(b) What was the result of the match between Dunrovia and Crittle?

(c) If Brindling beat Dunrovia, can you determine the results of all the matches?

2 Andy, Benita and Chico went out for a meal together. When the bill came, they originally decided to divide it equally between them. However, Chico admitted to having chosen more expensive dishes and noticed that his total was $3 more than the amount he would have paid if they split it equally.

If Andy and Benita's bills would have been $12 individually, how much was Chico's?

3 Conchita is making a quilt. The overall size is 1.7 m × 2.0 m. It will have a pattern of 6 × 5 patchwork squares in the middle and an equal border all the way around as shown below.

What size should the patchwork squares be?

4 Bill, Harry and Fred run a gardening business. Bill pays all the annual fixed costs (insurance, telephone line rental etc.) by instalments, which amount to $400 per week. Harry buys the materials for any job they do. Fred collects the payment for jobs. They split all profits evenly and settle up after every job is completed. They have just done a landscaping and re-fencing job for Mrs Fothergill that took the three of them exactly 2 weeks. Materials cost $1,400 and Mrs Fothergill paid Fred $4,900.

How much does Fred owe Bill and Harry?

Answers and comments are on pages 271–2.

40 Using other mathematical methods

Some types of question may be answered in a more straightforward manner by using mathematical techniques of a slightly higher level than those required so far. In particular, simple algebra can be used to give a clear statement of the problem, which can then be solved by standard mathematical methods. Other areas where some mathematical knowledge can help are those such as probability, permutations and combinations, and the use of highest common factors and lowest common multiples. Although these techniques are beyond the elementary methods we have used so far, they are dealt with in the early stages of secondary education, and most candidates for thinking skills examinations will have some knowledge and skill in these areas.

Consider the problem below. This is similar to one we encountered earlier. It can be solved using intuition or trial and error, but the algebraic method illustrated is quicker – use of such techniques can be a particular help when working on thinking skills questions under time pressure.

A ferry travels at 20 km per hour downstream but only 15 km per hour upstream. Its journey between two towns takes 5 hours more going up than coming down. How far apart are the two towns?

Before looking at the algebraic solution below, you may like to consider alternative ways of solving the question.

If the distance between the two towns is x km, we have:

Time upstream = $x/15$ hours
Time downstream = $x/20$ hours.

Thus, since the difference between these times is 5 hours:

$x/15 - x/20 = 5$

Multiplying both sides by 60:

$4x - 3x = 300,$

so x, the distance between the towns, is 300 km. Put this answer back into the question to check that it is right.

This was a very simple example and hardly needed the formality of a mathematical solution. However, similar methods can be used for more complex questions to reduce them to equations that can be solved quite easily. Try the problem below.

Kara has just left the house of her friend Betsy after visiting, to walk home. 7 minutes after Kara leaves, Betsy realises that Kara has left her phone behind. She chases Kara on her bicycle. Kara is walking at 1.5 m/s; Betsy rides her bike at 5 m/s.

How far has Kara walked when Betsy catches her?

Once again, there is more than one way of answering this question, but algebra can make it much more straightforward:

If Kara has walked x metres when Betsy catches her, the time taken from Kara leaving Betsy's house is $x/1.5$.

The time for Betsy to cycle this distance is $x/5$. We know that Kara takes 7 minutes (420 seconds) longer than Betsy, so:

$x/1.5 - x/5 = 420$

Multiplying both sides by 15:

$10x - 3x = 420 \times 15 = 6300$, and
$x = 900$ metres.

900 metres takes Kara 600 seconds and takes Betsy 180 seconds – a difference of 420 seconds or 7 minutes as required. We could also calculate that it takes Betsy 3 minutes to catch Kara.

Another example follows of a problem that can be solved using a simple mathematical technique:

From a boat at sea, I can see two lighthouses. The Sandy Head lighthouse flashes every 6 seconds. The Dogwin lighthouse flashes every 8 seconds. They have just flashed together. When will they flash together again?

There is a straightforward way of solving this with little mathematics: just list when the flashes happen:

Sandy Head: 6, 12, 18, 24, 32 seconds later

Dogwin: 8, 16, 24 seconds later.

So they coincide at 24 seconds. Those with a little more mathematical knowledge will spot that this is an example of a lowest common multiple (LCM) problem. The answer is the LCM of 6 and 8. The prime factors of 6 are 2 and 3; the prime factors of 8 are 2, 2 and 2. One of the 2s is common to both so the LCM is $2 \times 2 \times 2 \times 3 = 24$, the same answer as before.

In this case there is little to choose between the two methods, but if the counting method gave no coincidence for 30 or 40 values, the LCM method would be much faster. There is another lighthouse example in the end-of-unit assignments, but with a twist. Problem-solving question-setters often use such twists to take problems out of the straightforwardly mathematical so that candidates must use their ingenuity rather than just knowledge. Even so, using the mathematics you do know can often reduce the time necessary for a question.

Another area where a little mathematics can help is in problems involving permutations and combinations. Here is another simple example:

Three married couples and three single people meet for a dinner. Everybody shakes hands with everybody else, except that nobody shakes hands with the person to whom they are married.

How many handshakes are there?

Without the twist of the married couples, this would be very straightforward – the answer is 9 × 8 / 2 = 36. You have to divide by 2 because the '9 × 8' calculation counts A shaking hands with B and B shaking hands with A. The married couples can be taken care of easily, because they would represent 3 of the handshakes, so the total is 33.

The alternative way to do this is to count: AB, AC, AD, AI, BC, BD etc. This is very time-consuming.

The activity below is a probability problem with a slight twist.

Activity

At a village fair one stall has a game of chance that involves throwing two dice. The dice are normal, numbered 1 to 6. One is red and one is blue. The number on the red die is multiplied by 10 and added to the number on the blue die to give a two-digit number. (So, if red is 2 and blue is 4, your score is 24.) You win a prize if you get more than 42.

What are the chances of winning?

There are 36 (6 × 6) possible throws in all. If the red die shows 1, 2 or 3, whatever the blue die shows, you lose (18 of the throws). If the red die shows 5 or 6, whatever the blue die shows, you win (12 of the throws). This leaves 6 possible throws with the red die showing 4: you lose with 2 of these (blue 1 and 2) and you win with 4 (blue 3, 4, 5 and 6).

So the number of ways of winning is 12 + 4 = 16 out of 36. (The number of ways of losing is 18 + 2 = 20 out of 36). So the probability of winning is 16/36 = 4/9.

Summary

This unit has shown how knowledge of a few relatively simple mathematical techniques can make the solution of some problem-solving questions quicker and more reliable.

The use of algebra, permutations and combinations, and simple probability can aid the finding of methods of solution and shorten the work required for some problems.

1 At my local baker's, the price of bread rolls is 25¢ and I went with exactly the right money to buy the number I needed. When I got there, I found they had an offer giving 5¢ off all rolls if you bought 8 or more. Consequently, I found I could buy 3 more for exactly the same money.

How many was I originally going to buy?

2 From my boat at sea I can see three lighthouses, which flash with different patterns:

- Lighthouse A flashes 1 second on, 2 seconds off, 1 second on, 1 second off then repeats.

- Lighthouse B flashes 1 second on, 3 seconds off, 1 second on, 2 seconds off, 1 second on, 3 seconds off then repeats.

- Lighthouse C flashes 2 seconds on, 1 second off, 1 second on, 2 seconds off then repeats.

They have all just started their cycles at the same time. When do they next all go on at the same time?

3 Four friends have a photograph taken with them all throwing their graduation hats in the air. Afterwards they pick up the hats and find they all have the wrong hat. How many different combinations of hats are there? In how many of these combinations do they all have the wrong hat?

4 My wife has sent me to the bank with her cash card. I do not know the four-digit number I have to enter into the machine to withdraw money. I know the first two digits are the two digits of her month of birth, in the right order. The last two digits are the date in the month of her birthday. There are no zeros and I have forgotten my wife's birthday.

What are the chances of my getting it right first time? What are the chances of my getting it right in the three attempts I am allowed?

Answers and comments are on page 272.

41 Use of more complex diagrams

Venn and Carroll diagrams were introduced in Unit 33. The problems considered there were relatively simple and could have been solved without the diagrams, just by using a bit of clear thinking.

In this unit we are going to look at problems that are more complicated and, although they could be solved without the use of diagrams, the diagram makes the solution much more straightforward.

Taking a problem of a similar nature to that which we used to introduce Venn diagrams, the extension to one more category makes analysis of the problem much more complex, as in the following example.

Elections have just been held in the town of Bicton. There were two parties, the Reds and the Blues. Turnout to vote was 70%. The Reds got 60% of the vote and the Blues the remaining 40%. An exit poll showed that 30% of women voting voted Red, whilst 70% voted Blue (there are equal numbers of men and women registered to vote and the percentage turnout was the same for men and women).

What proportion of men in the total electorate voted Blue?

The rectangle represents all those who voted. We do not need to consider the non-voters as the exit poll does not categorise whether non-voters can be defined as Blue, Red, Men or Women. We just need to remember that only 70% of the electorate voted.

The left circle represents the Red voters and the right circle represents Women voters. R represents Red, B represents Blue, W represents Women and M represents Men.

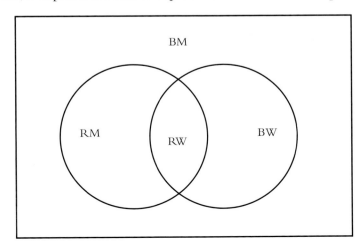

We know that the Red vote was 60% of those who voted, so the areas:

RM + RW = 0.6 × 0.7 = 0.42, i.e. 42% of the electorate, and

BM + BW = 0.4 × 0.7 = 0.28, i.e. 28% of the electorate.

We know that 50% of the electorate were women, 70% of these voted, of these 30% voted Red and 70% voted Blue so:

RW = 0.5 × 0.7 × 0.3 = 0.105, i.e. 10.5% of the electorate, and

BW = 0.5 × 0.7 × 0.7 = 0.245, i.e. 24.5% of the electorate.

We can now calculate the proportion of the electorate in each area of the diagram:

RW = 10.5%, BW = 24.5%, RM = 31.5% and BM = 3.5%.

(We can check that this is correct as these add up to 70% – the turnout, and both men and women add to 35% – equal numbers. The proportion of women voting Red is 10.5/(10.5+24.5) = 30% and the proportion of Red voters is (10.5 + 31.5)/70 = 60%.)

The area BM indicates that 3.5% of the electorate were men who voted Blue. Since half the electorate are men, we can now answer the original question: 7% of men voted Blue.

As was shown in Unit 33, this can also be solved using a Carroll diagram – Venn and Carroll diagrams become more complicated when there are more categories of things involved but a problem involving more than three categories is unlikely to appear in a thinking skills examination.

The Carroll diagram for three categories may be drawn with an inner rectangle expressing one level of the third category (e.g. non-voters) and, for the problem above, would appear as in the diagram.

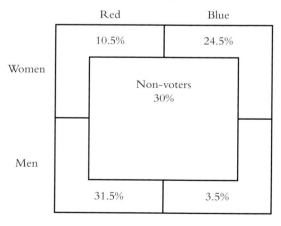

The inner rectangle is not subdivided as it represents the non-voters. In this case (and, in fact, in many cases) the Carroll diagram is easier to understand than the Venn diagram and the various subdivisions and sums may be more easily seen and totalled.

Activity

A general household repairs business has 15 workers. 2 are managers and do not have specialised skills. 5 are plumbers and do not do other jobs. There are 6 electricians and a number of carpenters. Of these, 3 can work as either electricians or carpenters. How many are carpenters but not electricians?

The Venn diagram for this problem is shown here. As none of the plumbers are either electricians or carpenters, their area does not intersect with the other two. The entire outer box represents the 15 workers. The '2' shown on the diagram outside the circles is the two managers who do

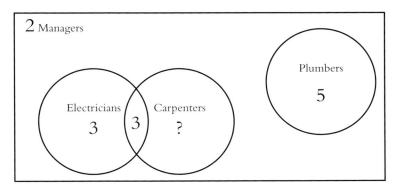

not fit any of the other categories. The 5 plumbers are shown in their circle. The intersection between electricians and carpenters represents those 3 falling into both categories. As there are 6 electricians, there must be 3 who are not also carpenters. We now have 13 accounted for so the remainder, 2, must be carpenters but not electricians.

Certain problems, especially those in probability that are not absolutely straightforward, can be solved using a tree diagram. This enables probabilities for certain combinations of events to be evaluated and allows probabilities to be divided between all possible circumstances. Here is an example:

I have 6 coins in my pocket, 4 of 5¢ and 2 of 10¢. If I take 3 coins out of my pocket at random, what are the chances of the total being 20¢?

The method of solution of this problem using a tree diagram is shown below. At each stage (i.e. as each coin is drawn from the pocket) the branches of the tree show the possibilities (in this case only the withdrawal of a 5¢ or 10¢ coin) and the numbers beside the branches show the probability of each outcome. After three coins are withdrawn, all possible combinations of coin may be calculated (by adding along the branches) and the probability of that combination obtained (by multiplying along the branch). After making the calculations, you may check whether you are correct as the sum of the probabilities should be 1.

Coin 1	Coin 2	Coin 3	Total	Probability
		5¢	15¢	$\frac{2}{3} \times \frac{3}{5} \times \frac{1}{2} = \frac{1}{5}$
	5¢	10¢	20¢	$\frac{2}{3} \times \frac{3}{5} \times \frac{1}{2} = \frac{1}{5}$
		5¢	20¢	$\frac{2}{3} \times \frac{2}{5} \times \frac{3}{4} = \frac{1}{5}$
5¢	10¢	10¢	25¢	$\frac{2}{3} \times \frac{2}{5} \times \frac{1}{4} = \frac{1}{15}$
		5¢	20¢	$\frac{1}{3} \times \frac{4}{5} \times \frac{3}{4} = \frac{1}{5}$
	5¢	10¢	25¢	$\frac{1}{3} \times \frac{4}{5} \times \frac{1}{4} = \frac{1}{15}$
		5¢	25¢	$\frac{1}{3} \times \frac{1}{5} \times \frac{1}{1} = \frac{1}{15}$
10¢	10¢	10¢	30¢	$\frac{1}{3} \times \frac{1}{5} \times \frac{0}{1} = 0$

The problem may now be solved. Reading from the top, combinations 2, 3 and 5 lead to a sum of 20¢. The sum of the probabilities for these three combinations is $\frac{1}{5} + \frac{1}{5} + \frac{1}{5}$ or $\frac{3}{5}$ — a 60% chance.

Summary

In this unit we have seen how Venn, Carroll and tree diagrams may be used to represent and solve more complicated problems in categorisation, logic and probability.

End-of-unit assignments

1 My drawer contains 8 blue socks and 6 black socks. If I take 4 socks out at random, what are the chances that they will make up two matching pairs?

2 Draw a Venn diagram for three categories to sort the numbers from 1 to 39 according to whether they are even, multiples of three or square numbers. Write each number in the appropriate part of the diagram.

3 The island of Nonga has two ferry ports: Waigura and Nooli. All ferries from Waigura go to Dulais on the island of Soria. Some ferries from Nooli also go to Dulais. Some of the ferries that serve Dulais are fast hydrofoil services, those going elsewhere are slow steamboats.

Which of the following statements can safely be concluded from the information given above?

A   No hydrofoils go to Dulais from Nooli.

B   All hydrofoils going to Dulais leave from Waigura.

C   Some hydrofoils from Nooli go to places other than Dulais.

D   Some steamboats from Waigura go to Dulais.

E   All hydrofoils from Waigura go to Dulais.

4 A fairground game involves taking three throws to get a ring over two poles in the ground at different distances from the throwing position. Throws must be taken alternately at the two poles, but you may start with either one. You win a prize if your ring lands over a pole in two successive throws out of the three.

Clearly, it is easier to throw the ring over the nearer pole than the farther one. Is it better to make your attempts in the order 'near, far, near' or 'far, near, far' or doesn't it matter?

Answers and comments are on pages 273–5.

42 Modelling and investigating

The modelling problems described in Unit 38 involved choosing the correct model of a given situation. More advanced modelling questions can require the solver to use a model to draw conclusions or actually to develop a mathematical model for a given situation and make inferences from the model derived. Some of the problems we have already seen are in this category, but the model is so simple that you are usually unaware that you are using it. For example, the activity in Unit 33 about Reeta's telephone bill involved recognising that the bill, made up of a fixed monthly charge and an amount per minute, could be represented by:

Cost = fixed charge + m × minutes used

where m is the charge per minute. This equation is a simple mathematical model.

An investigation is a problem where a set of information is given and the student is asked to consider various scenarios, either to find which is the best or just to consider the results of various options. Investigations are closely related to modelling, in that a model may be developed to help with the investigation. Some investigations can be quite open-ended – some students will be able to take problems further, extract more detail, illustrate the results better etc.

Here is an example that leads to a fairly simple model.

Perfect Pots is a company making decorative plant pots. Its overheads (rent on premises, insurance etc.) are $15,000 per year. There are four administrative staff (manager, accountant, sales director and secretary) earning a total of $85,000 per year. The pots are made by a number of skilled workers – each can produce up to 5000 pots a year and earns $20,000 per year. Materials, power etc. cost $1000 per 10,000 pots.

How will the company's profits vary with the number of pots made and sold (assuming they only make pots to supply orders) and the selling price of the pots?

The model depends on the number of workers, and it must be remembered that each one cannot produce more than 5000 pots per year.

The mathematics of this model are quite simple, depending only on multiplication, addition and subtraction. If the number of workers is n, the number of pots produced and sold is m and the selling price per pot is p, the profit can be calculated as follows:

Income = mp

Expenditure = $100\,000 + 20\,000n + 1000m/10\,000$

Profit = $mp - 100\,000 - 20\,000n - m/10$.

The table shows how this varies, assuming the number of workers employed is controlled by the number of pots produced.

Annual production	Workers employed	Selling price per pot ($)			
		10	12	14	16
1 000	1	−110 100	−108 100	−106 100	−104 100
2 000	1	−100 200	−96 200	−92 200	−88 200
3 000	1	−90 300	−84 300	−78 300	−72 300
4 000	1	−80 400	−72 400	−64 400	−56 400
5 000	1	−70 500	−60 500	−50 500	−40 500
6 000	2	−80 600	−68 600	−56 600	−44 600
7 000	2	−70 700	−56 700	−42 700	−28 700
8 000	2	−60 800	−44 800	−28 800	−12 800
9 000	2	−50 900	−32 900	−14 900	3 100
10 000	2	−41 000	−21 000	−1 000	19 000
11 000	3	−51 100	−29 100	−7 100	14 900
12 000	3	−41 200	−17 200	6 800	30 800
13 000	3	−31 300	−5 300	20 700	46 700
14 000	3	−21 400	6 600	34 600	62 600
15 000	3	−11 500	18 500	48 500	78 500
16 000	4	−21 600	10 400	42 400	74 400
17 000	4	−11 700	22 300	56 300	90 300
18 000	4	−1 800	34 200	70 200	106 200
19 000	4	8 100	46 100	84 100	122 100
20 000	4	18 000	58 000	98 000	138 000

This type of model is useful to the accountant and sales director in producing sales targets. This leads to the type of 'what if?' analysis that is commonly used in economics. Note that there are points at which selling extra pots means employing an extra worker, which can lead to a fall in profits.

The example below is more investigative – you have to consider various options and their effect on the result.

I mow my lawn (as shown in the diagram) using a push-along mower. My speed when mowing is 1 m/s. My mower cuts a strip 0.5 m wide. When I reach the edge, I must turn the mower around. If I turn it through 90° it takes me 5 seconds; if I turn it through 180° it takes me 8 seconds. Every 30 m, I need to empty the grass box, which takes 1 minute. Each time I start a stretch, I must start 1m into the lawn (as I don't want to stand in the flower beds), but I can mow right to the edge in front of me. I only mow in straight lines.

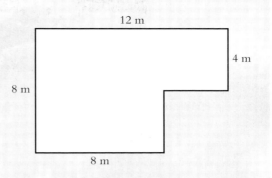

There are various strategies I can use. I can do it all side-to-side as in the orientation shown in the plan or top to bottom (in both cases remembering to cover any bits I may miss by starting 1 m inside the edges). Alternatively, I can go right round the outside, then do the next strip in etc. until I get to the centre.

How long will it take me using the best strategy?

This is a realistic problem and requires both data processing and a search (of possible strategies). In cases like this, it is not always possible to be absolutely sure that you have found the optimum – but the investigative process will often make the best strategy clear.

We consider only one possibility here; you should go on to look at others for yourself.

Side-to-side strategy: If I start in the bottom-left corner, each strip on the short bit will be 7 m long (starting 1m inside the lawn). 4 m requires 8 strips – 56 m in total (56 seconds) and 8 × 180° turns (the last one makes me ready to do the long section) taking 64 seconds. I will have emptied the grass box once (1 minute), so this takes 3 minutes.

The long section will take 11 m × 8 strips = 88 seconds and 7 × 180° turns (56 seconds). I had 26 m worth of grass left in the box after the first section, so the total is 88 + 26 = 114 m, needing emptying 3 times. The total time for this section is 88 seconds + 56 seconds + 3 minutes = 5 minutes 24 seconds.

I must now consider the bits I left by starting inside the edge. The left-hand edge is easy, as I am now at the top-left corner. To do this, I do a 90° turn and mow the 7 m back to the start: 5 + 7 = 12 seconds. This was only 0.5 m, so I must do it again, 0.5 m in from the edge, another 180° turn and 7 m mowing: 8 + 7 = 15 seconds. However, I had 24 m worth of grass in the box, so need to empty it once. The total is 1 minute 27 seconds.

The bits I missed on the right-hand edges are more complicated. There are two 4 m sections. It is most efficient to mow these when I get there. When I get to the bottom-right (after the first strip) I do a 90° turn, mow 3 m, another 180° turn and 3 m back. I then need to turn 90° to be ready for the next strip (note that this saved me one 180° turn in the first section). I will not need to empty the grass box (it now has 14m worth of grass in it). This takes me 5 + 3 + 8 + 3 + 5 − 8 = 16 seconds (the −8 is for the time saved on the first section).

The top-right 4 m strip will take exactly the same time (if done after the first long strip): 16 seconds. I will then have to finally empty the grass box at the end.

The total is: short section – 3 minutes; long section – 5 minutes 24 seconds; left edge – 1 minute 27 seconds; right edges – 2 × 16 seconds; emptying box at the end – 1 minute. The total is 11 minutes 23 seconds.

You should now be able to convince yourself (without doing much more work) whether the up-and-down method would be better or worse. This leaves only the round-and-round, or spiral, method to investigate – you can do this for yourself.

This exercise was surprisingly complicated – it required quite a lot of calculation and needed great care, both in deciding the order of actions and arithmetically. This is typical of investigative problems, in real life as well as in examinations.

Summary

We have seen how models can be developed for a variety of situations that allow the prediction of what will happen if certain variables change.

A model can be used as part of an investigation to carry out 'what if?' analyses.

End-of-unit assignments

(A calculator or computer spreadsheet will be useful for these assignments.)

1 Duane and Mervin are going to town, a distance of 12 km. They have only one bike between them, so they decide that one should ride a certain distance while the other walks. The cyclist will then leave the bike by the side of the track for the walker to pick up when he arrives, and continue on foot. The walker will then ride the same distance and they will repeat the process until they get to town. Duane rides at 15 km/h and walks at 6 km/h. Mervin rides at 20 km/h and walks at 4 km/h.

How long does it take until they both reach town if they use the best strategy?

If you have time, you may consider what would happen if they cycle different distances – can the time for them both to arrive in town be improved?

2 A Grand Prix motor race consists of 60 laps of 5 km each. Some of the specifications for the Marlin team car are as follows:

Fuel consumption: 1 litre/km

Fuel tank capacity: 160 litres

Refuel rate: 15 litres/second

Pit stop time: 10 seconds plus time to refuel

Average speed (no fuel): 75 seconds/lap

Speed with fuel: 0.12 seconds slower/lap for each 5 litres of fuel carried

It may be seen that the car cannot carry enough fuel to complete the race without a pit stop. However, the car goes slower if it carries more fuel. The fuel gauge is very accurate, so it can effectively be run down to zero before refuelling. (Hint: in order to calculate the average lap time for each section you may use the average fuel load. Assume the race is broken into equal distances between pit stops.)

How many pit stops should the car make to complete the race as fast as possible, 1, 2 or 3?

3 A supermarket sells three types of nuts:

Brazil nuts: 80¢/kg

walnuts: 70¢/kg

hazelnuts: 40¢/kg

The shop makes 50% profit on each type of nut. They wish to sell mixed nuts at 60¢ per kg. What proportion should the mix of the three nuts be if they are to make 50% profit on the mixed nuts? Is there one answer or a range of answers? If so, which contains the most even mix of nuts? Can you generalise the result?

Answers and comments are on pages 275–6.

43 Analysis: hypotheses, reasons and inference

We have seen that problems involving making inferences from data or suggesting reasons for the nature of the data may appear in either the critical thinking or the problem-solving sections of thinking skills examinations.

Such examples are usually based on quantitative (numerical or graphical) data and may arise from such areas as finance or science. They require analysis of the data given in order to reach some conclusions that may be drawn from the data or to suggest reasons for the nature of the data.

The example below shows an example based on a scientific scenario. While this requires a little understanding of basic scientific concepts, most of the skills involved in coming to a solution depend on clear, logical thinking. This graph shows the results of an experiment to determine the growth of a culture of yeast in a nutrient medium. The liquid containing the nutrient was made up and a small amount of yeast introduced. At regular intervals afterwards, the solution was stirred, a small sample taken and the concentration of yeast measured. The graph represents a smooth line drawn through the results.

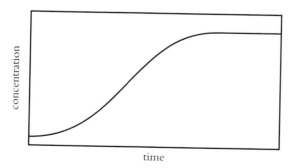

Which of the following explanations are consistent with the shape of the curve? (Answer as many as apply.)

A Yeast cells divide when they have grown enough, so grow exponentially if they have enough nutrient.
B The rate of increase of yeast cells depends only on the amount of nutrient.
C Eventually, the growth of yeast cells is limited by lack of nutrient.
D Yeast cells die when there is insufficient nutrient.
E The shape of the curve is explained by a linear growth in yeast and a linear decrease in nutrient.

Looking at the statements in turn:

A This statement explains the initial increase in growth rate – the increase looks exponential.

B This statement would not explain the initial growth, it would start at a finite growth rate, which would then decrease all the time.

C This statement would explain the drop to zero growth after a time, linked to a lack of nutrient.

D There is no indication of death – the population would fall.

E Any combination of two linear processes would itself be linear:
$(a + bt) + (c - dt) = (a + c) + (b - d)t$: another linear function.

So A and C are the explanations for the shape of the curve.

Longer questions at A-level can involve analysing quite complex data and determining what conclusions may be drawn from it. The activity below is of this type.

Activity

The graph shows which types of charities benefit from donations from the general public.

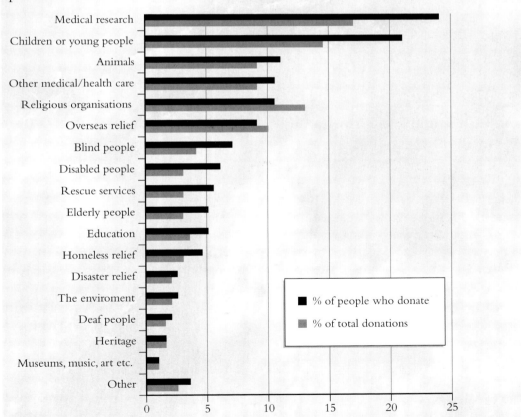

Source: NCVO

The sources of income for charities (as a whole) are shown in the pie chart.

Where income comes from

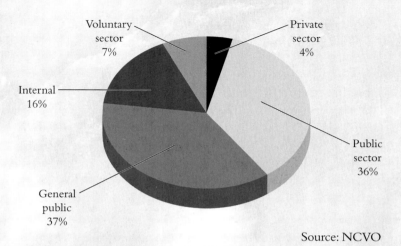

Source: NCVO

Answer the following questions and give brief explanations of your answers:

1 For which type of charity do individuals donate the largest average amount?

2 For which type of charity do individuals donate the smallest average amount?

3 What percentage of total charity income is the general public's donations to medical charities?

4 6% of charities receive 90% of the total income, yet medical research accounts for 17% of donations. Explain this.

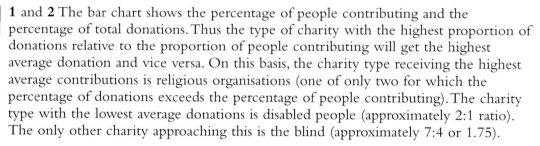

1 and **2** The bar chart shows the percentage of people contributing and the percentage of total donations. Thus the type of charity with the highest proportion of donations relative to the proportion of people contributing will get the highest average donation and vice versa. On this basis, the charity type receiving the highest average contributions is religious organisations (one of only two for which the percentage of donations exceeds the percentage of people contributing). The charity type with the lowest average donations is disabled people (approximately 2:1 ratio). The only other charity approaching this is the blind (approximately 7:4 or 1.75).

3 The general public donates 37% of total charity income (pie chart). Of this, 17% goes to medical charities. Thus donations to medical charities from the public represent 6.3% of all charity income.

4 This is explained by the fact that a small number of charities receive very large incomes – there will be a large number of medical research charities, some of which will be very small so will not contribute to the 6% that receive 90% of the income. The 6% will be made up of a small number of charities in the top few categories. In the lower parts of the chart, there will be a huge number of very specialised charities receiving very small incomes. The numbers on the chart do not relate to the numbers of charities, only to the proportions.

Summary

We have encountered more complex examples where we are required to suggest a hypothesis or a reason for the nature of variation in data.

We have seen that extended examples where more data are supplied can require analysis that may lead to a range of conclusions.

End-of-unit assignments

1 In order to treat a particular disease effectively, patients are initially given two drugs. Drug A alone has the effect shown on the graph below (10 = total relief from symptoms. 1 = no relief).

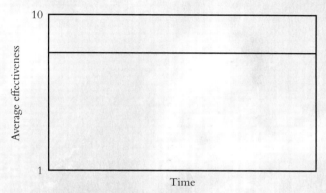

The effect of drug B as a function of time is shown in the graph below (on the same effectiveness and time scales).

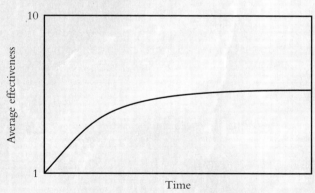

The reason the patients are given two drugs is that drug A, whilst being very effective, has long-term deleterious side effects. Drug B takes some time to become effective, and has a lower eventual effect but can be taken indefinitely. The regime used by doctors is to give both drugs starting at the same time, then to withdraw A linearly until, at half the time shown in the graphs, patients have stopped taking it.

Assuming that the effects of the two drugs are independent, what would be the expected shape of the graph of effectiveness for a patient on the regime described above?

2 The graphs show estimates of world fossil-fuel reserves, world energy consumption and regional energy consumption by source.

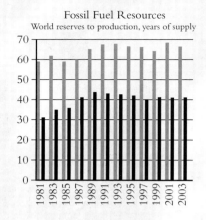

Fossil Fuel Resources
World reserves to production, years of supply

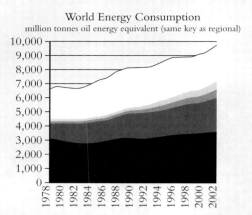

World Energy Consumption
million tonnes oil energy equivalent (same key as regional)

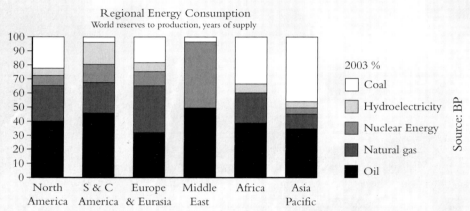

Regional Energy Consumption
World reserves to production, years of supply

2003 %

☐ Coal

Hydroelectricity

Nuclear Energy

Natural gas

■ Oil

Source: BP

(i) The first graph shows gas and oil reserves as a function of time; the second graph shows energy consumption as a function of time and the third graph shows the percentage consumption of various fuels in different regions of the world. Are the following statements true, false or can they not be confirmed? Give a brief reason for your answer in each case.

(a) The world's oil supplies will run out in about 40 years, and the gas supplies in about 70 years.

(b) There are about 50% more gas reserves than oil reserves.

(c) Over recent years, new discoveries of oil and gas have just about matched consumption.

(d) Oil and gas reserves are being discovered at an increasing rate.

(e) Energy consumption is increasing, while the known available reserves are fixed.

(ii) Known oil reserves rose during the 1980s and have been roughly constant since. Over all this period, world consumption of oil has risen little. Consider what might have caused the reserves graph to show this behaviour.

(iii) In the article accompanying these charts, the author states:

Higher priced energy will slow global economic growth and that damages living standards everywhere ... the big issue is the extent to which high-priced fossil fuels stimulate the quest both for greater efficiency in energy use and the development of alternative sources ... it typically takes 30 years for a development to get from the initial invention to widespread global application ... there isn't anything likely to change the world. If that is right, the only way forward is the quest for greater efficiency ... the lesson of the 1980s may be helpful ... higher prices are really the only weapon that works ... in the medium term we should hope that the oil price does not fall back too far and the complacency of the 1990s sets in again.

The Independent, June 2004

Given that reserves are finite and world energy consumption is rising, what would be the implications of higher prices and less use of fossil fuels on world energy reserves and consumption?

3 In the group stages of the Euro 2004 football tournament, teams were in groups of 4 in which all played each other, making 6 games in total. The first two teams in each group after this stage went through to the quarter-finals. Teams were awarded 3 points for a win, 1 for a draw and 0 for losing.

After 4 matches in Group 1, the situation was as follows:

Team	Played	Points	Won	Drawn	Lost	Goals for	Goals against
Greece	2	4				3	2
Spain	2	4				2	1
Portugal	2	3				3	2
Russia	2	0				0	3

The remaining two games are: Spain versus Portugal and Greece versus Russia.

(a) Can you reconstruct the missing data (games won, drawn and lost for each team)? How much further can this be taken: can the results of individual games be established; can the scores be deduced?

(b) Which teams can still qualify for the next stages and for what results of the final two matches will each possible pair of teams go through?

(Note: in the event of a draw on points between two teams, the results of the match between those two teams will decide who goes through; if this was a draw, the difference between goals scored and goals conceded decides and, if this is equal, the team with the most goals scored will go through. If all else fails, qualification will be decided by drawing of lots.)

Answers and comments are on pages 276–8.

44 Have you solved it?

This unit considers how you may check and be sure that your answer to a problem-solving question is correct. In real life, there might be several possible answers, or even no answer to a problem (can you fit a square peg into a round hole?). However, in examinations, especially those with multiple-choice answers, there must be a correct answer. One of the options in some cases might, of course, be that the task cannot be done. This means that, when you have an answer, you must have a way of being sure that it is correct.

Different problems need to be checked in different ways. Sometimes it is possible to put the answer back into the question and see if it 'fits'. This is probably the easiest way.

For example, look at the question in Unit 30 on Geeta selling toothpaste. She sells one tube for $1.20 and two for $1.80. She makes the same profit on both transactions. How much does she pay her wholesaler per tube? The answer we came to was 60¢. If we put this answer back into the question we see that she made $1.20 − 60¢ = 60¢ profit on one transaction and $1.80 − 2 × 60¢ = 60¢ profit on the other. They are both the same, so the answer is right. Similarly, the first problem in Unit 31, with the table showing personal music player ownership, could be checked by putting the correct answer into the table and seeing whether all the rows and columns added up correctly.

You can go back and check the answers for a lot of the activities and examples in this section of the book by using the 'put it back in' method.

However, the next problem in Unit 31, with graphs showing rainfall, cannot be checked in this way. We are simply being asked to extract the right value from the graph and there is no way of putting this back in to see whether it is right. In cases like this, the answer simply has to be checked carefully. What exactly was the question asking? Is this what we answered? Is the numerical value of the answer about what we would expect?

The same applies to questions requiring a search. 'Putting the answer back' will tell you whether your answer fits the criteria asked for in the question but will not tell you whether it is the lowest (or largest) possible answer. If the search is not too large, you can sometimes check, if you are looking for the least of something, that all smaller answers will not work. This can be time-consuming and unpractical if the search is large. It is often better to check your method and be sure that it will come up with the correct answer.

Approximation, or a feel for the magnitude of results are skills that can be refined by doing a lot of this type of question. This is particularly valuable when questions depend on getting the decimal point in the right place. A minimum temperature of 10 °C might be acceptable when 100 °C would not.

The end-of-unit assignment considers several problems that may have a variety of ways of checking. It is always preferable to use a different method for checking the problem from that which you originally used to solve it. If you simply repeat your original calculation, it is possible that any mistake you made in the first instance you will make again.

Checking the answers of questions involving searches (Unit 34) can be more difficult. There can often be more than one may of searching but, if you have done the question efficiently, any other way may be time-consuming. It is often more important to ensure that your method of searching is 'cast-iron' and will not produce an incorrect answer unless you make a slip.

Multiple-choice questions

There are some particular aspects of answering multiple-choice questions that can help in getting the correct answer. One is elimination. This is especially useful in answering questions involving spatial reasoning and identifying similarity between two sets of data. Even if you are guessing an answer, you can increase your chances of getting it right by eliminating one or two of the options.

It is not always necessary to check every aspect of a drawing, graph or table to be sure that it is wrong. Sometimes one needs only to check a single part – one plotted point on a graph – to eliminate it as a possible answer. This means that the time available for the question can be concentrated on the more likely answers and in checking that your final answer is correct. You can try this in the activity below.

Activity

Consider the activity in Unit 35 on page 211 about the different views of a puzzle piece. How many of the options can you eliminate by looking at just one feature on the three-dimensional drawing? Look at another feature and see whether this will eliminate more. How many different things do you need to look at until you have only one possible answer left? Can you then check that your final answer is right? – try drawing a three-dimensional view of the solid from another direction.

Although thinking skills questions in examinations have to be done under a certain amount of time pressure, it is important that you have some certainty that your answers are correct. Some checking can only take a few seconds or, if you can use methods of solving problems which give a good degree of certainty that the answer will be correct, you will stand a much better chance of doing well. Even on questions where you are uncertain of the answer, elimination of some options will increase your probability of getting the right answers and thus improve your score. Good examination technique is as important in thinking skills tests as in anything else.

Summary

We have seen how an answer may be checked by 'putting it back' into the question.

This method may not work for all questions and other ways of checking may be needed for other types of question.

Elimination of incorrect answers can help in finding the correct solution to multiple-choice questions.

End-of-unit assignment

Reconsider some or all of the following problems from the end-of-unit assignments. See whether you can find ways of checking that your answer is correct. Try to use a different method from the one originally used for solving the question. Look at how you might eliminate some of the options in multiple-choice questions.

Unit 30, problem 2

Unit 31, problem 2; problem 4

Unit 32, problem 2

Unit 33, problem 1; problem 4

Unit 34, problem 3

Unit 35, problem 4

Unit 36, problem 3

Unit 38, problem 2

PART 3 End-of-unit assignments: answers and comments

End-of-unit assignments
Answers and comments

1   What is an argument?

1 A suitable conclusion would be: 'The next ice age should begin in the next few thousand years.'

2 There are many possible answers. These are suggestions:

    (a) All students receive the same education from their college or university.

    (b) A car with one person in causes as much pollution and congestion as a car with four occupants.

    (c) It requires hard work and complete dedication to reach the top levels in sport.

3, 4 *Variable*

2   Recognising arguments

1 B is the only passage that can be understood as a reasoned argument. It can be rearranged, and the 'therefore' test applied, as follows:

> Aspirin, which is a safe and effective painkiller for most humans, is fatal to the domestic cat. Penicillin poisons guinea pigs. These examples alone show that differences do exist between species with regard to drugs. Therefore the public should not expect the safety of drugs to be guaranteed by animal testing.

A similar test makes no sense of the other two passages.

2 Not complete. The author obviously thinks that the MTR should follow the lead of the KCR and have announcements in Mandarin as well as Cantonese and English, but this is not a stated conclusion.

3   Responding to arguments

Variable

4   Analysing arguments

1 Three reasons are given for the conclusion.

    R1 There have been health alerts about the chemicals found in bottled water.

    R2 It is absurdly expensive.

    R3 Tap water is improving in quality.

    Therefore

    C People should not be so ready to spend their money on bottled mineral water.

Each of the reasons adds to the argument, without relying on the other reasons.

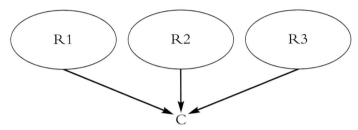

2 Two reasons combine to support the conclusion.

    R1 At the highest levels of sport drugs can make the difference between winning gold and winning nothing.

    R2 The rewards are so huge for those who reach the top that the risk will seem worth taking.

    Therefore

    C There will always be some athletes who will give way to the temptation.

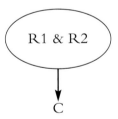

It is because R1 and R2 are *both* true that the conclusion follows. If drugs did *not* make a difference, or if the rewards did *not* make the risk worth taking, there would not be the same temptation.

3 There are three reasons, all closely interdependent:

    R1 No sport should be allowed in which the prime object is to injure an opponent.

    R2 No sport should be allowed in which the spectators enjoy seeing competitors inflict physical harm on each other.

    R3 What boxers have to do, in order to win matches, is to batter their opponents senseless in front of large, enthusiastic crowds.

    Therefore

    C Boxing should be one of the first sports to be outlawed.

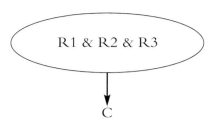

Note that this argument could be unpacked more thoroughly by breaking R3 down into two separate premises and pairing them with R1 and R2:

R3 What boxers have to do, in order to win matches, is to batter their opponents senseless.

R4 They do this in front of large, enthusiastic crowds.

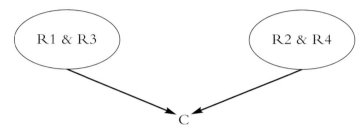

5   More complex arguments

1

Context

Recently the operators of a cruise liner were fined $18m for dumping oil and other hazardous waste at sea. This may seem substantial, but...

R1 In the same year the ship earned profits of $340m.

R2 The company could well afford the fine.

R3 Dumping saved them the considerable expense of storing and legally disposing of the waste.

(therefore)

IC: R4 Emptying their tanks into the ocean was probably a risk worth taking.

R5 In the last decade only a handful of companies have been fined.

R6 Every year there are unsuccessful attempts to prosecute.

(therefore)

IC: R7 Dumping is not much of a risk.

R8 The oceans of the world are in danger of becoming open sewers.

Therefore

C   We must give the authorities greater powers and demand that they use them.

The two intermediate conclusions, together with R8, are given as reasons why the authorities ought to have and use greater powers.

2

Context

Scientists have discovered some three-million-year-old leaves preserved in the ice (at the South Pole).

R1 They are so undamaged, and preserved in such fine detail, that they could not have been carried there by wind or sea.

(therefore)

IC: R2 They can only be from trees that once grew there.

R3 The leaves belong to a species of beech tree that grows only in warm or temperate regions.

R4 Beeches do not evolve quickly enough to adapt to changes in climate.

Therefore

C The South Pole must once have been much warmer than it is today.

6 Claims

1 (a) Sentence 1: reason, factual; Sentence 2: conclusion, recommendation
(b) Sentence 1: reason, factual; Sentence 2: conclusion, prediction
(c) Sentence 1: reason, factual; Sentence 2: reason, factual; Sentence 3: conclusion, recommendation.
2 Postal voting has been found to increase the number of votes cast in general elections. However, the opportunities for cheating with postal voting are greater than with the traditional ballot-box procedure, and cheating almost certainly does more harm to the electoral process than low turn-outs.
3 *Variable*

7 Conclusions

1 The correct selection is C. Note that C is actually a conjunction of two sentences, one recommending the abolition of charging, the other recommending an alternative solution. Neither of these is a reason for the other: they are like parallel claims, or two sides of the same coin; and they both follow from the other claims that are made.
Distractors: A is introductory; B is one of the reasons (premises); D is not stated at all. On a casual reading it looks like the last sentence (which is a premise), but it omits the crucial word 'equally', which makes it a very different claim.
2 The correct selection is A. The argument begins half-way through, after 'But…'. It states the conclusion first, then gives reasons to support it, including the intermediate conclusion that differing fares are the only way the system can work.
Distractors: B is the intermediate conclusion, and therefore a premise; C and D are part of the introductory information which provides the target for the main argument; E is one of the reasons which supports the intermediate conclusion.

3 The correct selection is A. The actual sentence that states the conclusion is: 'This is nonsense', but when you are asked to express the conclusion you obviously need to say what 'This' is. 'This' refers to the target claim, 'We must be carnivores', as A correctly includes.

Distractors: B would be a premise, if it were correctly interpreted. The actual claim in the passage is that these foods are the natural diet of our nearest ancestors; C and D are premises; E is implied in the introductory sentence.

8 Drawing conclusions: inference

1 The correct selection is D. The trees tend to get shorter the higher up they are planted, for whatever reason.

Distractors: A generalises about all trees on hillsides. The graph only relates to fir trees on one particular hillside. B claims that the growth can be accurately predicted from the altitude, whereas the graph shows only a rough correlation. (The crosses would have to lie on a straight line for an accurate prediction to be possible.) C and E both draw inferences about what has caused the growth rates to be different (soil quality and air temperature respectively). There is nothing in the graph to say which, if either, of these is the cause (or correct explanation). There is only a correlation between altitude and growth.

2 The correct selection is E. The passage tells us that once at least a small army beat a very large one. That makes E true.

Distractors: A would only follow if there was evidence that small armies usually beat large ones. We have no information to that effect and it would be very surprising if it were true. B, C and D all make claims about why the Macedonians won, i.e. the cause of their victory. There is no support for any one of these rather than another, and possibly none of them is the true explanation.

3 It has been said that 'every picture tells a tale'. That may be so, but we need to be very careful what tale we read into a picture. Can we conclude that the person nearer to the camera is trying to steal the car? Or, alternatively, that she is doing something perfectly innocent? Does the position and behaviour of the other person tell us anything? Indeed, can it be assumed that the two people in the picture have any connection with each other at all? Can we conclude anything useful from the fact that both are wearing coats with hoods? Lastly, what significance, if any, has the tool-box on the wall?

If you have considered all or some of these questions, and have not jumped to over-hasty conclusions about guilt or innocence, you have adopted the right critical approach. If you have presumed guilt or innocence, you have inferred too much.

9 Assumptions

1 *Variable*

2 A and B are both underlying assumptions; C is not. It is implied that Raisa likes novels, but it is not necessary to assume it to support the conclusion that she won't like this book (a documentary).

3 A is the underlying assumption.

4 C is the missing premise.

10 Sound or unsound?

1 (a) is invalid, and therefore unsound. Lemons, as it happens, *are* citrus fruits, but many things with a sharp, acidic taste – e.g. pickled onions – are not. Therefore having sharp and acidic taste is not a good enough reason to say that something is a citrus fruit.

(b) on the other hand is valid and sound. Its premises are both true and the conclusion follows from them. If citrus fruits have a particular taste, then lemons, which are citrus fruits, must have that taste.

2 This is a valid argument. You can show this by simplifying it as follows: 'If this is a diamond it would scratch glass. It doesn't scratch glass. So it isn't a diamond.' As for the premises, the first is true: diamonds do scratch glass. The second *we are told* is true. Therefore the argument is sound as far as we can tell.

3 This argument is also valid. If it is true that the president really would be in prison if he were guilty, and he is not in prison, then he is not guilty. What makes this argument seem unconvincing is not that the conclusion doesn't follow from the premises but that the first premise is open to question. An awful lot of presidents have been guilty of corruption and escaped prison. That doesn't alter the *logical* fact that if the premises were true the conclusion would have to follow; but it does cast doubt on the overall soundness of the argument.

4 *Discussion*

11 Finding flaws

1 (a) B is the correct selection. The flaw is mistaking correlation for cause.

(b) A and B both expose the flaw. If true, both would show that unhappiness in the workforce was not the cause of higher profit, as assumed in the argument, but that arguably higher profit was the cause of the unhappiness. C does not show up a flaw. If anything C supports the argument by suggesting that, conversely, worker happiness may cost a company financially, not help it.

2 B exposes the flaw. The argument implies that lack of exercise was the cause of the writer's long life and good health. B raises the possibility that it may have been genetic, inherited from her parents.

12 Challenging an argument

1 C is the correct selection. The argument considers only the superior strength and effort involved in the men's game. It does not consider whether or not the men entertain the spectators any more than the women do, which arguably should be taken into account (since the spectators pay to watch). C claims that the women entertain more than the men, and therefore weakens the argument. None of the other options deals with the central issue of whether the men *deserve* the bigger prizes.

2 The correct selection is B. The argument claims that there is no justification for rejecting over-qualified applicants and that companies benefit if they appoint them. B points out that over-qualified employees are likely to move on as soon as they can, which challenges both these claims: it shows that the companies don't benefit; and it gives them a good reason not to appoint such people.

Distractors: A considers what the applicant should do, not what the employer does; C supports the argument; D misses the point: it is not about earnings, but about the fairness of the selection process.

3 The conclusion is that severe punishment is not an effective deterrent. The reasoning is that it did not deter pickpockets who operated at public executions (on the assumption that the deterrent should have been at its most effective on such occasions). The comment offers a different explanation for the alleged 'extraordinary fact': the pickpockets simply didn't expect to be caught when they stole at executions. This does not mean that under different and more normal circumstances severe punishment is ineffective as a deterrent. Therefore the comment could be said *either* to weaken the argument *or* to raise a different issue that neither strengthens nor weakens it.

13   Lending support

1 The correct selection is B.
2 The correct selection is A. The argument is that general elections will never produce desirable leaders, because vote-winning is competitive and ruthless. The statement adds the claim that the voters won't even get a chance to vote for someone with the right qualities, which, if true, more or less clinches the argument.

14   Explanation

1 (a) *Variable*
   (b) *Variable*
   (c) None of them. Though all four are possible explanations for the outcome, and some of them are plausible ones, there isn't one which is clearly the cause. Therefore none can be inferred from the information alone. Even if we take the likeliest explanation, which is the first one, we can't be sure that it is a fact without an independent experiment to find out. The difference in overall density may be due to the container rather than the liquid, or to the amount of air inside.
   (d) Any of these could be an explanation for can R sinking and can D floating.
2 A is an explanation for the fact that the sea around icebergs remains in a liquid state. If you didn't know that seawater had a lower freezing point than fresh-water ice, you might expect it to freeze too, or the iceberg to melt; B is also an explanation for the fact that ice forms on the surface of water; C is an argument. The conclusion is that in science we have to preserve the distinction between mass and weight. This is quite a tricky question because there is a sense in which the argument is explaining why you have to keep a distinction between the two words. But the reasons also support the conclusion *that* you must preserve the distinction, and it is that which makes it an argument.

15 Looking at evidence

1 There is no obvious reason to suggest Mrs Short made up her story, or that she might have been mistaken about what she saw. Given where she lives, she would have every chance of seeing someone arrive at the house. She may have seen him through a window or passed him in the hall or on the stairs. Of course, we know nothing about her relationship with Mr Green: if she happened to be a close friend as well as a neighbour, she might just be saying whatever Green wants her to say, though this is merely a possibility. A bigger problem with Mrs Short's evidence is that it is so vague. 'She saw a man answering White's description' could mean nothing more than seeing someone of similar age or height. Mrs Short supplies no times of arrival or departure, so that even if she is telling the truth we don't really know that the man she saw 'on that Saturday' was the one who allegedly visited her neighbour. There are many more questions you would want her to answer before you placed too much weight on this evidence. It offers some corroboration, but nothing solid.

2 The restaurant owner is not a reliable witness because of his relationship with the accused man. That does not mean he is lying or mistaken, only that his association with White means that he is not neutral or independent. If the men had had no connections, this would be strong evidence, especially if it were supported by other staff or by customers at other tables etc. But on his own this witness is not in a position to provide White with a convincing alibi.

3 Mr Long, by contrast, doesn't know White, or so we are told. However, he has seen a photograph of him, and his car, and knows that White has been accused of a crime against a person living opposite. This weakens his evidence greatly because the information Long gives could all have been gathered from the newspaper. Mr Long may just be seeking attention, as some people unfortunately do in these situations. Or he may have seen a white car and jumped to the conclusion that it was the same car as the one in the photograph. Also, the car he says he saw was outside *his* house, a detail that Mrs Short does not mention, though she doesn't specify where the car was parked at all. Nor does Long notice a parking ticket. These are small differences that do not prove the main claims false; but they do add a little uncertainty.

4 As already noted in the answer to the first question, there are further questions to be asked about the relationship between Mr Green and Mrs Short. It might also be worth investigating whether anyone else saw White or his car at the restaurant. But the most obvious lead to follow up is the parking ticket, because, if Mrs Short was correct, there would be hard evidence about the car's whereabouts at a certain time. If the ticket was issued near Green's house this would be very difficult for White to explain, especially as it would show he had also lied.

16   More about evidence

1 Emilio's statement is most unreliable. To begin with Emilio has an obvious reason to challenge the story given by the tourist, because that would make the café responsible for the tourist's injuries and the damage to the door as well. However, this doesn't tell us that Emilio's account is not accurate: only that it is contested. The real deficiency in Emilio's evidence is that it is second-hand, or hearsay. The waiter, who would have been an eye-witness, is not around to question (which itself is a bit suspicious), and Emilio, who was upstairs when the incident took place, is simply reporting what he (the waiter) supposedly said and did. The words 'They appeared at the door, kicking…' etc. are not the waiter's, they are Emilio's. Not only do we not know whether the waiter told the truth; we don't even know whether Emilio accurately repeated what the waiter told him. That is the problem with hearsay evidence.

2 *Variable*

17   Case study: who's telling the truth?

Variable

18   Case study: collision course

Variable

19   Introducing longer arguments

1 If the bored and disadvantaged young men knew that the police were banned from chasing stolen cars, they might not find the theft of a car so exciting, and a ban may not, after all, lead to an increase in car thefts.

2 *Variable*

20   Applying analysis skills

The main conclusion is the first sentence: that sport's governing bodies are right to prohibit drugs and not to tolerate their use.

The main reasons are:

> R1 *(para. 1)* Performance-enhancing drugs are harmful to health.
>
> R2 *(para. 2)* Sport's governing bodies have a duty of care not to let athletes harm themselves.
>
> R3 *(para. 3)* If drugs are driven out we will know who the real champions are.
>
> R4 *(para. 6)* Drug-taking by top athletes encourages other young people to do it.

There is also a counter-argument that is anticipated and replied to. It is the argument that drug-taking is no different from special diet, equipment, etc., and that these, arguably, are cheating too. The writer's response, which could be given as a fifth reason, is:

> R5 *(para. 5)* Drug-taking is different from other ways of improving performance because drugs are banned and the other practices are not.

Notice that the reasons that have been picked out are the main, or *direct*, reasons. There are other claims made in the passage that contribute to the argument by supporting one of these main reasons. Paragraph 2, for example, is really a subsidiary argument and R2 is its conclusion:

> Athletes are reckless about their health;
>
> the rewards are very large (implying that they are a temptation); and
>
> it would be irresponsible to stand by and allow drug use.
>
> *(therefore)*
>
> IC: R2 The governing bodies have a duty not to let athletes harm themselves.

Similarly, paragraph 3 gives several reasons to support R3:

> The purpose of sport is to find out the best.
>
> The only way to do this is to have a 'level playing field'.
>
> You can't say who is best if some athletes cheat.
>
> *(therefore)*
>
> IC: R3 If drugs are driven out we will know who the real champions are.

Your analysis of the argument may have varied in certain details from the one suggested here. But, however you mapped it out, you should at least have identified the main conclusion and listed all or most of the main reasons. You should also have noticed that there was a counter-argument and reply. If you are unsure that you have correctly interpreted it, read it again now with the above analysis to help you. We will be returning to it from a different angle in the next unit.

21 Critical evaluation

1 *Variable*
2 The argument is blatantly circular. It uses the claim that the dinosaurs were made extinct by a sudden catastrophe to draw the intermediate conclusion that they disappeared almost overnight. But then it argues, from that, back to the first claim that the cause must have been an event rather than a process. This can also be called 'begging the question'.

22 Further argument

Variable

23 The appliance of science

Variable

24 Conditions

1 (a) Reading the book is a necessary but not a sufficient condition for passing the exam.

(b) B is the correct answer, because reading the book was a necessary condition only; A treats reading the book as a sufficient condition, whereas it is only necessary; C could be reliably inferred only if reading the book guaranteed passing, but it doesn't. In fact everyone could fail, readers of the book included, and the tutor's prediction would not have been wrong; D turns the prediction round and makes passing the exam a condition for having read the book. This does not follow from the prediction; E does not have to be true because reading the book was not a sufficient condition for passing the exam.

2 (a)

(b) A is correct. 'Yes' to being within the city and 'Yes' to 200+ members lead straight to 'Grant'. But 'No' to being within the city and 'No' to 300+ lead to 'No grant'; B is correct. Even outside the city limits, 'Yes' to 300+ and 'Yes' to public transport lead to 'Grant'; C is incorrect. Access to transport is not necessary for any club inside the city limits with 200+ members; D is incorrect. The first part is true: that it is not necessary for a club with 300 members to be in the city. But it is not sufficient either, because the club may have no access to transport.

25 Principles

Variable

26 An argument under the microscope

Variable

27 Synthesis

Variable

28 Critical marking

Essay 1 – Maria

The examiner's mark was C.

The selection of material was good but not as thorough as it needed to be for an A or B. Some, but not all, of the inferences were sound. For example, her claim that an end to the bidding process would mean less danger to the participants is not strongly supported. A lot of Maria's claims are simply her own views, or Ms Sender's. But she does generally make it clear when she is expressing opinion and when she is presenting facts from the documents.

She offers some evaluation of evidence, for instance where she discusses a possible contradiction in paragraph 2. She brings together information from different sources and uses this to support her views. Her overall conclusion – agreement with Janet Sender – is clearly stated and she gives reasons to support it.

It is fair to say that all of the C-grade descriptors are met by Maria's essay, but it would be unrealistic to award her three or more credits at the next level.

Essay 2 – Gudrun

The examiner's mark was E.

There is certainly reference to the documents but not all of it is relevant to the argument. A lot of this essay is taken up with simply recounting historical or other information from the texts, without really drawing any conclusions from it – the only real exception being paragraph 3. The evaluation is very weak – little more than an unsupported comment at the end. There is also a conclusion, but it too is little more than Gudrun's statement that she agrees with the author.

At least 3 of the 4 E-grade descriptors are met, but none at the C-grade level.

Essay 3 – James

James's essay was awarded a B, but it was very close to an A.

By contrast with both the other two, this essay is critical in all the best senses of the word. There is a very thorough analysis and evaluation of Ms Sender's arguments, picking up many of the weaknesses and contradictions in her reasoning. Sound inferences are drawn from the texts provided, for instance that Athens, strictly speaking, is no more the historic site of the games than other cities outside Greece. There is a well-supported conclusion at the end; and the essay brings together (synthesises) information from more than one document in a generally well-organised way.

The point on which the examiner was critical of James was that he was a bit too selective with the information at his disposal. He tended to use what suited his argument and dwelt mostly on opposing Janet Sender, instead of looking at all the evidence and balancing pros and cons. For instance, he did not deal with the glaring imbalance between different continents in the choice of host cities. Nor did he address the problem of corruption, alleged or actual. This is not to say that he should have modified his conclusion: only that he should have acknowledged these potential counter-arguments and had some answers for them.

This was a very competently written essay, and if you gave it an A you would not have been over-generous. However, it is worth noting that to be sure of the top grades in an A-level assignment, you need to read the question and accompanying documents very carefully, and make certain that you cover them thoroughly.

29   What do we mean by a 'problem'?

1 *Variable*
2 *Variable*
3 The key here is to be systematic: did you look at *all* the possibilities? Could you save some time by eliminating some orders?
4 (a) The answer is 3. If the first two you pick out are of different colours (the 'worst-case scenario'), the third must match one of them.
  (b) The answer is 2. As for the situation above, if the first two are different, the third must match one of them.
  (c) The answer is 9. The first 8 you pull out could all be black – the ninth must then be blue so you will have one of each.
  (d) The answer is 8, as above – all the first 8 you take out could be the same.
  (e) The answer is 10 (note the difference from 4 (a)). The first 8 you take out could all be black. You would then need to take out 2 more to get a blue pair.

30   How do we solve problems?

1 The efficiency (in km/litre) is distance driven divided by petrol used. The calculations may be approximated as shown in brackets.
In order the cars are:
Riviera: 8
Roamer: 8.8 (just under 9)
Stella: 9.375 (just under 10)
Montevideo: 12
Carousel: 14.375 km/l (over 14)
2 If, as each bottom candidate is withdrawn, all their votes are transferred to their next lowest, we keep as many as possible in with a chance. As they are withdrawn we get the following results:

	original	after first withdrawal	after second withdrawal
Patel	323	323	323
Brown	211	211	211
Walshe	157	157	157
Ndelo	83	83	158
Macpherson	54	75	
Gonzalez	21		

At this stage, either Walshe or Ndelo could be withdrawn, depending on the distribution of the votes of the lower candidates. The one who survives could go on to receive Brown's vote and win, so 4 candidates can still win.

3 This is a problem where we need to work backwards. If we look at each dish in turn, we can find out its timing so that it is ready at 7 p.m.

Chicken: 15 minutes rest after 2 hours of cooking. Cook for 15 minutes after heating the oven.

Rice: 15 minutes cooking after 30 minutes soaking.

Broccoli: 5 minutes cooking after 5 minutes preparation.

Sauce: 15 minutes cooking after 10 minutes preparation.

Working out each event time and putting them in order, we have:

Turn on oven	4.30 p.m.
Put in chicken	4.45 p.m.
Soak rice	6.15 p.m.
Prepare sauce	6.35 p.m.
Cook rice	6.45 p.m.
Cook sauce	6.45 p.m.
Remove chicken from oven	6.45 p.m.
Prepare broccoli	6.50 p.m.
Cook broccoli	6.55 p.m.
Eat	7.00 p.m.

4 As the length of the shelves is 1.6 m, they must be cut lengthwise from the sheet of wood. The 1.2 m end pieces can be cut either way. This leaves only two reasonable options. The left-hand one clearly leads to the larger uncut rectangle (in area).

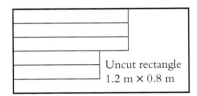

Uncut rectangle 2.0 m × 0.6 m

Uncut rectangle 1.2 m × 0.8 m

31   Selecting and using information

1 This graph can be drawn as either a bar chart or a pie chart.

2 In 1984, vinyl singles were 44% of 170 million, or 74.8 million; in 1994, vinyl singles were 26% of 234 million, or 60.8 million; A is correct, they fell by 14 million.

3 He lost his initial grid position in seven races: Alency, Euroland, Saint Croix, Castelle, Fertoux, Belle Plage and Grunlande.

In five of these he regained at least one place: Alency, Euroland, Saint Croix, Fertoux and Belle Plage.

5 is the correct answer.

4 Each shelf requires 30 mm gap, 210 mm for books and 20 mm for the shelf thickness, or 260 mm in total. The available gap is 2.5 m less 300 mm (as the bottom shelf must not be too close to the ground), or 2200 mm.

A maximum of 8 shelves at 260 mm total can be fitted into 2200 mm.

32 Processing data

1 If you buy goods to the value of $100 or more, you receive a discount of 60%. Therefore the cheapest possible price you could pay for goods at this discount rate is $100 × 0.4 = $40.

So it will be worthwhile to buy more goods if your purchase at the lower discount rate will be more than $40. This is the case if your purchase has a total marked value of more than $40/0.6 = $66.67, but less than $100.

In other words, one can select goods to a value of $100 without paying over $40. Any purchases with a marked price between $66.67 and $99.99 will cost more than $40.

2 Her total time for the first 5 laps is 5 × 73 = 365 seconds. The time she is trying to achieve is 14 minutes 35 seconds or 875 seconds, so she must run within 875 − 365 = 510 seconds for the last 7.5 laps or 68 seconds (1 minute 8 seconds) per lap.

3 The savoury pancakes come in these types: egg; ham; tomato; egg and ham; egg and tomato; ham and tomato; and egg, ham and tomato − 7 in total.

The sweet pancakes come in 3 types (orange, lemon or strawberry) times 2 toppings (cream or ice-cream), 6 in total.

The number sold by the stall is 6 + 7 or 13.

4 If we look at the cost over 8 years:

Conventional bulbs cost 4 × 60¢ = $2.40, electricity is 8 × 600 × 2 = 9600¢ or $96.

Energy-saving bulb (1 needed) costs $6, electricity is 8 × 600 × 0.2 = 960¢ or $9.60.

The saving is $98.40 − $15.60 = $82.80. The saving per year is $82.80 / 8 = $10.35.

33 Finding methods of solution

1 Each additional link adds length of the overall length of the link minus twice the metal thickness (this can be seen from the diagram). Thus, if 10 extra links add 8 cm to the length, the effective added length per link is 0.8 cm, so the actual length of a link must be 1.2 cm. Thus the number of links in the 33.2 cm length is:

(33.2 − 1.2)/0.8 + 1 = 41

(as you must add the full length of the end link). The number of links in the 25.2 cm length is:

(25.2 − 1.2)/0.8 + 1 = 31.

The total number of links is 72.

2 In 1 hour, the ferry travels 1/5 as far upstream as it does downstream, so the upstream speed must be 1/5 of the downstream speed. If the speed of the river is 4 km/h, the speed of the ferry must be 6 km/h (2 km/h upstream and 10 km/h downstream). Thus the distance between the towns is 10 km.

3 For every stride Joe takes, Jim takes $1\frac{1}{4}$ (when Joe has taken 4, Jim will have taken 5). This means that, after 4 of Joe's strides, Joe's left foot will hit the ground at the same time as Jim's right foot. It will take 4 more of Joe's (8 in total) or 5 more of Jim's for their left feet to coincide again − 10 in total.

4 This appears to be a Venn diagram problem, and one could be used to solve it. However, there is an easier analysis. If we add the number with neither (5) to the number with a dog (13) and the number with a panda (12), we get 30. There are only 23 children in the class, so the difference (7) must be the overlap, or those with both a dog and a panda. You might like to draw a Venn or Carroll diagram to show all the subdivisions.

34 Solving problems by searching

1 There are a large number of ways of paying, but clearly 1 adult + 1 pensioner + 2 children (total $32) comes to more than the family ticket ($30), so some combination using a family ticket must be used.

Family ticket ($30) + 2 extra children ($10) = $40
1-adult family ticket ($20) + extra pensioner ($5) + 2 extra children ($10) = $35.

The latter is the best option.

2 The options to search involve dividing the books as 7 (6+1 would be silly), 5+2 or 4+3. The prices, respectively, are $3.20, $2.15 and $2.10. The last of these is the best.

3 One can start listing the piles systematically:
$20 \times 5¢$; $16 \times 5¢ + 1 \times 20¢$; $12 \times 5¢ + 2 \times 20¢$
continuing to $5 \times 20¢$; thus there are piles containing 0 to $5 \times 20¢$ coins, or 6 in total.

35 Spatial reasoning

1 The letters should look as follows:

ƆℲ2

2 *Variable*

3 It is best to draw lines on the drawing to show where the changeover points are. As you walk from left to right, the orders will be:

RYBOGW
RBYOGW
RBYGOW
BRYGOW
BRGYOW
BGRYOW
BGRYWO
GBRYWO
GBRWYO
GBWRYO

10 different orders in total.

4 Since the minute hand behaves normally, the time is quarter past something. We must imagine the hour hand reflected about the centre, so the time is 2.15. D is correct.

5 A and D will work. If you have doubts, try them.

6 B is correct. Again, you can try it to make sure.

36 Recognising patterns

1 *Variable*

2 The numbers of my birth date could be from 01 to 31 (these are then reversed). The numbers of my birth month can be from 01 to 12 (these are also reversed). We can then look at the options in turn:

A   with the respective parts reversed becomes 23 12 – this is possible (23 December).
B   becomes 05 06 (5 June).
C   becomes 11 14 (impossible – the month cannot be more than 12).
D   becomes 12 12 (12 December).
E   becomes 21 09 (21 September).
So C is the only impossible number.

3 The first table shows the situation after four of the six matches have been played. The Britons have drawn 2 games, so the matches B vs. D and B vs. S must have been draws. The Normans had lost one other game, so this must have been to the Danes, the remaining game already played must have involved the Normans beating the Saxons. This means the two games to be played are B vs. N and D vs. S. There are nine combinations of results. The final league tables in each case are:

	B wins/ D wins	B draws /D wins	B loses/ D wins	B wins/ D draws	B draws/ D draws	B loses/ D draws	B wins/ D loses	B draws /D loses	B loses/ D loses
B	5	3	2	5	3	2	5	3	2
D	7	7	7	5	5	5	4	4	4
N	3	4	6	3	4	6	3	4	6
S	1	1	1	2	2	2	4	4	4

All of the final points situations given in the table are possible except D.
This question could also have been done backwards: looking at each option given and seeing whether that combination was possible.

4 The price structures for each option are:

Books	A	B	C	D	E
1	$3	$5	$3	$3	$5
2	$6	$7	$6	$6	$7
3	$9	$9	$9	$9	$9
4	$12	$11	$12	$12	$11
5	$15	$13	$14	$10	$14
6	$18	$15	$16	$12	$17
7	$21	$17	$18	$14	$20

C represents the graph shown.

37   Making choices and decisions

1 If you have 17, the possible outcomes (only allowing one more throw) are:

No extra throw		win 3
One extra throw	1	win 3
	2	win 6
	3	win 8
	4	win 10
	5	lose 4
	6	lose 4

Averaging the outcomes with the extra throw (all scores are equally possible):

$(3 + 6 + 8 + 10 - 4 - 4)/6 = 19/6$, so the average is a win of just over 3.

The score with no extra throw is a win of 3, so it is marginally better to throw again.

2 If she spends $29.99, she will get a 2¢ voucher that will save her 60¢ on petrol, so her effective spend is $29.39. Any spend over $30 in the shop will get her a 3¢ voucher, saving her 90¢ on petrol, so she can spend up to $30.29 (an extra 30¢) without increasing her overall bill. Similarly, if she spends $49.99, she could spend up to $50.29 without increasing the bill.

3 D is not possible as there is no subject from the third column.

4 34¢ can be made up as 22¢ + 9¢ + 2¢ + 1¢; any other combination needs at least one more denomination. 67¢ can be made up as 3×22¢ + 1¢, so no extras are needed. $1.43 can be made up as 6×22¢ + 9¢ + 2¢, so 4 denominations are needed in total: 22¢, 9¢, 2¢ and 1¢.

38 Using models

1 At 3.45, the clock will appear as in the diagram. The left tube will be nearly 1/3 full (3.75 hours out of 12) and the right tube will be 3/4 full (45 minutes out of 60).

2 Jerome's bottle must last either from the base to the spring, the spring back to the spring, or the spring back to the bottom. The last of these is clearly shorter than the first, so we can ignore it.
Base to spring takes $10/2 = 5$ hours, needing 2.5 litres.
Spring to spring takes $5/2 + 0.25 + 5/5 = 2.5 + 0.25 + 1.0 = 3.75$ hours needing 1.875 litres.
The journey up to the spring takes the longest, so he needs a 2.5-litre bottle.

3 The cost of calls is as follows:

Time	1	2	3	4	5	6
Total cost	60	60	60	66	72	78
Average per minute	60	30	20	16.5	14.4	13.0

B is correct.

39 Combining skills — using imagination

1 Dunrovia has 6 points – this can only be obtained by 2 wins and one loss. Similarly, Arbadia and Brindling's 4 points can only be achieved by one win, one draw and one loss. Crittle's 2 points can only be obtained by 2 draws and a loss.

(a) Crittle drew two matches. Two other teams drew a match each; thus Crittle must have drawn with both Arbadia and Brindling. 2 matches were drawn.

(b) Crittle drew two and lost one, Dunrovia won two and lost one. Thus Dunrovia must have beaten Crittle.

(c) This leaves 3 games unaccounted for: D vs. A, D vs. B and A vs. B, none of them draws. If Brindling beat Dunrovia, Dunrovia must have beaten Arbadia and Arbadia must have beaten Brindling.

2 If Chico's bill was $3 more than the average, Andy and Benita would have paid $13.50 each ($12 + $3/2) if all had paid the average. Thus Chico's bill was $16.50.

3 If the border is the same all the way around, and there is one more square vertically than horizontally, the difference between the two dimensions must be the same as one square. Thus the squares are 0.3 m × 0.3 m. The border is 0.1 m on each side.

4 The total expenses were 2 × $400 (two weeks' fixed costs) + $1,400 for materials, or $2,200 in total. Thus the profit was $2,700, or $900 each. Bill had paid out $800, so Fred owes him $1,700, Harry had paid out $1,400, so Bill owes him $2,300, leaving $900 for himself.

40 Using other mathematical methods

1 If I originally would have bought n rolls, I took $25n$ cents. The reduced price is 20 cents and I can buy 3 more, for $20(n+3)$ cents. These two amounts are the same, so: $25n = 20(n+3) = 20n + 60$ so $5n = 60$ and $n = 12$.
I was originally going to buy 12 rolls.

2 This is most easily solved with the aid of a diagram (each box represents 1 second and black is on):

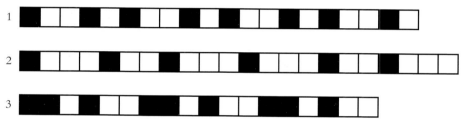

Thus they all flash together at 15 seconds after starting their sequences.

3 The total number of ways they can pick up the hats is 4 × 3 × 2 × 1 = 24. We must subtract from this the number where 1 or more has the right hat.
Look first at only 1 having the right hat. If A has the right hat, there are 6 combinations of hat for B, C and D (BCD, BDC, CBD, CDB, DBC, DCB). Of these, only 2 have all BCD wrong (CDB and DBC). The same applies if B, C or D has the right hat, making 8 in total.
Look now at 2 people having the right hat: this could be AB, AC, AD, BC, BD and CD. In each case, there is only one way the other two could be wrong, making 6 in total.
It is impossible for exactly 3 people to have the right hats. There is only 1 way all 4 people can have the right hats.
This makes 8 + 6 + 1 = 15 ways of at least one person having the right hat, leaving 9 ways that everyone has the wrong hat. You could try to list these.

4 The first two digits are 11 or 12. The second two digits can be 11–19 or 21–29 (for either combination of the first two digits) or 31 (but only if the first two digits are 12). There are 37 possibilities, so the chances of getting it right the first time are 1/37. The chances of getting it right the second time are 1/36 and the third time are 1/35. The total chance in three attempts is 1/37 + (36/37 × 1/36) + (36/37 × 35/36 × 1/35) = 3/37 or 6.1%.

41 Use of more complex diagrams

1 This can be solved using a tree diagram.

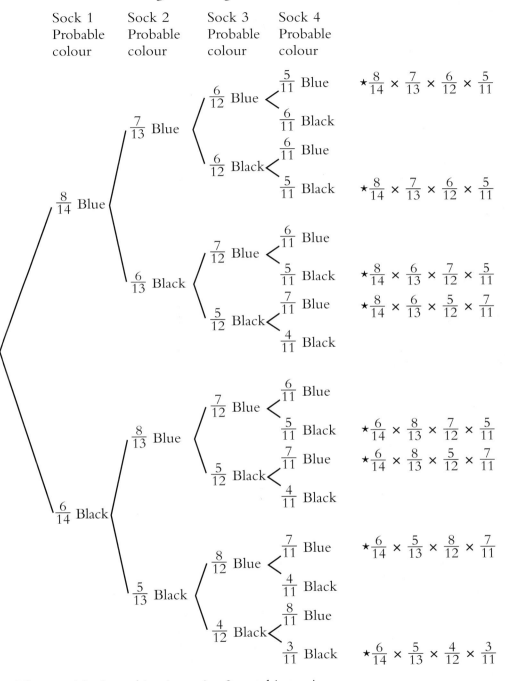

The asterisked combinations give 2 matching pairs.

There are 8 possibilities and the probabilities of all but the last are the same. The probabilities need to be worked out with a calculator and are as follows:

$7 \times 0.0699 + 0.5045 = 0.549$.

Thus the chance of drawing two pairs is approximately 50%.

2 The Venn diagram is as shown here. The top-left circle represents even numbers, the top-right circle multiples of 3 and the bottom circle square numbers. Those outside the three circles do not fit into any of the categories.

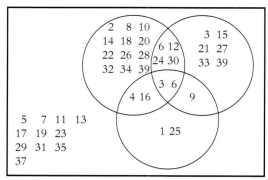

3 These statements may be represented as a Carroll diagram.

	Leave from Waigura	Leave from Nooli
Go to Dulais		
Do not go to Dulais	X	X	X

The inner square shows the fast hydrofoil services, the outer square the slow steamboats. The Xs mark the cells that are empty (represent no service). These are all ferries going from Waigura to anywhere other than Dulais and fast hydrofoil services to anywhere other than Dulais. All other cells may contain services.

We can now answer the statements:

A Hydrofoils from Nooli to Dulais are represented by the inner, top-right and are possible. So this statement cannot be concluded.

B As the inner, top-right is possible, this statement cannot be true; hydrofoils could leave from Nooli.

C This is not true – hydrofoils from Nooli to places other than Dulais are represented by the inner, bottom-right box, which is empty.

D Steamboats from Waigura to Dulais are represented by the outer, top-left box, so this statement is possible, but it cannot be concluded from the data, as it could be that all the ferries from Waigura to Dulais are hydrofoils.

E This is true, since no hydrofoils from Waigura go elsewhere.

4 Let us suppose that the probability of hitting the nearer pole is $\frac{1}{2}$ and the probability of hitting the farther pole is $\frac{1}{3}$. (If the question can be answered, it clearly does not matter what the exact probabilities are or we would have been given them.)

If we throw near, far, near, the probabilities of throwing two in a row are as follows:

Hit, hit, miss: $\frac{1}{2} \times \frac{1}{3} \times \frac{1}{2} = \frac{1}{12}$

Miss, hit, hit: $\frac{1}{2} \times \frac{1}{3} \times \frac{1}{2} = \frac{1}{12}$

Hit, hit, hit: $\frac{1}{2} \times \frac{1}{3} \times \frac{1}{2} = \frac{1}{12}$

The total probability of winning is $\frac{3}{12}$ or 25%.

If we throw far, near, far, the probabilities of throwing two in a row are as follows:

Hit, hit, miss: $\frac{1}{3} \times \frac{1}{2} \times \frac{2}{3} = \frac{2}{18}$

Miss, hit, hit: $\frac{2}{3} \times \frac{1}{2} \times \frac{1}{3} = \frac{2}{18}$

Hit, hit, hit: $\frac{1}{3} \times \frac{1}{2} \times \frac{1}{3} = \frac{1}{18}$

The total probability of winning is $\frac{5}{18}$ or about 28%. The second strategy is better. Some may regard this as counter-intuitive as it involves two throws at the harder target. Did you expect this answer? Can you rationalise why the second strategy should be the best? Can you prove that it works for all probabilities (as long as the farther target is harder to hit)?

42   Modelling and investigating

1 Let us assume that Duane walks x km. It doesn't matter whether this is done as a single stage or they swap bike and walk several times – it is only important how far in total each walks and rides.

Duane's total journey time is $x/6 + (12 - x)/15$.

Mervin's total journey time is $x/20 + (12 - x)/4$.

If they arrive at town at the same time:

$x/6 + (12 - x)/15 = x/20 + (12 - x)/4$.

Multiplying both sides by 60:

$10x + 4(12 - x) = 3x + 15(12 - x)$ or $10x + 48 - 4x = 3x + 180 - 15x$.

Simplifying: $18x = 132$ or $x = 7.33$ km. The total time is:

$x/6 + (12 - x)/15 = 1.22 + 0.31 = 1.53$ hours.

We still have to convince ourselves that arriving at the same time is the best strategy. Suppose Duane (the faster walker) walks the whole way. It takes him 2 hours. Clearly any strategy in which Duane walks more than 7.33 miles will result in a slower time (nearer to 2 hours). It is even worse if Mervin walks further as he is a slower walker.

2 We need to calculate the total race time for the various numbers of pit stops.

For 1 pit stop, 150 litres of fuel are required for each half of the race. The average lap time (0.12 seconds slower than 75 seconds for each 5 litres of fuel) is, therefore:

$75 + 0.12 (75/5) = 76.8$ seconds

so 60 laps takes $60 \times 76.8 = 4608$ seconds.

The time for the pit stop is $10 + 150/15 = 20$ seconds, so the total race time is 4628 seconds (77 minutes 8 seconds).

For two stops, the calculation is based on an average fuel load of 50 litres, so the average lap time is 76.2 seconds and the pit stop time is 16.7 seconds.

The total time is $60 \times 76.2 + 2 \times 16.7 = 4605.4$ seconds (76 minutes 45.4 seconds).

For three stops, the average fuel load is 37.5 litres, the average lap time 75.9 seconds and the pit stop time 15 seconds.

The total time is $60 \times 75.9 + 3 \times 15 = 4599$ seconds (76 minutes 39 seconds), so 3 stops is optimum. Should you consider 4?

As a further exercise you might consider how the problem could be tackled if the distance between pit stops was not constant (for example, it might be worth filling the car right up at the start to save on refuelling time, although this would make it slower).

3 Suppose we have x% of Brazil nuts, y% of walnuts and $(100 - x - y)$% of hazelnuts. Their cost for this mix is $0.4x + 0.35y + 0.2(100 - x - y)$. They wish to make 50% profit, so they sell it at 60¢, which is twice this value. We now have a model:
$0.4x + 0.35y + 0.2(100 - x - y) = 30$.
Simplifying:
$0.2x + 0.15y = 10$.
This cannot be solved explicitly for x and y, so we must investigate different values. We can note that $x = 50 - 0.75y$, so this gives a relationship between the two (and implies the proportion of the third ingredient).
Putting some values into this:

x	0	10	20	30	40	50	60	70
y	50	42.5	35	27.5	20	12.5	5	–ve
z	50	47.5	45	42.5	40	37.5	35	–

Thus there is a range of mixes that fulfil the conditions, from 0 to 60% walnuts. We can test one of these answers: 1 kg is made up of 40% walnuts costing 14¢, 20% Brazil nuts costing 8¢ and 40% hazelnuts costing 8¢, a total of 30¢, so the shop makes 50% profit when selling at 60¢.
The most even mix is around 30% walnuts – can you define it more closely?

43   Analysis: hypotheses, reasons and inference

1 The effectiveness of drug A, allowing for the gradual withdrawal, is shown in the first graph.

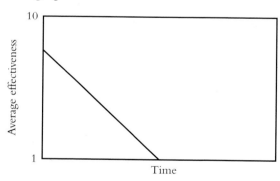

The overall effectiveness will be the sum of the first graph and that for drug B. It will appear as in the second graph.

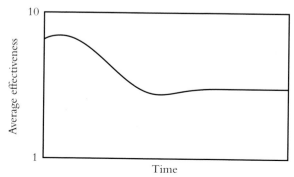

The sizes and positions of the peak and dip will depend on the exact values for the original two curves.

2   (i) (a) This statement cannot be confirmed. Over the last 12 years, the discovery of new resources has matched the rate of depletion for both oil and gas. Whether this will continue to happen in the future, and for how long, is not certain.

   (b) This is true if stated in terms of years of potential supply. The current gas reserves will last 65 years and the oil just over 40.

   (c) As stated under (a): this is true, the graphs of potential years of supply are approximately horizontal.

   (d) This is also true. Energy consumption is rising (graph 2) so, if the reserves are constant in terms of years of supply, the rate of discovery must be increasing in a similar manner to the rate of usage.

   (e) This is not true. It would lead to the potential years reserves in graph 1 falling.

   (ii) In the 1980s there must have been a surge of exploration and discovery of new reserves. As the usage was fairly constant, this led to an increase in the known years of supply. Since then, discoveries have just matched consumption. Other factors may be involved.

   (iii) If the discovery of new reserves fails to match consumption, prices will rise. This will lead to a variety of things, one being a search for alternative energy sources (which will become more attractive as the price for energy is higher), another is a recession in world trade (this would reduce consumption and ease prices) and a third is a search for increased energy efficiency. You should comment on these, their implications and any other factors you can think of which are relevant. This is a good topic for class discussion.

3   (a) Greece and Spain have 4 points: this could only be achieved by one win and one draw. Portugal have 3 points – only a win and a loss would give this. Russia have lost both their games. These results are shown in the table.

Team	Played	Points	Won	Drawn	Lost	Goals for	Goals against
Greece	2	4	1	1	0	3	2
Spain	2	4	1	1	0	2	1
Portugal	2	3	1	0	1	3	2
Russia	2	0	0	0	2	0	3

Russia have lost to both Spain and Portugal (they have yet to play Greece). Spain must have drawn with Greece (only one match was drawn). Greece must have beaten Portugal (this is the only game not accounted for).
Russia lost one game 1–0 and the other 2–0 (the only way of making 3 goals against). They could not have lost 2–0 to Spain as Spain would then have lost their other game (their total is 2 for and 1 against). Thus Russia lost 2–0 to Portugal and 1–0 to Spain. We can now work out all the results and scores:

Greece 2 Portugal 1
Greece 1 Spain 1
Spain 1 Russia 0
Portugal 2 Russia 0

(b) There are 9 possibilities for the remaining 2 games (either team can win, or the game can be drawn). Russia cannot finish in the first two, but the three other teams can. The situation can be analysed backwards (e.g. if Greece win or draw they are through, as Spain are playing Portugal and both cannot get 3 points). The full analysis is given in the table (GbR means Greece beat Russia).

	SbP	SbP	SbP	SdP	SdP	SdP	PbS	PbS	PbS
	GbR	GdR	RbG	GbR	GdR	RbG	GbR	GdR	RbG
Greece	7	5	4	7	5	4	7	5	4
Spain	7	7	7	5	5	5	4	4	4
Portugal	3	3	3	4	4	4	6	6	6
Russia	0	1	3	0	1	3	0	1	3
Qualify	G S	G S	G S	G S	G S	G S	G P	G P	P★

The result is clear in all but two columns. In column 6, Greece and Portugal finish level on points but Greece qualify as they beat Portugal.

In column 9, Greece and Spain finish equal and they drew their game. The scores of the two games will determine who goes through on goal difference, goals scored or drawing of lots. Can you determine which scores will lead to which outcome? The actual result was column 9 (Spain 0 Portugal 1, Russia 2 Greece 1), Greece and Portugal went through. Portugal had the only positive goal difference and Greece had scored more goals than Spain.

Index